Integrated Mathematics 1

Practice Bank

The Practice Bank includes a page of practice exercises for every section in the textbook, plus a page of cumulative practice at the end of each unit. Answers are provided on annotated reduced facsimilies following the last practice page.

Houghton Mifflin Company • Boston

Atlanta • Dallas • Geneva, Ill. • Palo Alto • Princeton

ISBN: 0-395-69812-X

123456789 - BW - 98 97 96 95 94

Contents

Name ______________________ Date ______________

Practice 1

For use with Section 1-1

For Exercises 1–4, use the graph at the right, which shows average weekly television viewing time for various age groups in a rural community.

1. Does the graph show that men generally watch television more than women?

2. Which age group of both men and women watches the most hours of television?

3. Which age group of both men and women watches the fewest hours of television?

4. **True or false** Viewing time for both sexes goes down steadily with increasing age.

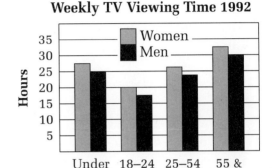

Weekly TV Viewing Time 1992

Women
Men
Hours
35
30
25
20
15
10
5
Under 18
18–24
25–54
55 & over
Age

For Exercises 5–9, use the chart at the right. The road mileage between two cities can be found where the row of one city crosses the column of the other city.

	L.A.	Det.	Den.	Dal.	Cle.	Chi.	Bos.
Atlanta	2182	699	1398	795	672	674	1037
Boston	2979	695	1949	1748	628	963	
Chicago	2054	266	996	917	335		
Cleveland	529	170	1321	1159			
Dallas	1387	1143	781				
Denver	1059	1253					
Detroit	2311						

What is the mileage between each pair of cities?

5. Boston and Detroit

6. L.A. and Dallas

7. Denver and Chicago

8. Which two cities are farthest apart?

9. Which two cities are closest together?

For Exercises 10–12, use the concept map at the right.

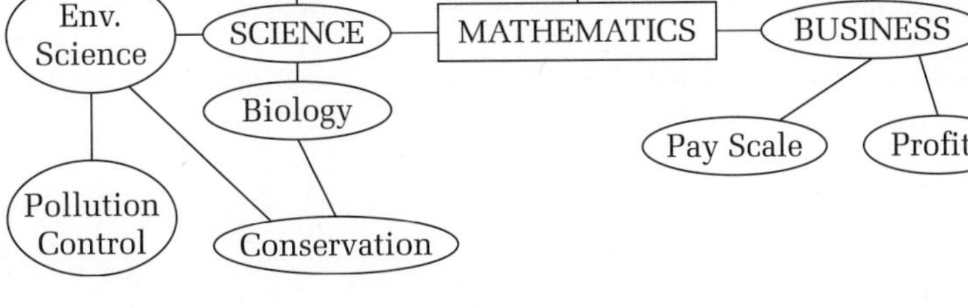

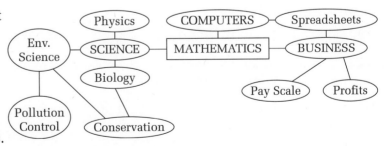

10. What are the three large categories directly related to mathematics?

11. Name a concept that is related to both computers and business.

12. ***Writing*** Describe all the relationships you can that are illustrated by the concept map.

Name ______________________ Date ______________

Practice 2

For use with Section 1-2

Draw Shapes 4 and 5 in each pattern. Make a table of the perimeters of the shapes. Then write a variable expression for the perimeter of Shape *n*.

1.

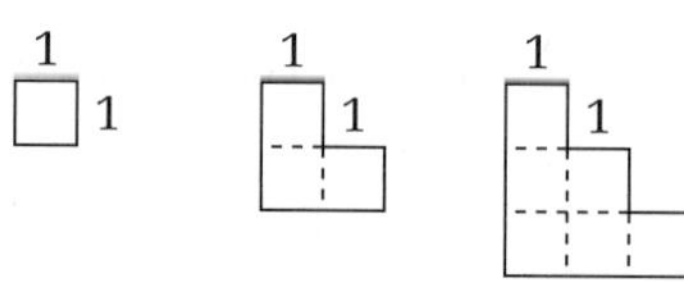
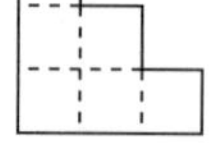

Shape 1 Shape 2 Shape 3

2.

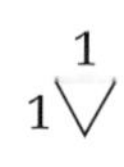

Shape 1 Shape 2 Shape 3

Write a variable expression for each phrase.

3. the number of fielders x plus the number of pitchers y

4. 10 times the rate r

5. the mass m multiplied by the velocity v

6. 0.25 times the number of quarters q

Evaluate each variable expression for $x = 3$ and $y = 15$.

7. $x + y$

8. xy

9. $\frac{y}{x}$

10. $2x + y$

11. $y - x$

12. $0.5y + x$

13. $3y - 2x$

14. $4xy$

Write a variable expression for the perimeter of each shape.

15.

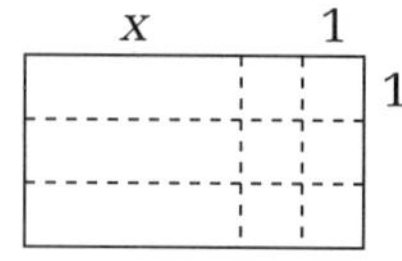

16.

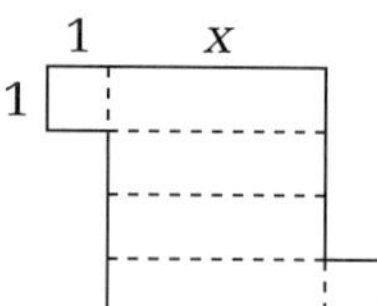

17.

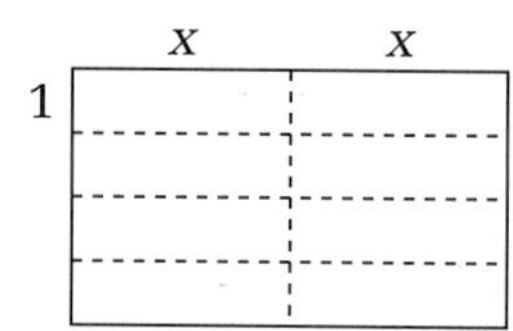

A car can go 28 mi on one gallon of gas. Find how far the car can go on each amount of gas.

18. 5 gal

19. 10 gal

20. 50 gal

21. n gal

22. There are 1.6 km in one mile. Write a variable expression for the number of kilometers in p miles.

23. Suppose a car can go 28 mi on 1 gal of gas. How many kilometers can it go on 1 gal?

24. How many kilometers can the car go on x gal?

Name ______________________ Date ______________

Practice 3

For use with Section 1-3

Write the product as a power. Then write how to say it.

1. $10 \cdot 10$

2. $5 \cdot 5 \cdot 5$

3. $2 \cdot 2 \cdot 2 \cdot 2 \cdot 2 \cdot 2$

4. $3 \cdot 3 \cdot 3 \cdot 3 \cdot 3$

5. $7 \cdot 7 \cdot 7 \cdot 7$

6. $8 \cdot 8 \cdot 8 \cdot 8 \cdot 8 \cdot 8 \cdot 8$

7. $n \cdot n$

8. $x \cdot x \cdot x \cdot x \cdot x$

9. $y \cdot y \cdot y$

10. $w \cdot w \cdot w \cdot w$

11. $k \cdot k$

12. $m \cdot m \cdot m \cdot m \cdot m \cdot m$

Write using exponents.

13. 5 to the fourth

14. 3 squared

15. 4 cubed

16. the fifth power of 7

17. the sixth power of 2

18. 5 squared

19. n to the sixth

20. b cubed

21. p to the seventh

22. q squared

23. y to the fourth

24. the fifth power of z

Write an expression for the area covered by each group of tiles. Evaluate each expression when $x = 3$.

25.

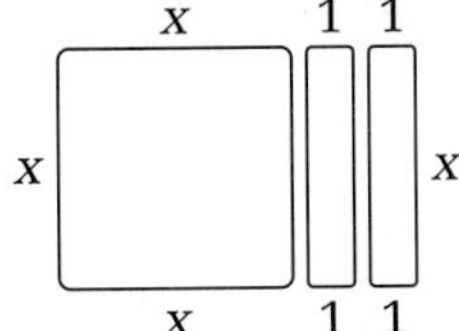

26.

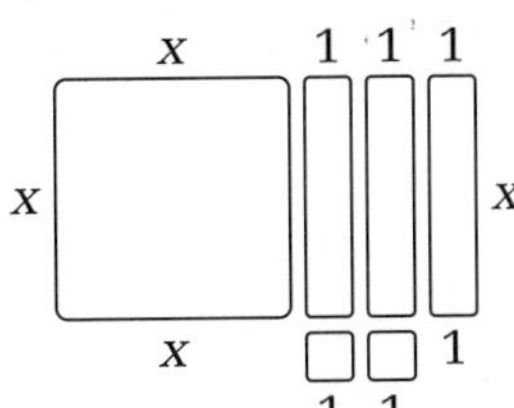

27.

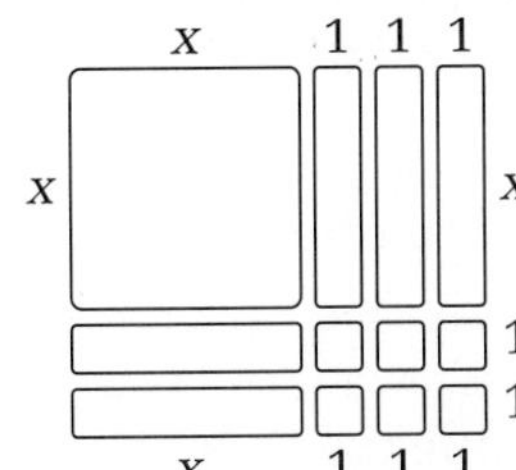

Write as a power of ten.

28. $10^2 \cdot 10^3$

29. $10^5 \cdot 10^4$

30. $10^8 \cdot 10$

31. $10^6 \cdot 10^6$

32. $10^{15} \cdot 10^{15}$

33. $10 \cdot 10^{12}$

34. $\frac{10^3}{10^2}$

35. $\frac{10^6}{10}$

36. $\frac{10^{13}}{10^8}$

37. ***Open-ended*** Write as a power of 10: $(10^3)^2$, $(10^3)^3$, and $(10^3)^4$. Make a conjecture about what power of 10 you get for $(10^a)^b$.

Name ______________________ Date ______________

Practice 4

For use with Section 1-4

Calculate according to the order of operations.

1. $10 \cdot 3 + 5$

2. $6 + 12 \div 3$

3. $4 \cdot 2^3$

4. $25 - 3^2 \cdot 2$

5. $4^3 \div 8 - 2$

6. $54 - 6^2 \div 3$

7. $3 \cdot 5 - 2^2$

8. $5^3 \cdot 10 \div 2$

9. $10^4 \div 5 + 15$

10. $5 + 20 \cdot 3 - 1$

11. $5 \cdot 2^5 - 20 \div 5$

12. $108 - 12 \cdot 3^2$

13. $200 - (11 - 3)^2$

14. $200 - 11 - 3^2$

15. $200 - (11 - 3^2)$

16. $24 + 8 \div 2^3$

17. $(24 + 8) \div 2^3$

18. $24 + (8 \div 2)^3$

19. $(3 \cdot 10)^2 \div 5 - 4$

20. $3 \cdot 10^2 \div 5 - 4$

21. $3 \cdot 10^2 \div (5 - 4)$

22. $[(5 + 3)^2 \div 4]^2 - 3$

23. $27 - [6^2 \div (10 - 6)]$

For each group of tiles, (a) write a variable expression for the perimeter, (b) write a variable expression for the area, and (c) evaluate the expressions when $x = 5$.

24.

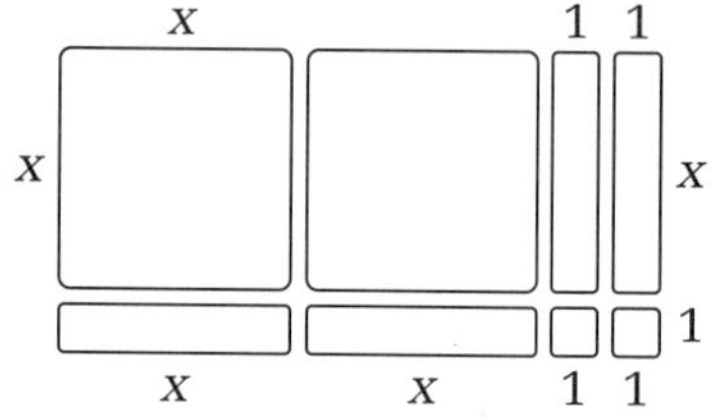

25.

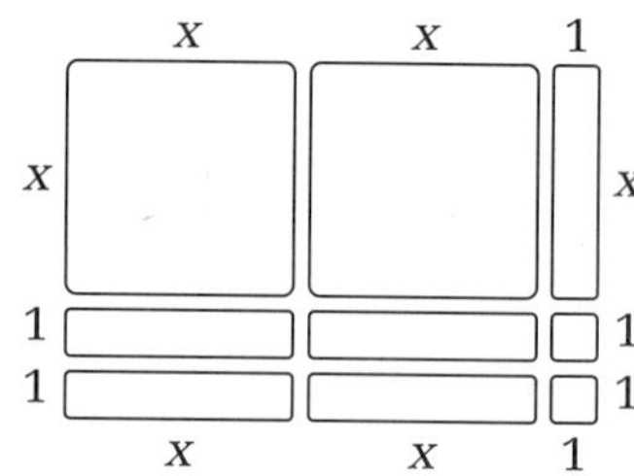

Insert parentheses to make each statement true.

26. $90 \div 5 + 4 \cdot 2 - 1 = 19$

27. $90 \div 5 + 4 \cdot 2 - 1 = 22$

28. Samia asked her friend, "What's 48 divided by 3 plus 5?" Her friend wondered whether she meant "48 divided by 3 ... plus 5" or "48 divided by ... 3 plus 5". Write these two interpretations as expressions and evaluate them.

29. ***Open-ended*** By inserting one pair of parentheses at different places in $100 - 3^2 + 5 \cdot 4 - 6 \div 2$, find as many different ways of evaluating the expression as you can.

Name ______________________ Date ____________

Practice 5

For use with Section 1-5

Rewrite each product as a sum or difference. Do not calculate.

1. $3(50 + 25)$

2. $6(200 - 30)$

3. $7(100 + 10)$

4. $5(200 - 30)$

5. $2(140 - 50)$

6. $4(500 + 15)$

7. $9(400 - 40)$

8. $8(100 + 60)$

Use the distributive property to find each sum or difference mentally.

9. $19 \bullet 6 + 19 \bullet 4$

10. $22 \bullet 13 - 22 \bullet 3$

11. $170 \bullet 35 - 70 \bullet 35$

12. $17 \bullet 28 + 3 \bullet 28$

13. $45 \bullet 21 - 45$

14. $15 \bullet 93 + 15 \bullet 7$

Use the distributive property to rewrite each expression without parentheses.

15. $3(x + y)$

16. $5(p - 2q)$

17. $7(3a - b^2)$

18. $\frac{1}{2}(4w - 12)$

19. $\frac{1}{7}(7u + 56v)$

20. $\frac{1}{3}(24 - 15n)$

Combine like terms.

21. $5x - 2x$

22. $7a^2 - 3 + 2a^2$

23. $8y + 5y^3 - 3y$

24. $6(r + 8) - r$

25. $10m + 4(3 - m)$

26. $9(2j^2 - j) - 3j^2$

27. $2(3x + 2y) + 10(x + 2y)$

28. $5(2a - 3) + 7(a + 6)$

For Exercises 29 and 30, use the diagram.

29. The diagram contains a large rectangle and small rectangles. Write expressions for the areas of the small rectangles and for the whole figure.

30. Write expressions for the length and width of the whole figure. Using these expressions, write an expression for the area of the whole figure. Is this expression equal to what you got in Exercise 29?

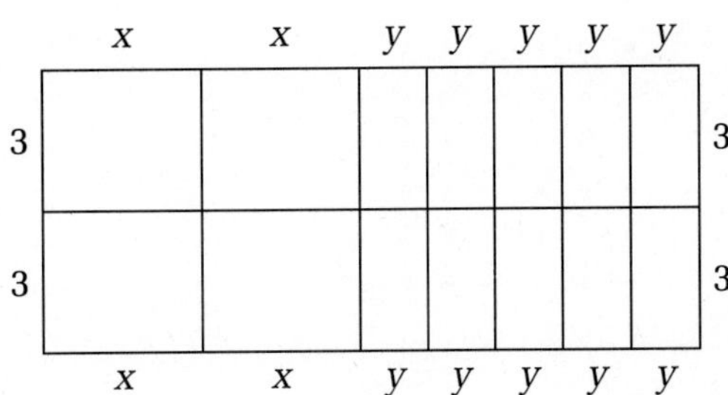

Name ______________________ Date __________

Practice 6

For use with Section 1-6

What kind of (*slide*, *turn*, or *flip*) shows that the two shaded polygons are congruent?

1. 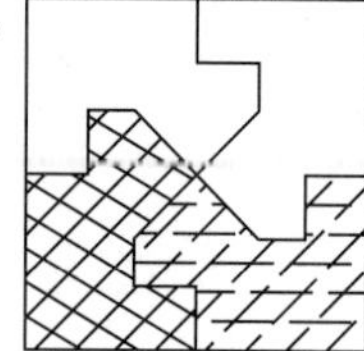

2. 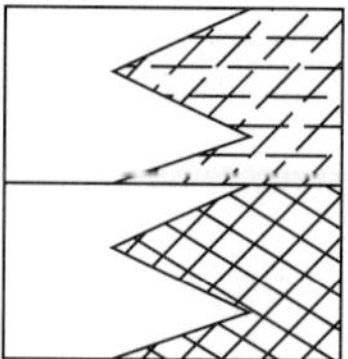

3. 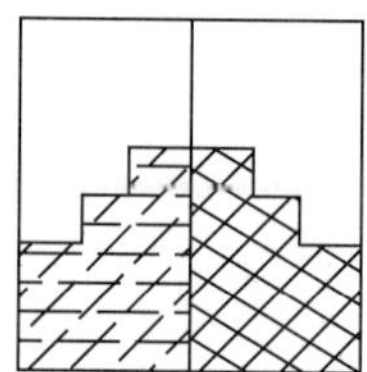

4. 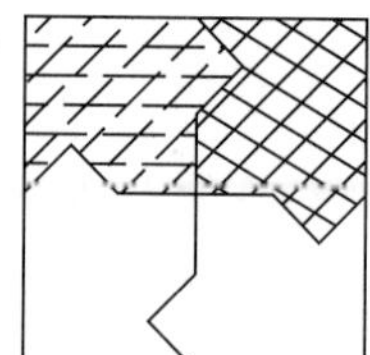

What kind of movement (*slide*, *turn*, or *flip*) shows that the two symbols are congruent?

5. $\leq$ $\geq$

6. NZ

7. MM

8. ? ¿

9. 9 6

10. ó ò

11. $\pm$ $\mp$

12. ” ”

For Exercises 13 and 14, name the two congruent polygons and name three pairs of congruent sides.

13. 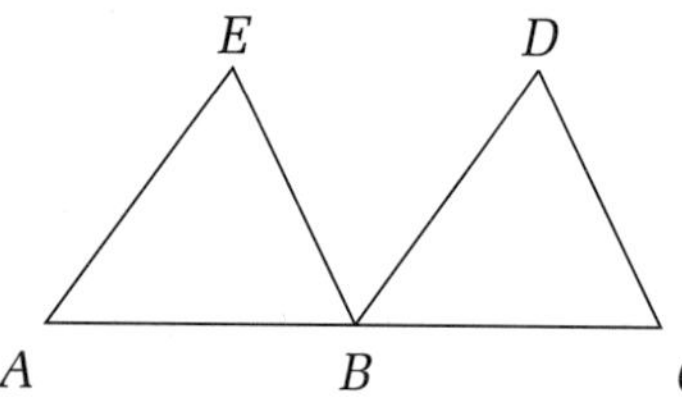

14. 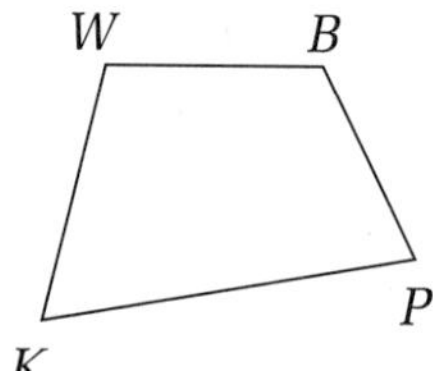

Q M

Y

C

For Exercises 15–17, mark congruent lengths with tick marks and with letters, and write a variable expression for the perimeter of the polygon.

15. 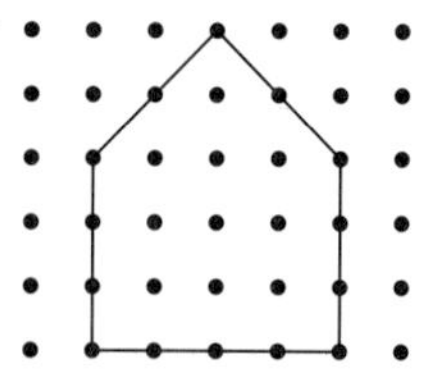

16. 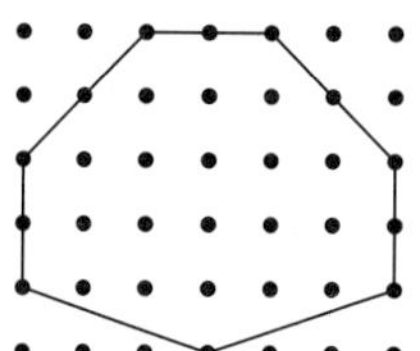

17. 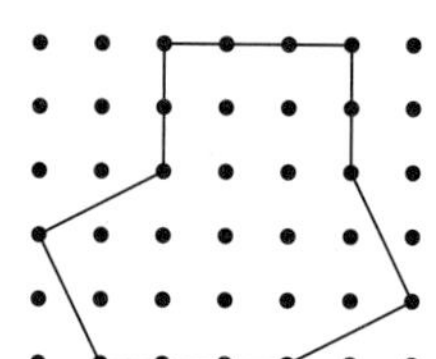

18. ***Writing*** Suppose you are shown a diagram of two congruent polygons. Explain how you would decide which vertices and which sides are corresponding.

Name ______________________ Date ______________

Practice 7

For use with Section 1-7

What name best describes each quadrilateral?

1. 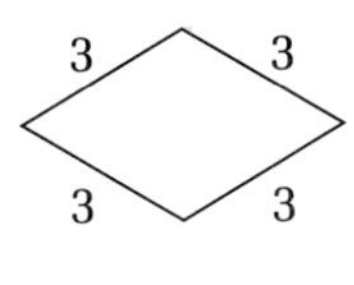

2. 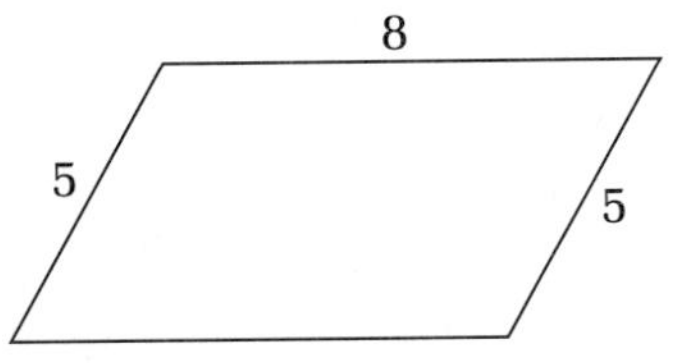

3. 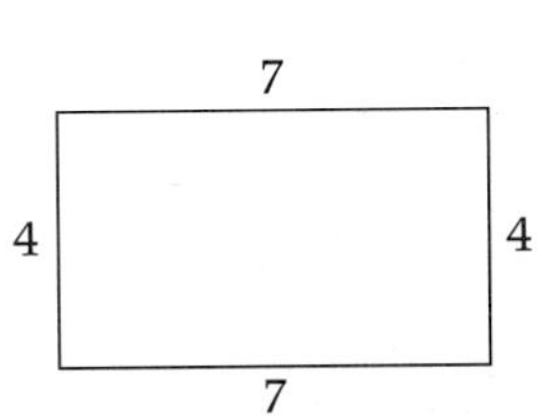

4. 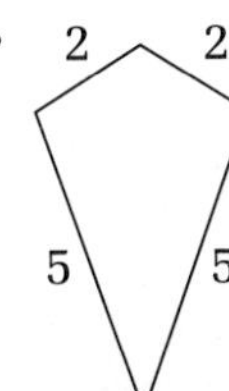

Copy each diagram. Draw the lines of symmetry for each polygon, or write *no symmetry*.

5. 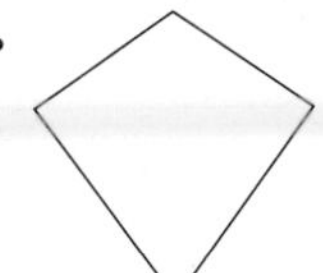

6. 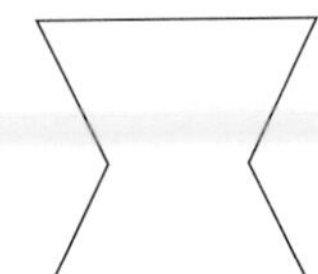

7. 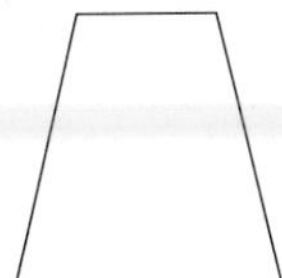

8. 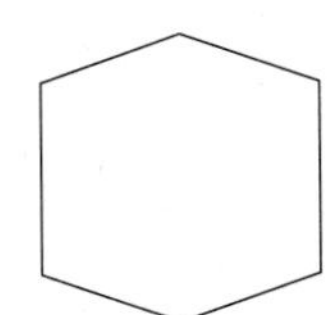

9. 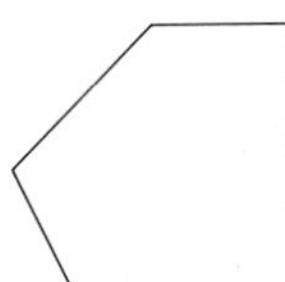

10. 

For each pair of triangles, name all the quadrilaterals from the list below that can be made by putting the triangles together, without flipping.

a. parallelogram **b.** rhombus **c.** rectangle **d.** kite

11. 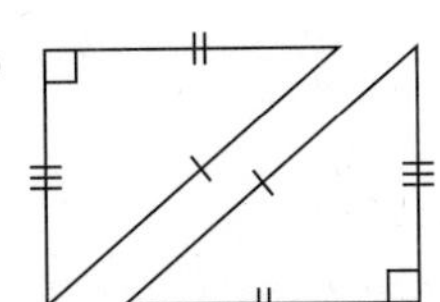

12. 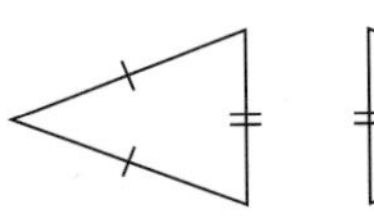

13. 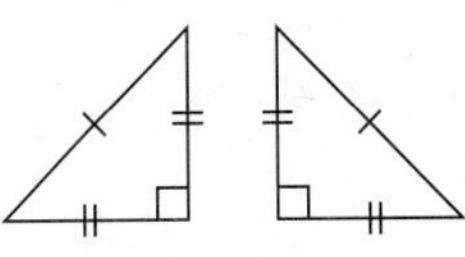

Draw a quadrilateral of each type. Draw one line that divides the quadrilateral into two congruent triangles.

14. rectangle **15.** kite **16.** parallelogram

17. ***Writing*** Suppose you have two congruent triangles cut out of paper, and suppose neither triangle contains a right angle. Can you put the two triangles together to make a rectangle? Tell how, or explain why you cannot do it.

Name ______________________ Date ______________

Practice 8

Cumulative Practice through Unit 1

Write a variable expression for each phrase.

1. Angelo's weekly earnings s divided by the number of hours h that he works each week.
2. Miao's speed r times the numbers of hours h she drove.

Evaluate each variable expression for $x = 12$ and $y = 25$.

3. $x + 2y$ 4. $\frac{x}{y}$ 5. xy 6. $\frac{0.3y}{x}$

Write as a power of ten.

7. $10^8 \cdot 10^3$ 8. $10 \cdot 10^5$ 9. $\frac{10^7}{10^3}$ 10. $\frac{10^{20}}{10^{12}}$

Calculate according to the order of operations.

11. $4 + 6 \div 2 + 5$ 12. $37 - (8 + 5)$ 13. $7 \cdot 2 - 3(10 - 9)$

Combine like terms.

14. $3c + 4d - c + 2d$ 15. $5x^2 + (x - 3x^2)$ 16. $8(m + n) + 2(m + 2n)$

Name the congruent polygons. Then list three pairs of congruent sides.

17. 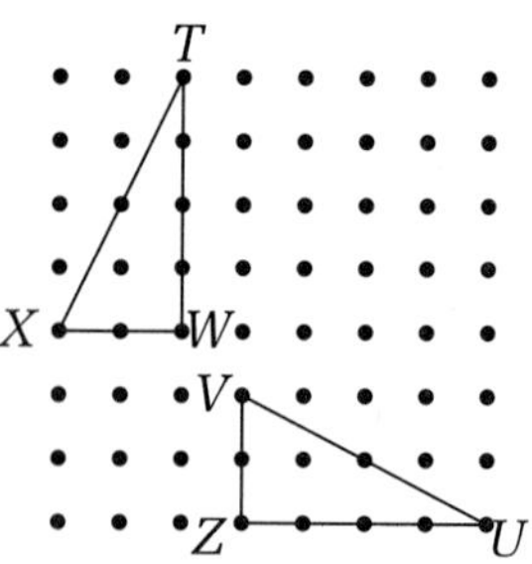

18. 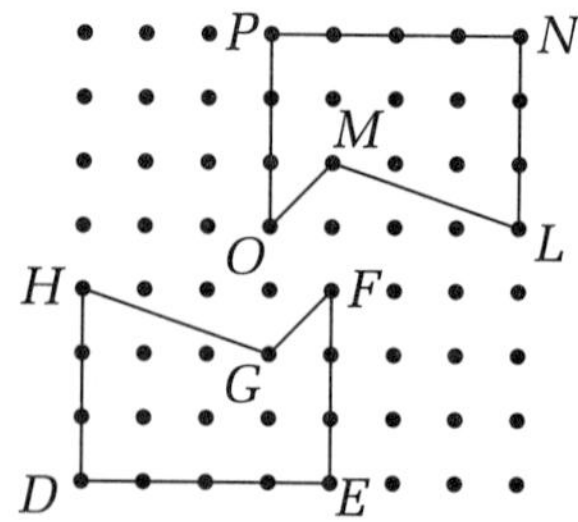

Draw all lines of symmetry for each figure or write *no symmetry.*

19. 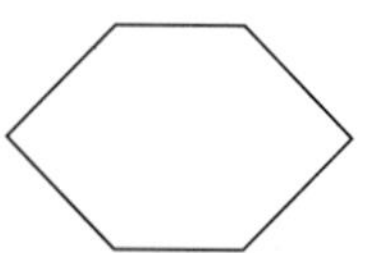

20. 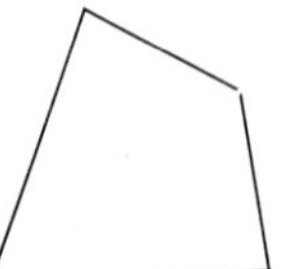

21. 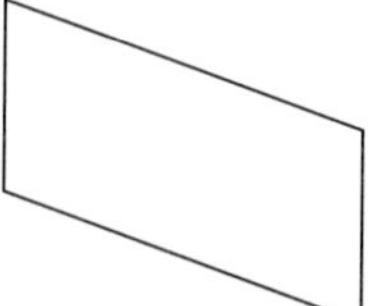

22. 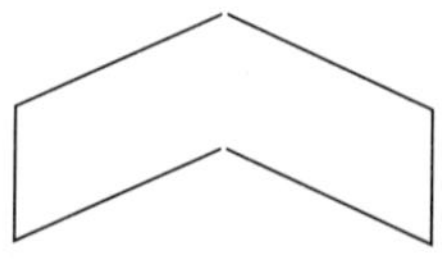

Name ______________________ Date ______________

Practice 9

For use with Section 2-1

Tell whether each number is used for *identifying,* or *ordering,* or as a *count* or a *measure.* Tell whether each number is likely to be exact or estimated.

1. The population of Austin, Texas
2. The position of a song in the Top 40
3. The distance traveled by a home-run ball
4. A score on a science true-false quiz
5. The land area of Earth
6. The attendance at a free outdoor concert

Classify each quantity as *discrete* or *continuous.*

7. An amount of rainfall
8. The attendance at a football game
9. The number of stars you can see
10. A person's weight

Exercises 11–13 refer to the diagram at the right.

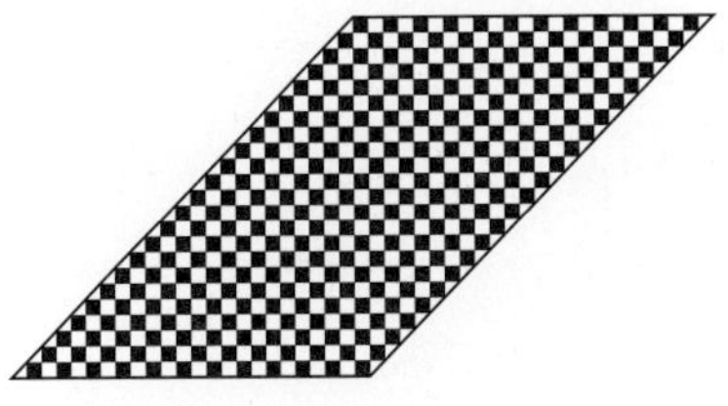

11. Without counting black squares, is the number of black squares in the tens, hundreds, or thousands?
12. Describe a method for estimating the number of black squares.
13. Use your method to estimate the number of black squares.

For Exercises 14–16, refer to the following scale.

impossible	unlikely	possible	likely	certain
0%	25%	50%	75%	100%
0	0.25	0.5	0.75	1

Use a number anywhere along the scale to estimate the probability of each event.

14. One of your teachers will be absent tomorrow.
15. It will be dark at 11:00 P.M. tomorrow night.
16. A coin that you toss will land heads up.
17. ***Writing*** Arlene wanted to estimate the number of words in the English language. She counted all the words in her pocket dictionary that started with the letter Z. Then she multiplied by 26. Was this a good plan? Explain your answer.

Name ______________________ Date ______________

Practice 10

For use with Section 2-2

Find the opposite and the absolute value of each number.

1. 5

2. $-\frac{2}{3}$

3. -4.7

4. 0

5. 8.4

6. $-5\frac{1}{2}$

Simplify.

7. $|-3|$

8. $|4.3|$

9. $|-0.6|$

10. $|-17|$

11. $-5 + 17$

12. $-22 + 9$

13. $15 + (-16)$

14. $4 - (-1)$

15. $-7 - 29$

16. $33 - (-33)$

17. $12 - 12$

18. $19 + (-23)$

19. $-5.8 + 100$

20. $-4.2 + (-5)$

21. $-3 - (-7.8)$

22. $-6.2 + 10.3$

23. $(3)(-7)$

24. $(-4)(-13)$

25. $(180)(-1)$

26. $(-2.5)(16)$

Simplify. Show every step.

27. $-5 + (-3)(4) - 7$

28. $15 - (-9 + 4) - 2$

29. $-7 - 6(5 - 17)$

30. $16 - 7 \cdot 5 + 8$

31. $24 \cdot 3 - (9)(-8)$

32. $5 + 0.5(-28 + 12)$

33. $(0.2)(50) - (5 + 19)$

34. $-2(4 - 7) + 15$

35. $(-1.5)(6) - 2(3)(-8)$

36. $\frac{-17 + 9}{3}$

37. $\frac{5 \cdot 6}{3 - (-4)}$

38. $\frac{-1 + 10}{-3 - 11}$

Evaluate each expression for the given values of the variable.

39. $5 - c$ when $c = -12$

40. $\frac{-p - 13}{4}$ when $p = -6$

41. $x^2 - 3$ when $x = 4$

42. $-y^2 + y$ when $y = -2$

43. $\frac{n - 8}{7}$ when $n = 1$

44. $\frac{3 + k}{3 - k}$ when $k = 0$

45. $10 - ab$ when $a = 3$ and $b = -4$

46. $0.5xy - x^2$ when $x = 4$ and $y = 6$

47. $\frac{c + d}{cd}$ when $c = 5$ and $d = -2$

48. $\frac{5}{9}(F - 32)$ when $F = -40$

49. "Par for the course" in golf means the number of strokes a good golfer is expected to take to go around the course. One golfer shoots 5 strokes above par and another shoots 4 strokes below par. What is the difference between their scores?

Name ______________________ Date ______________

Practice 11

For use with Section 2-3

Write each number in scientific notation.

1. 567,000

2. 45.8

3. 0.0019

4. 0.0596

5. 7,000,000,000

6. 84

7. 453.5

8. 0.000228

9. 7050

10. 0.05

11. 50,600

12. 6,000,000

Write each number in decimal notation.

13. 3.62×10^{-3}

14. 5.8×10^{7}

15. 6.43×10^{3}

16. 1.98×10^{1}

17. 3.07×10^{-2}

18. 9.5×10^{-6}

19. 5.638×10^{0}

20. 8×10^{4}

21. 4.875×10^{-1}

Simplify. Write each answer in scientific notation.

22. $(1.2 \times 10^{3})(3 \times 10^{2})$

23. $(3.6 \times 10^{-4})(1.5 \times 10^{-3})$

24. $\frac{4.5 \times 10^{8}}{9 \times 10^{-3}}$

25. $\frac{8.4 \times 10^{-6}}{7 \times 10^{5}}$

26. $\frac{1.28 \times 10^{7}}{1.6 \times 10^{6}}$

27. $300(5.6 \times 10^{-4})$

28. $0.18(3.2 \times 10^{7})$

29. $16(1.8 \times 10^{-8})$

30. $\frac{4.9 \times 10^{6}}{7}$

31. $\frac{4 \times 10^{12}}{25}$

32. $\frac{2.7 \times 10^{-3}}{5000}$

33. Sound travels about 340 m in one second. How far would sound travel in a minute and a half? Express your answer in scientific notation.

34. An India paper edition of an unabridged dictionary is 2.75 inches thick, not including the covers. There are 3210 numbered pages in the dictionary. How many sheets of India paper is this (two pages are printed on each sheet)? What is the thickness of one sheet of India paper? Express your answer in scientific notation.

35. During the year 1988, the average American ate an average of 31 eggs. There were about 246 million Americans at that time. How many eggs were eaten by all Americans during 1988? Express your answer in scientific notation.

36. ***Writing*** Suppose you were given two numbers in scientific notation. Describe a method for deciding which one is larger. Describe a way to estimate quickly how many times larger one number is than the other.

Name ______________________ Date ______________

Practice 12

For use with Section 2-4

Estimate the length of each side of quadrilateral *ABCD* in both U.S. customary units and metric units.

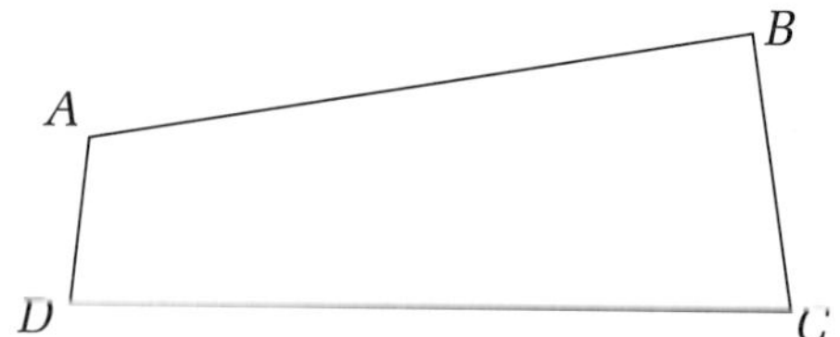

1. *AB*
2. *BC*
3. *CD*
4. *AD*

Estimate each distance by using the map at the right. Each grid square is 5 mi on a side.

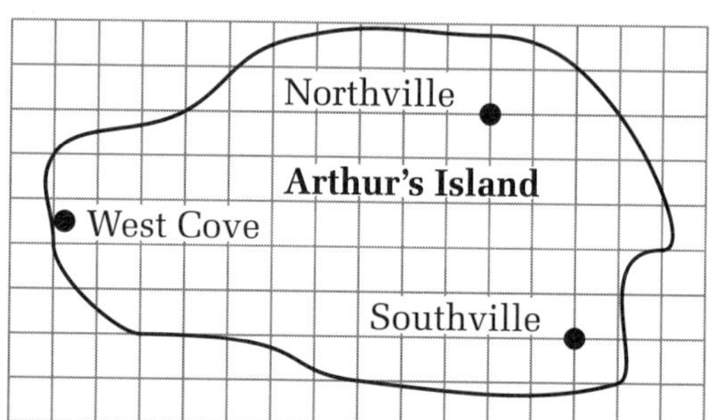

5. Northville to Southville
6. Southville to West Cove
7. Northville to West Cove
8. Estimate the area of Arthur's Island.

In the diagram for Exercises 9–12, *P* is the midpoint of $\overline{JK}$ and *Q* is the midpoint of $\overline{KL}$.

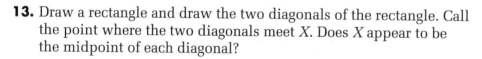

9. Suppose *JK* = 18. What is *PK*?
10. Suppose *KQ* = 10. What is *KL*?
11. Suppose *JK* = *KL*. Will *PK* equal *KQ*?

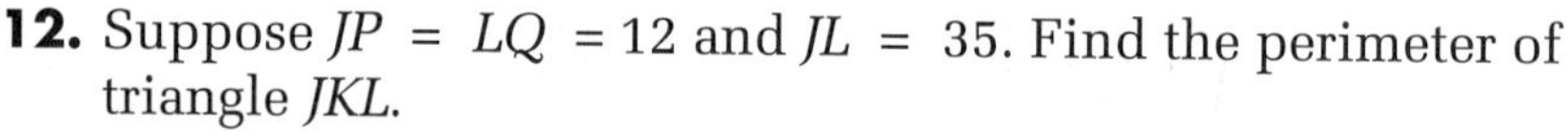

12. Suppose *JP* = *LQ* = 12 and *JL* = 35. Find the perimeter of triangle *JKL*.
13. Draw a rectangle and draw the two diagonals of the rectangle. Call the point where the two diagonals meet *X*. Does *X* appear to be the midpoint of each diagonal?
14. The Tigers plan to have a stitched block letter "T" on their baseball uniforms, as shown at the right. What area must be covered by stitching? (You can sketch a figure like this on graph paper if you wish.)

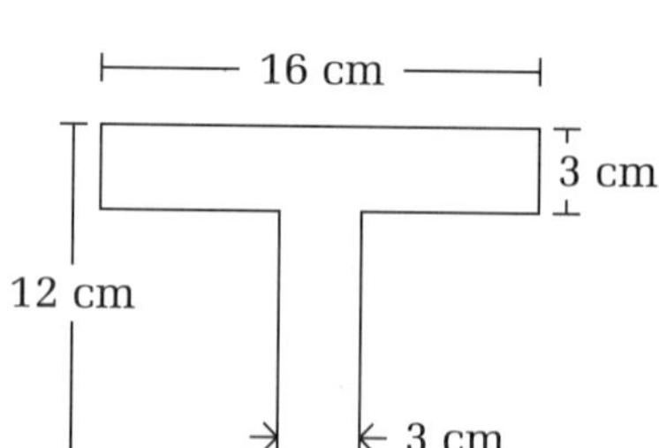

15. ***Open-ended*** On graph paper, draw several rectangles with the same perimeter. Do your rectangles all have the same area? Draw another rectangle with the same perimeter, but make the area as large as you can. How large can it be? Draw one more rectangle with the same perimeter, but make the area as small as you can. How small can it be?

Name ______________________ Date ____________

Practice 13

For use with Section 2-5

Exercises 1–5 refer to the diagram at the right.

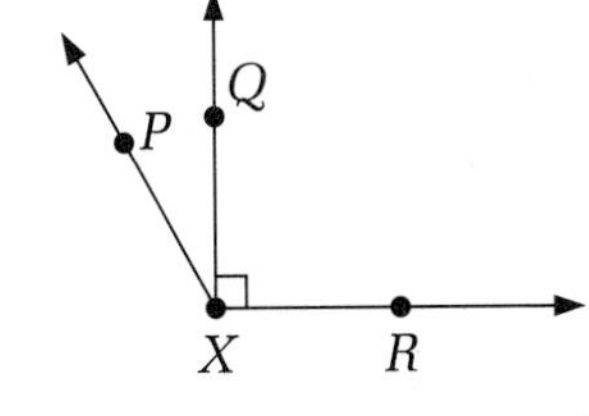

1. Name a right angle.
2. Name an obtuse angle.
3. Name an acute angle.
4. Estimate the measure of $\angle PXQ$.
5. Suppose $\angle PXQ$ has measure 32°. Find the measure of $\angle PXR$.

In the diagram, $\angle CKD$ is a right angle, and $\overrightarrow{KE}$ bisects $\angle DKF$. Find the measure of each angle without estimating or using a protractor.

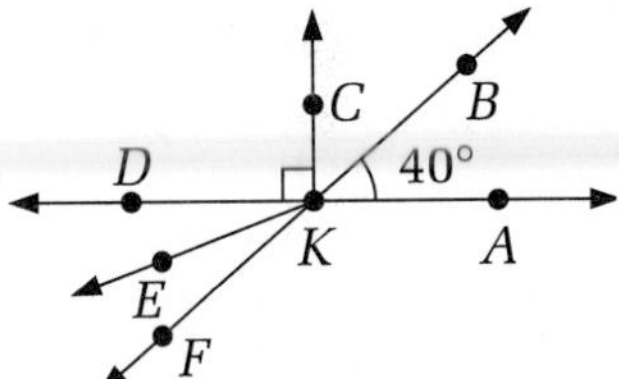

6. $\angle CKB$
7. $\angle FKA$
8. $\angle DKF$
9. $\angle DKE$
10. $\angle CKF$
11. $\angle BKE$

For each set of given information, find the missing angle measure.

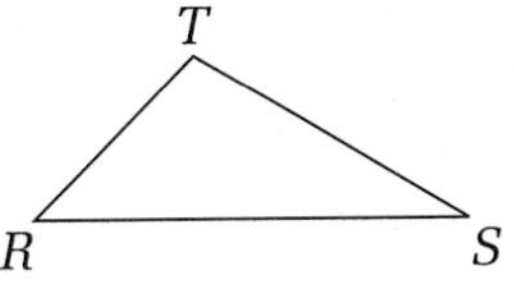

12. $\angle R = 45°; \angle T = 100°; \angle S = \underline{?}$
13. $\angle S = 32°; \angle T = 108°; \angle R = \underline{?}$
14. $\angle R = 56°; \angle S = 33°; \angle T = \underline{?}$
15. $\angle XPW = 75°; \angle WPY = \underline{?}$
16. $\angle XPV = 115°; \angle XPW = \underline{?}$
17. $\angle WPY = 125°; \angle VPX = \underline{?}$

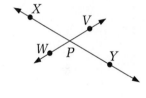

The circle graph at the right shows the distribution of household electricity use in the United States in 1987.

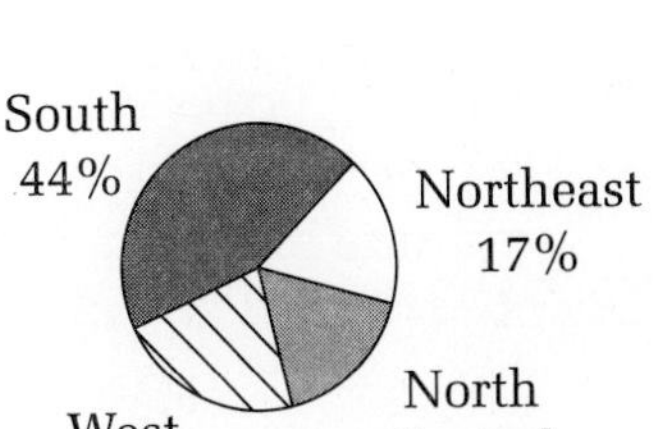

18. Which region is shown by an obtuse angle?
19. Which regions have central angles of equal measure?
20. Which region's angle is closest to a right angle?
21. *Open-ended* Draw a scalene triangle or cut one out of paper. Measure the three sides and list the measures in a column from largest to smallest. Do the same for the three angles. What do you notice about the side-angle pairs that are in the same slot in each list? Try the same procedure for several more triangles. Make a conjecture.

Name ______________________ Date ____________

Practice 14

For use with Section 2-6

Simplify.

1. $(3x)(3x)$
2. $(5a)(6b)$
3. $(-2p)(7q)$
4. $5(3n^2)$
5. $(2r)(2r)(2r)$
6. $(-4t)(6t)(-2t)$
7. $7x + 2x$
8. $9y - 6y$
9. $-8z^2 + 3z^2$
10. $3n - 5n^2 + 8n$
11. $-2k^2 + k - k^2 + 5k$
12. $x^3 - 4x^2 - 3x^3 + 7x + 4x^2$
13. $2y^2 - 3y + 4y - y^2 + 10$

Write and simplify an expression for (a) the perimeter and (b) the area of a rectangle with the given dimensions.

14. $3n, 5n$
15. $7v, 4$
16. $6t^2, 3t$
17. $6y, 4y + 5$

Write and simplify an expression for the volume of a box with the given dimensions.

18. $3c, c, 2c$
19. $5, w, 3w$
20. $4, a, a^2$
21. $d, 2d, 3d + 1$

Write and simplify an expression for the sum of the angles in each figure.

22. 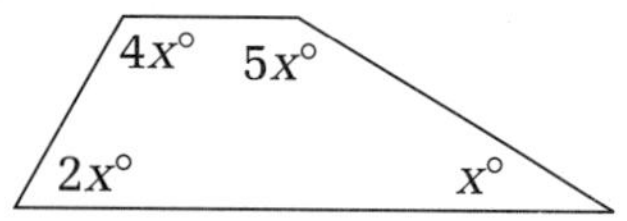

23.

24. Packing boxes are made with dimensions $6x$ in., $8x$ in., and x in., for various values of x. Write and simplify an expression for the volume of a box, and find the volume of boxes in which $x = 2$, $x = 3$, and $x = 5$.

The box at the right is to be made from six rectangles, two of each of the rectangles shown.

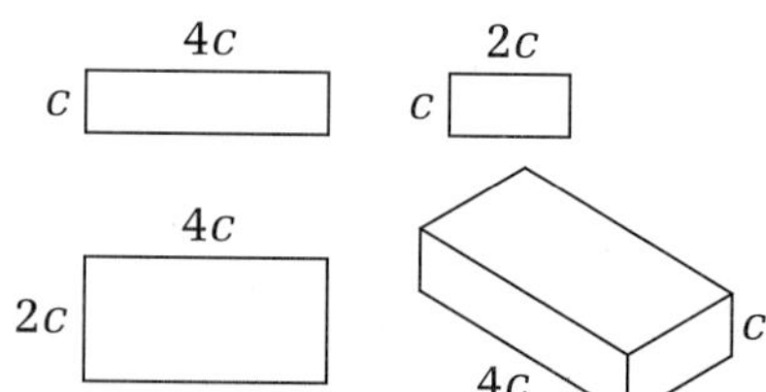

25. Write and simplify an expression for the total area of the outside of the box.
26. Write and simplify an expression for the volume of the box.

Name ______________________________ Date ______________

Practice 15

For use with Section 2-7

Solve each equation.

1. $a + 25 = 13$

2. $b + 12 = -8$

3. $r - 15 = -2$

4. $7 + d = 22$

5. $-3 + q = 5$

6. $u + 17 = 17$

7. $5j = 60$

8. $7p = 63$

9. $10y = 180$

10. $2n - 5 = 17$

11. $9 + 2m = 35$

12. $3x - 7 = 41$

13. $6 = 4k - 30$

14. $y + y - 9 = 55$

15. $c + 10 + c = 18$

16. $8 + 7w = 29$

17. $3b - b + 5 = 7$

18. $8t - 19 + t = 35$

Write and solve an equation to find each unknown angle measure in each figure. (*Note:* The sum of the measures of the angles of a quadrilateral is 360°.)

19.

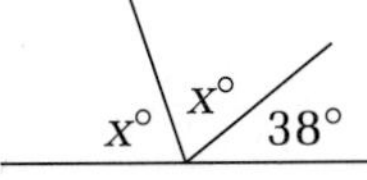

20.

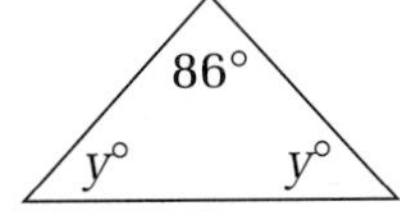

21.

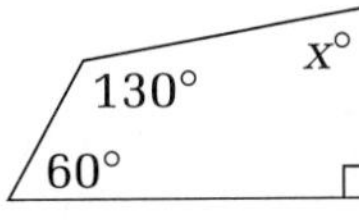

22.

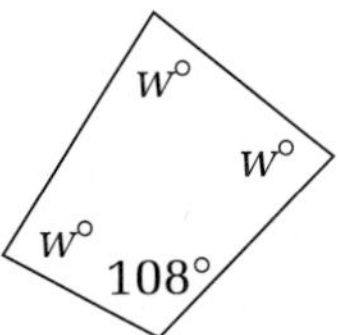

23.

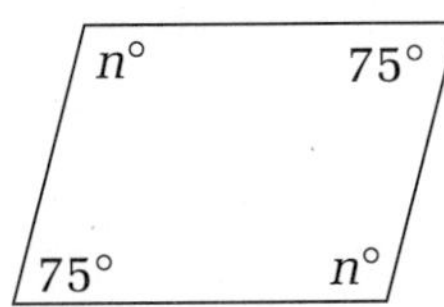

24.

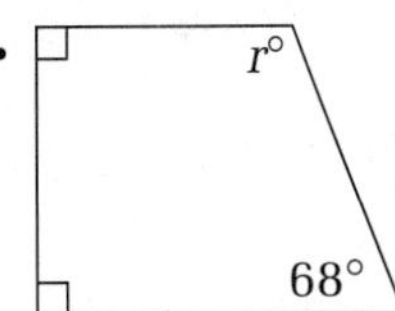

25. The perimeter of a trapezoid is 25 cm. Three sides of the trapezoid have length x cm. The fourth side has length 7 cm. Write and solve an equation to find the value of x.

26. Two sides of a kite are each 34 in. long. Each of the other two sides has length y in. Suppose the perimeter of the kite is 104 in. Write and solve an equation to find y.

Yi-Qian jogs around her block to keep in shape. Her block is a rectangle. She has found that one side of the rectangle is twice as long as the other. Suppose x stands for the length of the shorter side of the rectangle.

27. Write an expression for the length of the longer side, using x.

28. Suppose the perimeter of the rectangle is 1440 ft. Write an equation to find x, and solve the equation.

Name ______________________ Date ______________

Practice 16

For use with Section 2-8

Solve.

1. $4a + 3a = -35$

2. $2n - 17 = 15$

3. $-5c + 39 = -6$

4. $\frac{d}{2} + 6 = 8$

5. $5 + 3x = -19$

6. $\frac{y}{4} + 7 = 9$

7. $\frac{k}{3} - 5 = 4$

8. $-2n + 17 = -5$

9. $3a - 7a = 52$

10. $5p - 63 = 12$

11. $6q + 13 = -20$

12. $-9 = \frac{m}{6} + 2$

13. $1.2w - 5 = 10$

14. $5.5v - 3.3v = 7.7$

15. $8 - \frac{x}{4} = 2.5$

16. $3.2z + 4 = -0.8$

17. $-3.6t + 7.6 = 0.4$

18. $0.06x - 5 = 16$

19. $5.3y + 6.5y = 53.1$

20. $\frac{m}{2} - 3.4 = -6.5$

21. $-\frac{k}{5} + 0.8 = 1.2$

22. $\frac{x}{1.5} - \frac{x}{3} = 7$

23. $5.2b + 15 = 8.5$

24. $12a - 51 = -53$

25. $-6.4\text{k} + 3.5 = -7.7$

26. $\frac{c}{1.2} - 6.5 = 7$

27. $8 - \frac{m}{4.5} = 2.6$

28. Felipe bought two compact discs. He gave the cashier at the store \$30 and got \$2.10 change. One disc cost \$11.95. How much did the other disc cost? Let c = the cost of the other disc.

29. Mike Wei's construction company has a project that Mike figures will take his workers 182 hours to complete. His workers work 7 hours a day. How many working days will it take to complete the project? Let k = the number of working days to complete the project.

30. Sumi bought the same number of bran muffins and bagels at the bakery. Bran muffins cost \$.35 each, and bagels cost \$.45 each. Sumi spent \$5.60 altogether. How many of each item did she buy? Let n = the number of muffins or the number of bagels she bought.

31. Anna Gallagher and two friends want to rent an apartment. The three of them will split the rent evenly. Anna figures that food will cost her \$225 each month, and she can afford to spend a total of \$400 on food and her share of the rent. What should be the rent on an apartment in order for it to fit Anna's budget? Let r = the rent on the apartment.

Name ______________________ Date ______________

Practice 17

For use with Section 2-9

Find the square roots of each number.

1. 49 **2.** $\frac{1}{64}$ **3.** 1.69 **4.** $\frac{4}{81}$

5. 0.0036 **6.** 2500 **7.** 0.0121 **8.** 90,000

Find the cube root of each number.

9. 27 **10.** $\frac{1}{1000}$ **11.** $\frac{8}{125}$ **12.** 0.008

13. 0.027 **14.** 64,000 **15.** 0.125 **16.** 0.216

Tell whether each number is rational or irrational.

17. 23.6 **18.** $\frac{3}{7}$ **19.** $\sqrt{10}$ **20.** $1.6\overline{3}$

Estimate each square root within a range of two integers. Then use a calculator to find each square root to the nearest hundredth.

21. $\sqrt{30}$ **22.** $\sqrt{12}$ **23.** $\sqrt{106}$ **24.** $\sqrt{0.5}$

Estimate each cube root within a range of two integers. Then use a calculator to find each cube root.

25. $\sqrt[3]{15}$ **26.** $\sqrt[3]{35}$ **27.** $\sqrt[3]{5}$ **28.** $\sqrt[3]{1020}$

29. The current I (in amps) drawn by an appliance is given by the formula $I = \sqrt{\frac{P}{R}}$, where P is the power rating of the appliance (in watts) and R is its resistance (in ohms). What current is drawn by a 1500-watt toaster-oven with a resistance of 9.6 ohms?

30. The approximate time T (in seconds) for a pendulum L meters long to make a full swing is given by the formula $T = 6.3\sqrt{\frac{L}{10}}$. How many seconds will it take a pendulum 2 meters long to make a full swing?

31. ***Open-ended*** Convert several fractions to decimals on your calculator. First try fractions with small denominators, like 3, 7, 9, and 11. Then try fractions with larger denominators. Are all the numbers that you are using rational? Can you always tell from the calculator's display that the decimals are repeating? Explain.

Name ______________________ Date ______________

Practice 18

Cumulative Practice through Unit 2

Some Mayan numerals and their modern equivalents are shown below.

• • 2  8 ▬ ▬ 10  16

Tell what number each Mayan symbol represents.

1. • • •

2. • over ▬

3. • • • • over ▬ ▬

4. ▬ ▬ ▬ ▬

Write as a power of 10.

5. $10 \cdot 10 \cdot 10 \cdot 10 \cdot 10$ **6.** $10^5 \cdot 10^3$ **7.** $10 \cdot 10^8$

8. $10^5 \cdot 10^2 \cdot 10^3$ **9.** $\frac{10^7}{10}$ **10.** $\frac{10^{15}}{10^3}$

Simplify.

11. $-5 - 31$ **12.** $17 - (-12)$ **13.** $-26 \div 2$ **14.** $(-4)(-18)$

15. $(-29 + 8) \div 3$ **16.** $5 + (-3)(6) - 4$ **17.** $15 - 2(-8 + 14) \div 3$

Write and solve an equation to find each unknown angle measure.

18.

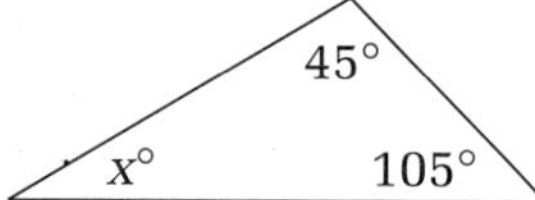

19.

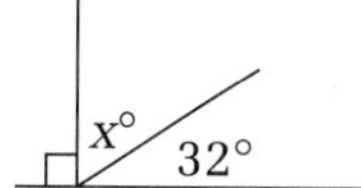

20.

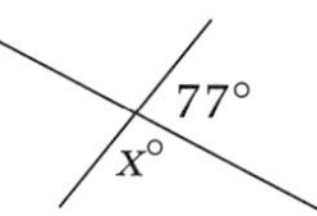

21. The edges of a rectangular box have lengths k cm, $3k$ cm, and $5k$ cm. Write and simplify an expression for the volume of the box.

22. A triangle has sides of length x^2 in., $2x^2$ in., and $5x$ in. Write and simplify an expression for the perimeter of the triangle.

23. Gregory Chan bought 10 ft of copper tubing and fittings to upgrade his hot-water system. The fittings cost \$5.25, and the total for the fittings and tubing came to \$12.75. What was the cost per foot of the copper tubing?

24. Felipe Peña brought 3 water bottles, all filled to the same level, on a day hike. During the hike, he drank 35 oz of water. At the end of the day, he had 16 oz of water left. At the start of the day, how many ounces of water were there in each water bottle?

Name ______________________ Date ______________

Practice 19

For use with Section 3-1

Federal Aid to Education (in billions of dollars)

	1984	1988	1990	1992
Elem. & Sec.	4.3	5.7	7.2	8.8
Handicapped	2.4	3.1	3.5	5.3
Voc. & Adult	1.0	1.0	1.1	1.9
College Aid	7.5	8.8	11.1	15.3

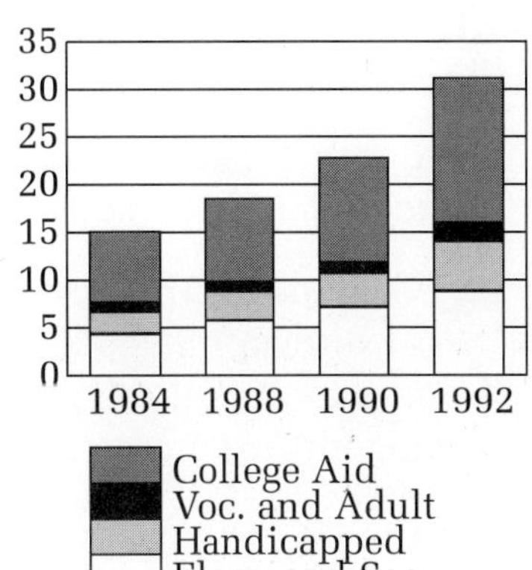

For Exercises 1–7 use the matrix and the stacked bar graph. The graph was drawn using the data in the matrix.

How much in rederal aid was spent in each category?

1. Elementary and wecondary aid in 1988

2. Aid for handicapped in 1992

3. Aid for vocational and adult education in 1984

4. Aid for college education in 1990

Tell what each number represents.

5. The second number in the fourth row

6. Which category of federal aid grew the least (in dollars) between 1984 and 1992?

7. Which category grew the fastest (in dollars)?

For Exercises 8–12 use the matrix and graph on population of U.S. cities.

Population of U.S. cities (in millions)

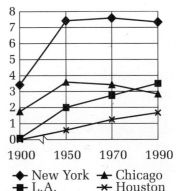

	1900	1950	1970	1990
New York	3.4	7.6	7.9	7.3
L. A.	0.1	2.0	2.8	3.5
Chicago	1.7	3.6	3.4	2.8
Houston	0.04	0.6	1.2	1.6

8
7
6
5
4
3
2
1
0
1900 1950 1970 1990
New York Chicago
L.A. Houston

8. Which two cities lost population between 1970 and 1990?

9. Did the same two cities lose population between 1950 and 1970?

10. Which city gained most in population between 1950 and 1990?

11. What was the ranking of the cities from largest to smallest population in 1970?

12. Which two cities traded rankings between 1970 and 1990?

Name ______________________ Date ______________

Practice 20

For use with Section 3-2

For Exercises 1–4, use the table of National League home run leaders.

National League Home Run Leaders (1985–1992)

Year	Leader	HRs
1985	Dale Murphy	37
1986	Mike Schmidt	37
1987	Andre Dawson	49
1988	Darryl Strawberry	39
1989	Kevin Mitchell	47
1990	Ryne Sandberg	40
1991	Howard Johnson	38
1992	Fred McGriff	35

1. Find the mean, the median, and the mode(s) of the home run data.

2. Which of the three numbers that you found in Exercise 1 gives the least accurate indication of the typical number of home runs hit by a home run leader?

3. Are there any outliers in the data?

4. What is the range of the data?

For each set of data, find the mean, the median, and the mode(s).

5. Judges' scores for one contestant at a diving competition: 7.8, 5.6, 8.3, 6.4, 8.3, 7.5, 7.8, 7.8, 3.2, 8.5, 8.3

6. Number of cars washed each day of a school event to raise money for a local charity: 35, 44, 31, 56, 53, 45, 60, 62, 56, 41, 56

7. Price of a pound of spaghetti at different supermarkets: $.89, $.79, $1.19, $.79, $.59, $.99, $.79, $.89, $.69, $.69

8. Attendance at school basketball games: 165, 230, 150, 185, 165, 110, 173, 224, 272

9. Normal precipitation for each month in Tampa, Florida (in inches): 2.2, 3.0, 3.5, 1.8, 3.4, 5.3, 7.4, 7.6, 6.2, 2.3, 1.9, 2.1

Ho Chan's scores on math tests so far this term are 86, 88, 68, 93, 84, 90, and 86.

10. What is the mean of her scores?

11. Name an outlier among the scores.

12. Suppose there is one more test in math this term. What will Ho Chan's score on this test have to be in order for her to end up with a mean score of 86?

13. ***Writing*** In a conversation with his math teacher, Mark argued that his score of 52 on one test was an outlier among the data and should not be counted in his average. Do you agree with his argument? How might his teacher counter this reasoning?

Name ______________________ Date ____________

Practice 21

For use with Section 3-3

Write an inequality that fits each graph.

1. 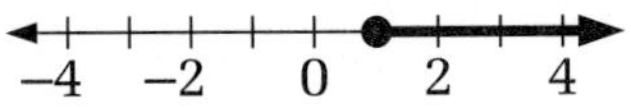

2. 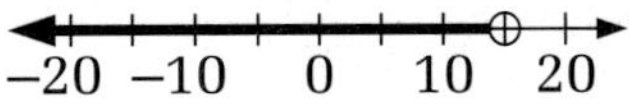

3. 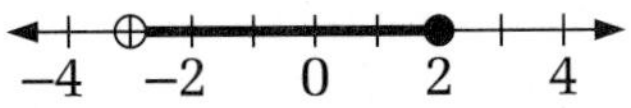

4. 

Graph each inequality on a number line.

5. $x \leq 5$

6. $x \geq -2$

7. $x \geq 3$

8. $-4 \leq x \leq 3$

9. $0 < x \leq 6$

10. $-5 < x < -1$

11. $x > 2.5$

12. $\frac{1}{3} \leq x < 1\frac{2}{3}$

13. $-\frac{1}{2} < x \leq 3\frac{1}{2}$

Write an inequality to describe the shortest interval of the number line than contains all the numbers in each group.

14. 5, –7, 3, –1, 8, 6, 2

15. 0, –1, 3, –9, –2, –4, –8

16. –1, –0.5, –1.6, –0.2, –1.2, 0

17. $\frac{1}{2}, -\frac{1}{3}, -\frac{1}{6}, \frac{1}{4}, -\frac{3}{4}, \frac{1}{5}$

Write an inequality to describe each statement.

18. All temperatures in the universe are above "absolute zero," which is –273°C.

19. In a school zone, cars can go no more than 20 mi/h.

20. Any year beginning with "19", such as 1956, is in the twentieth century.

21. The smallest distance between Earth and Mars is 35 million miles, and the greatest distance between the two planets is 248 million miles.

22. Altitudes in the Death Valley area range from 282 ft below sea level to about 11,000 ft above sea level.

23. Water can be in a liquid form between 32°F and 212°F.

24. Natural land formations on Earth vary from 29,028 ft above sea level (Mt. Everest) to 36,198 ft below sea level (the Mariana Trench in the Pacific Ocean).

Name ______________________ Date ______________

Practice 22

For use with Section 3-4

For Exercises 1–9, use the histogram at the right, showing the results of an experiment to find out the heights of specimens of a kind of tree after 3 years.

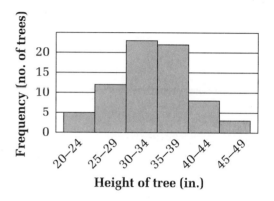

How many trees were in each interval?

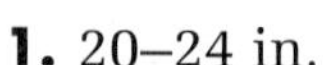

1. 20–24 in. **2.** 25–29 in.

3. 30–34 in. **4.** 35–39 in.

5. 40–44 in. **6.** 45–49 in.

7. What was the total number of trees in the experiment?

8. What interval contains the greatest number of trees?

9. What interval contains the smallest number of trees?

For Exercises 10–15, use the table below, listing the number of stories in buildings in Philadelphia, PA that are over 340 ft tall.

Number of Stories in Philadelphia Buildings							
30	29	34	30	61	52	54	53
30	33	32	44	50	40	40	7
29	37	20	33	40	40	38	39
27	33	22	18	36	38	32	25

10. Make a frequency table for the data.

11. Draw a histogram for the data.

12. What interval in your histogram has the tallest bar?

13. What numbers would you use for the stems of a stem-and-leaf plot?

14. List all the leaves for the stem 2.

15. Make a stem-and-leaf plot of the data in the table.

16. ***Open-ended*** Ask as many students in your school as you can how many hours they spend watching television in a typical week. Organize the data into intervals. Plot the data in a histogram. Think of other surveys you might make of numbers that each student might report. Construct a histogram or a stem-and-leaf plot of your data.

Name ______________________ Date ______________

Practice 23

For use with Section 3-5

Exercises 1–7 refer to the box-and-whisker plot below.

Brite-Glo Paint Employee Commuting Times (minutes)

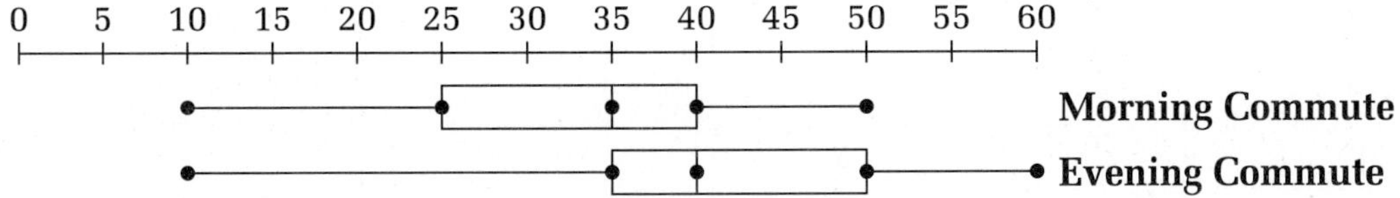

1. What were the median morning commuting time and the median evening commuting time?
2. What were the upper and lower extremes of the morning times?
3. What were the upper and lower extremes of the evening times?
4. About what percent of the morning commuting times fell between 25 and 40 minutes?
5. What percent of the evening commuting times fell between 40 and 50 minutes?
6. What percent of the evening commuting times fell above the median morning commuting time?
7. What percent of the morning commuting times fell below the lower quartile of the evening commuting times?

Henry Suarez grows two kinds of tomatoes, Great Northern and Red Giant. The tables at the right show the number of tomatoes produced by each of his plants.

8. Find the extremes, the upper and lower quartiles, and the median of the Great Northern data.
9. Construct a box-and-whisker plot for the Great Northern data.
10. Find the extremes, the upper and lower quartiles, and the median of the Red Giant data.
11. Copy the box-and-whisker plot you made for Exercise 9. Add to the copy a box-and-whisker plot for the Red Giant data.

Great Northern			
6	20	22	24
28	12	20	18
26	28	20	30
15	15	8	24
27	26	16	18
32	18	11	16
21	10	12	13
8	22	23	17

Red Giant			
15	18	16	22
19	21	22	16
17	21	12	23
28	25	16	26
22	14	19	15
18	25	26	25

Name ______________________________ Date ______________

Practice 24

For use with Section 3-6

For each kind of graph, tell whether or not each statement describes the given kind of graph.

Histogram:

1. Displays each item of data

2. Is good for data organized in intervals

3. Shows relationship of parts to whole

4. Displays frequencies

Circle graph:

5. Shows division of a whole into parts

6. Shows trends in the data

7. Angle of each "slice" indicates percent

8. Displays outliers clearly

Stem-and-leaf plot:

9. Shows trends in the data

10. Shows individual items of data

11. Shows the quartiles of the data

12. Shows the median of the data

Tell which type of graph best suits each situation.

13. A company's finance officer wants to show how the company spends its money and what percent is used for each purpose.

14. An agricultural researcher wants to compare the weights of feed consumed by six different kinds of farm animals in a month.

15. A bird-watching club wants to show the bird counts that its individual members achieved on a hike.

16. A city historian wants to display the changes in the population of two neighboring towns between 1900 and 1990. The graph should show upward and downward trends of the two populations clearly.

17. A statistician in a high school testing service wants to display the distribution of scores on a test, the median of the scores, and the interval that contained the middle half of the scores.

18. ***Writing*** Name two types of graph that you might use to display the data in the table at the right, and explain the advantages and disadvantages of each type.

Household Average Daily Electricity Usage (kWh)			
7.5	8.2	13.4	10.6
12.0	10.1	9.3	8.5
9.6	9.4	11.8	12.2
10.5	10.2	9.7	9.8

Name ______________________ Date ____________

Practice 25

For use with Section 3-7

The graph at the right compares the fuel economy of vehicles made by Consolidated Motors Company (CMC) with vehicles made by National Motors (NM). Use the graph for Exercises 1–8.

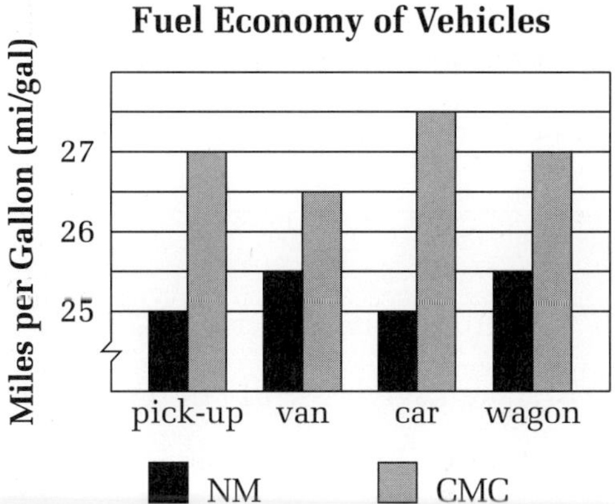

1. About how many times longer is the bar for the CMC pickup than the bar for the NM pickup?
2. What is the actual ratio of the CMC pickup's fuel economy to the NM pickup's fuel economy?
3. Does the graph give an accurate picture of the relationship between these two fuel economies?
4. How much greater is the fuel economy of CMC's car than the fuel economy of NM's car? Choose the correct letter.

   a. 1.5 mi/gal **b.** 2.5 mi/gal **c.** 25 mi/gal **d.** 27.5 mi/gal
5. What percent of the fuel economy of NM's car does the answer to Exercise 4 represent?
6. Does the graph give an accurate picture of the true relationship between the fuel economies of the two cars?
7. Do the other vehicle categories show accurately the relationship between corresponding fuel economies?
8. Suppose one of the two companies, NM or CMC, used this graph in a magazine ad. Which one do you think it was?

In Exercises 9–13, use the graph at the right, showing sales of computer disks in one area of the country.

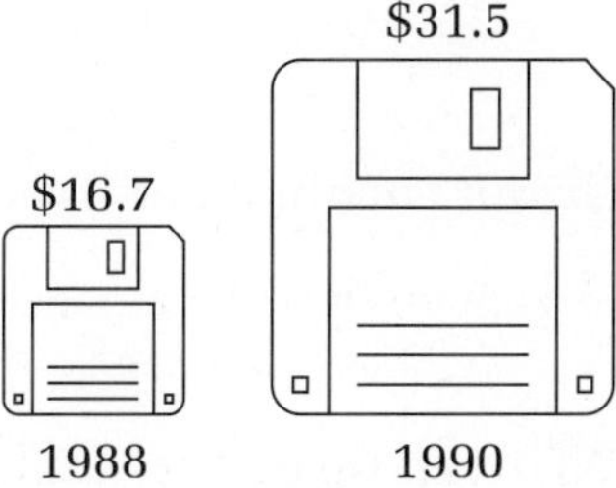

9. About how many times greater were the 1990 sales of disks than the 1988 sales?
10. Suppose the shapes are approximately square and that the width of the square for 1988 sales is x. Write an expression for the width of the square for 1990 sales, using x.
11. Using x, write expressions for the areas of the squares that represent 1988 sales and 1990 sales.
12. How many times greater is the area of the larger square?
13. Does the graph give an accurate picture of the relationship between the two sales figures?

Name ______________________________ Date ______________

Practice 26

Cumulative Practice through Unit 3

For Exercises 1–4, use a number anywhere along the scale below to estimate the probability of each event.

impossible	unlikely	possible	likely	certain
0%	25%	50%	75%	100%
0	0.25	0.5	0.75	1

1. A human being will walk on Mars within ten years.

2. Thanksgiving will fall on a Thursday this year.

3. You will have no homework in math for the rest of this year.

4. You will see a cat on the way home from school today.

For Exercises 5–9, use rectangle *ABCD* at the right. *M* is the midpoint of $\overline{AB}$ and *N* is the midpoint of $\overline{BC}$. Find each measure.

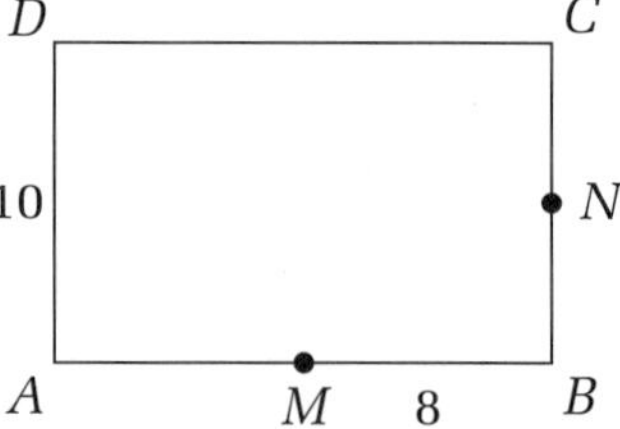

5. *AB* **6.** *BC* **7.** *CN*

8. the perimeter of *ABCD* **9.** the area of *ABCD*

Rewrite the numbers in order from least to greatest.

10. $\sqrt{10}$, 5, $\sqrt{22}$, $\sqrt{5}$, 4, 3, $\sqrt{15.1}$, $\sqrt{6}$

11. 6, $\sqrt[3]{29}$, 4, $\sqrt[3]{1001}$, $\sqrt{65}$, $\sqrt[3]{65}$, $\sqrt{75}$

Find the mean, the median, and the mode(s) of each set of data.

12. Sizes of men's shoes sold on a particular day at Walker's Shoe Store: 8, 7, 9.5, 10.5, 9.5, 6, 7.5, 7, 7, 8, 9.5

13. Points scored by a high school football team in each game: 9, 28, 20, 10, 16, 9, 17, 21, 20, 35

Graph each inequality on a number line.

14. $x > 5$ **15.** $x \leq 2$ **16.** $-1 < x \leq 3$

Write an inequality to describe each situation.

17. At sea level, water boils at or above 100°C.

18. A middleweight boxer must weight 160 lb or less.

19. Bus passengers over 12 and under 65 years of age pay full fare.

Name ______________________________ Date ______________

Practice 27

For use with Section 4-1

For Exercises 1–9, use the map below.

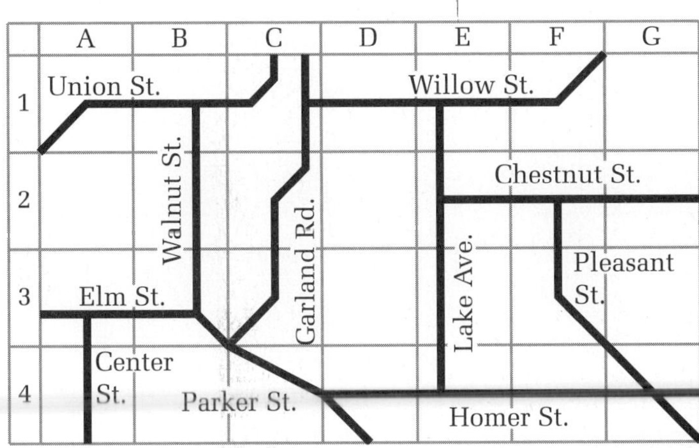

Name the street that goes through each group of squares.

1. C1, C2, C3 **2.** F2, F3, G4 **3.** B1, B2, B3

Name all the squares that each street runs through.

4. Elm St. **5.** Homer St. **6.** Union St.

7. Willow St. **8.** Parker St. **9.** Center St.

For Exercises 10–29, use the diagram at the right. Name the quadrant each point is in.

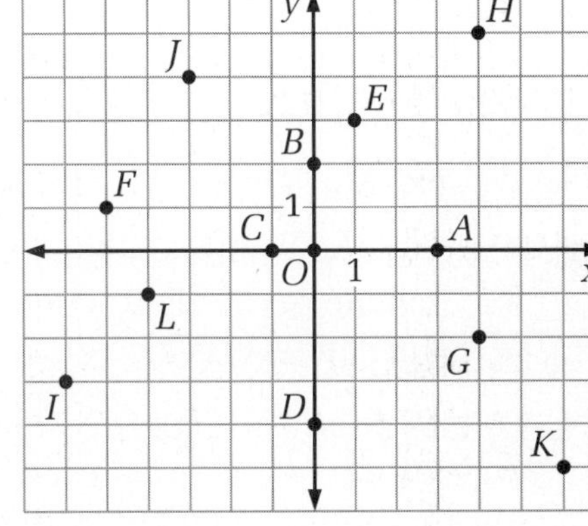

10. *E* **11.** *F* **12.** *G* **13.** *H*

14. *I* **15.** *J* **16.** *K* **17.** *L*

Name the coordinates of each point.

18. *A* **19.** *B* **20.** *C* **21.** *D*

22. *E* **23.** *F* **24.** *G* **25.** *I*

26. *J* **27.** *K* **28.** *L* **29.** *O*

30. ***Open-ended*** Draw a map of some of the streets near your home or school. Draw a grid and label your grid with letters across the top and numbers down the left side. Make up a street index, telling the labels of the squares through which each street runs.

Name ______________________________ Date ______________

Practice 28

For use with Section 4-2

Find the area of each polygon.

1.

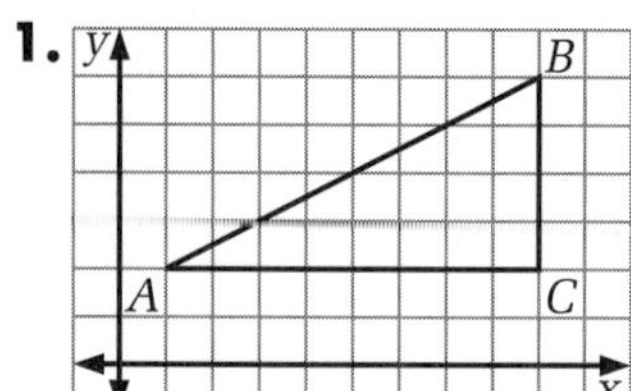

2.

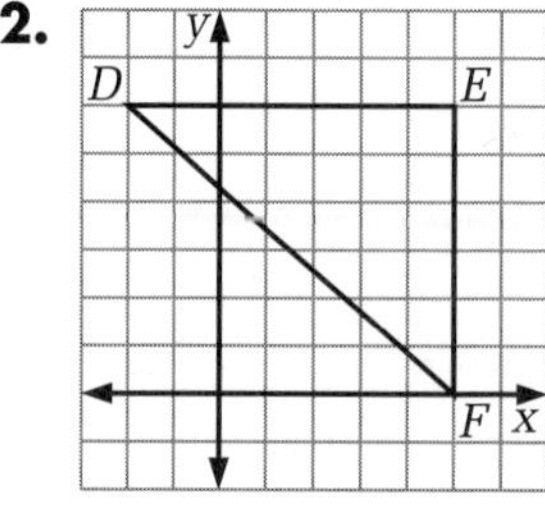

3.

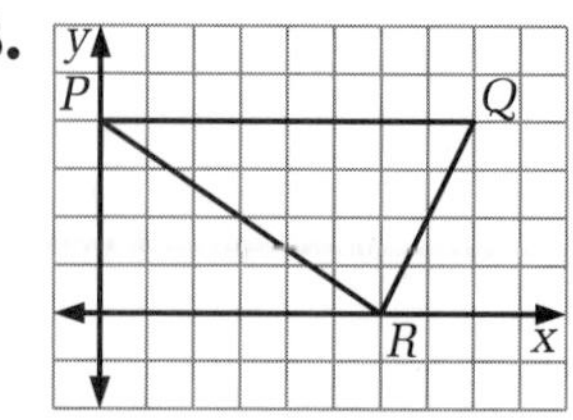

4.

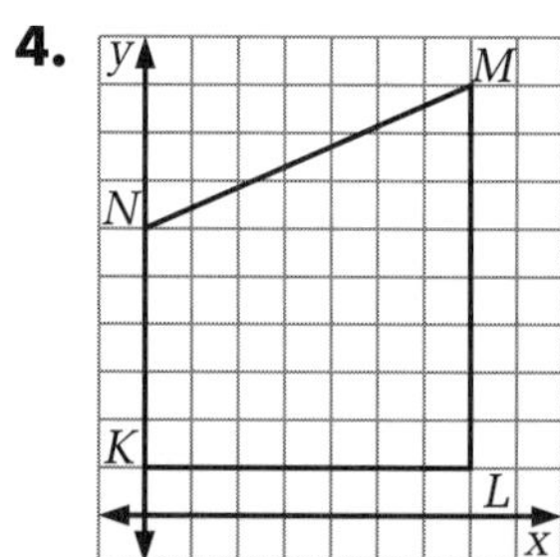

5.

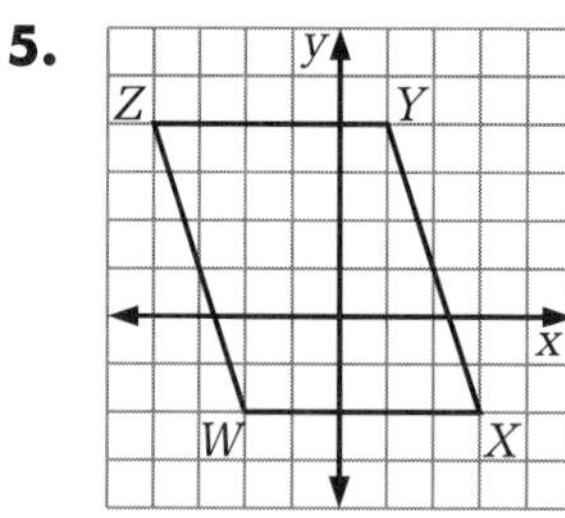

6.

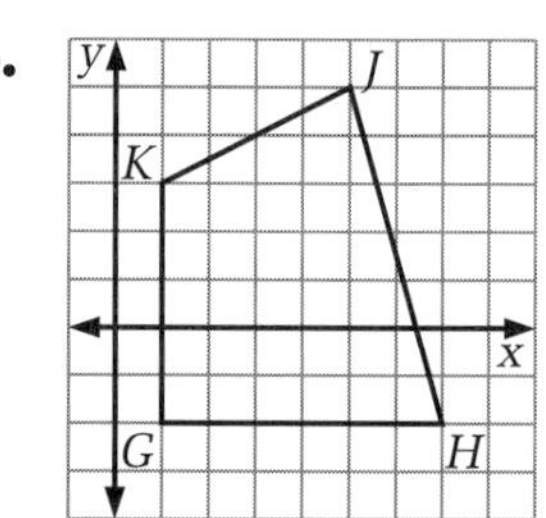

Follow these steps for Exercises 7–12.

a. **Plot the points on a coordinate plane. Connect the points in order and connect the last point to the first.**

b. **Write the specific name of the polygon you formed.**

c. **List all pairs of congruent sides.**

7. $A(1, -1)$, $B(7, -1)$, $C(4, 4)$

8. $U(-3, 4)$, $V(1, 1)$, $W(5, 4)$

9. $D(-1, 2)$, $E(3, 2)$, $F(3, 5)$, $G(-1, 5)$

10. $S(-3, 1)$, $T(5, 1)$, $U(3, 5)$, $V(-1, 5)$

11. $W(1, 0)$, $X(5, 2)$, $Y(4, 5)$, $Z(0, 3)$

12. $L(-1, 1)$, $M(2, -2)$, $N(5, -2)$, $O(-1, 4)$

13. Find the areas of the regions labeled I, II, III, and IV in the diagram at the right. Use these areas to find the area of quadrilateral *ABCD*.

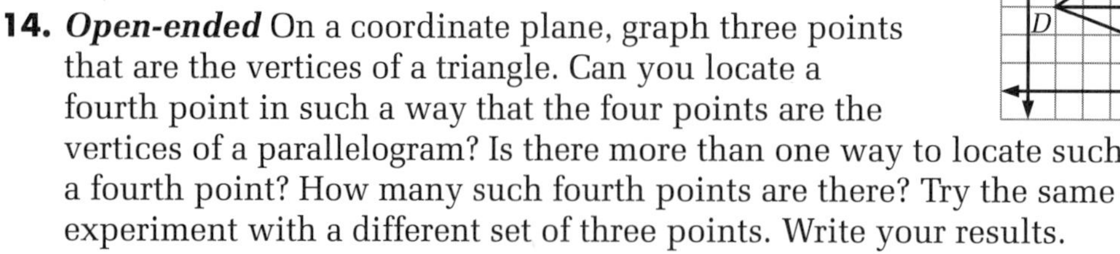

14. ***Open-ended*** On a coordinate plane, graph three points that are the vertices of a triangle. Can you locate a fourth point in such a way that the four points are the vertices of a parallelogram? Is there more than one way to locate such a fourth point? How many such fourth points are there? Try the same experiment with a different set of three points. Write your results.

Name ______________________ Date ______________

Practice 29

For use with Section 4-3

Find the coordinates of each vertex of $\triangle ABC$ after each translation.

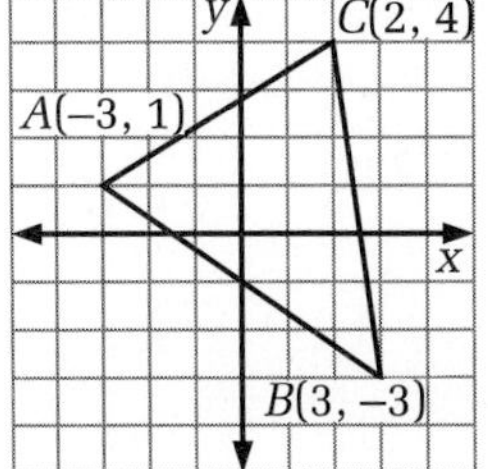

1. 1 unit right

2. 2 units down

3. 3 units up

4. 5 units left

5. 2 units right and 3 units down

6. 3 units left and 4 units up

7. 5 units right and 2 units up

Write the coordinates of P' after each translation of the given point P.

8. $P(4, 1)$; $(x, y) \rightarrow (x - 1, y)$

9. $P(3, 5)$; $(x, y) \rightarrow (x, y + 2)$

10. $P(2, 3)$; $(x, y) \rightarrow (x + 3, y - 5)$

11. $P(1, 4)$; $(x, y) \rightarrow (x - 2, y + 4)$

12. $P(-1, 5)$; $(x, y) \rightarrow (x + 2, y - 3)$

13. $P(0, -2)$; $(x, y) \rightarrow (x, y + 6)$

14. $P(-3, 0)$; $(x, y) \rightarrow (x - 7, y - 2)$

15. $P(1, 6)$; $(x + 4, y - 3)$

16. $P(-2, -4)$; $(x, y) \rightarrow (x + 5, y - 4)$

17. $P(-5, 1)$; $(x + 4, y - 1)$

Describe each translation by showing the change in the coordinates (x, y) of any point.

18. 2 units right

19. 3 units down

20. 5 units up

21. 1 unit left and 4 units up

22. 2 units right and 6 units up

23. 3 units right and 2 units down

24. 7 units left and 8 units down

25. $(3, 7) \rightarrow (4, 5)$

26. $(2, -9) \rightarrow (5, -7)$

Tell whether the pattern you find in each of the following has translational symmetry.

27. The rings of an archery target

28. The checkered flag at a car race

29. A straight brick wall

30. A basketball court

31. A maple leaf

32. A bicycle wheel

33. The lines on a page of ruled notebook paper

34. The wire fencing of a baseball backstop

Name ______________________________ Date ______________

Practice 30

For use with Section 4-4

The graphs show rotations around the origin. Describe the direction and amount of rotation of each graph.

1. 

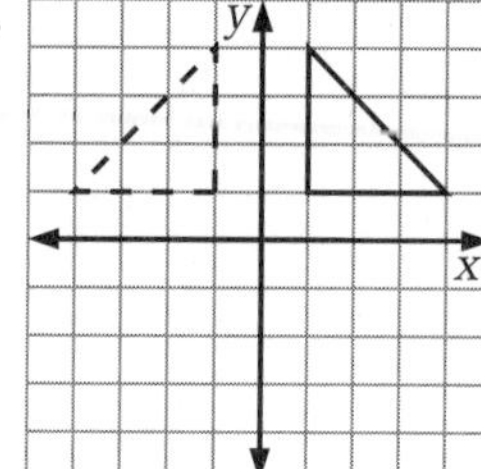

2. 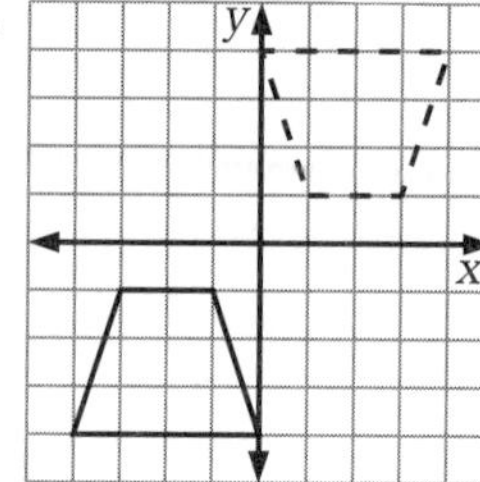

3. 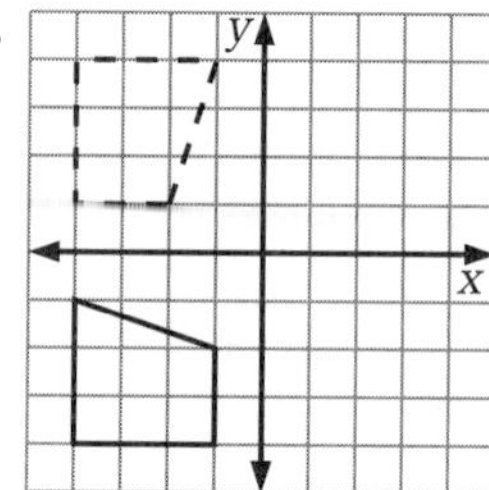

Copy the figure on polar graph paper. Draw each indicated rotation of the figure around the origin.

4. 30° counterclockwise

5. 90° clockwise

6. 180°

7. 90° counterclockwise

8. 120° clockwise

9. 60° clockwise

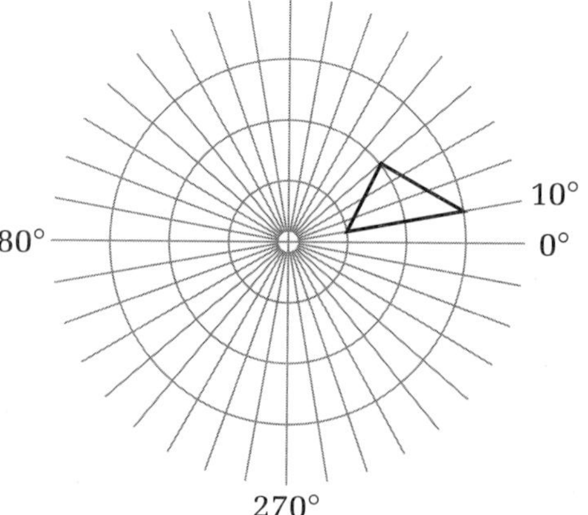

Tell whether or not each object has rotational symmetry. If it does, describe the symmetry.

10. The pattern of 5 dots on a die

11. The capital letter "N"

12. A window fan with three blades

13. The heads side of a penny

14. The outline of a stop sign

15. The head of a bolt with 6 sides

Tell whether or not each figure has rotational symmetry. If it does, describe the symmetry.

16. 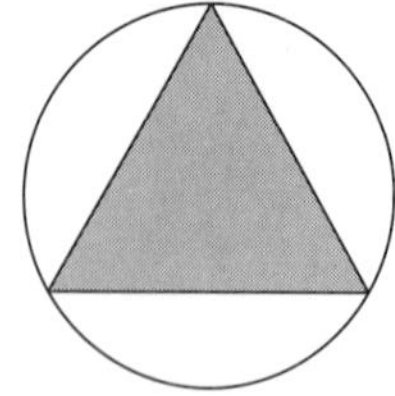

17. 

18. 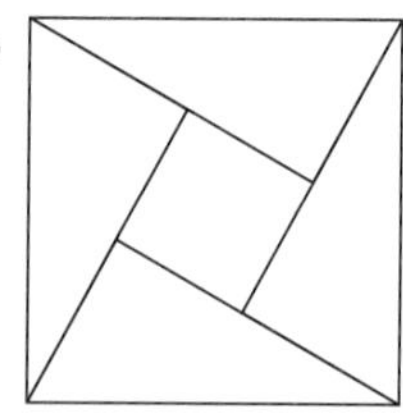

19. 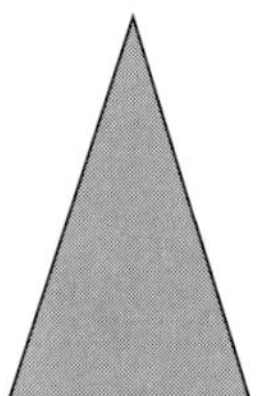

20. ***Open-ended*** Make up a table listing vehicles you see every day together with a description of the symmetry of their wheels. You can find the symmetry by counting the identical "pie slices" in the wheel and dividing 360° by this number.

Name ______________________ Date ______________

Practice 31

For use with Section 4-5

State whether each scatter plot shows a positive correlation, a negative correlation, or no correlation.

1.

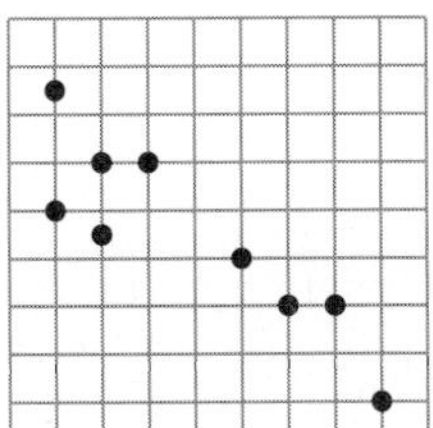

2.

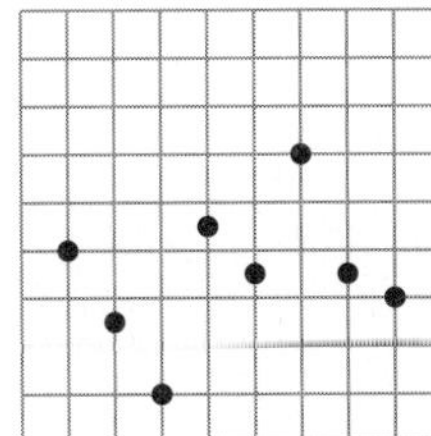

3.

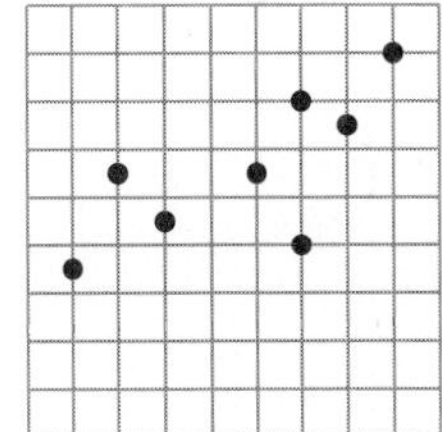

For Exercises 4 and 5, use the table at the right to make each scatter plot.

Date	Av. Temp. (°F)	Air Cond. Sales	Sweater Sales
March 10	35	3	45
March 20	40	1	42
April 1	52	5	35
April 12	63	10	21
April 30	55	16	12
May 5	76	22	5
May 15	72	26	8
May 25	85	35	2

4. Air conditioner sales versus average temperature

5. Sweater sales versus average temperature

6. State whether each of the scatter plots you made for Exercises 4 and 5 shows a positive correlation, a negative correlation, or no correlation.

For Exercises 7–11, use the table at the right, which lists data on laptop computers produced by various companies.
For Exercises 7–9, make a scatter plot of each relationship. State whether each scatter plot shows a positive correlation, a negative correlation, or no correlation.

Manufacturer	Price ($)	Weight (lb)	Ad Costs (mil. $)	Sales (units)
Leapfrog	1600	9.3	25	32,000
EZ Compr	2400	5.4	37	45,000
Link Inc.	1750	10.2	32	30,000
Future Pro	2900	6.0	50	47,000
Tec Trek	1300	11.5	20	18,000
Key Byte	2300	8.6	42	38,000
Disk Corp.	3000	5.2	24	19,000
Micro Power	2500	7.5	12	15,000
Star	2800	6.2	35	29,000
Laserkiss	1900	9.2	30	26,000

7. Price versus weight

8. Ad costs versus sales

9. Weight versus sales

10. For each of the scatter plots you drew in Exercises 7–9 that shows a positive or a negative correlation, draw a fitted line.

11. Based on your scatter plot for Exercise 7, predict the weight of a laptop computer that costs $2600.

12. ***Writing*** What conclusion can you draw from the scatter plot you drew in Exercise 9?

Name ______________________________ Date ______________

Practice 32

For use with Section 4-6

Tell whether each graph represents a function.

1.
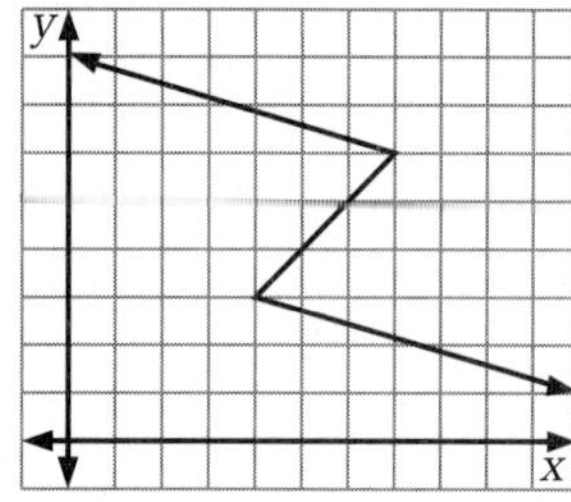

2.
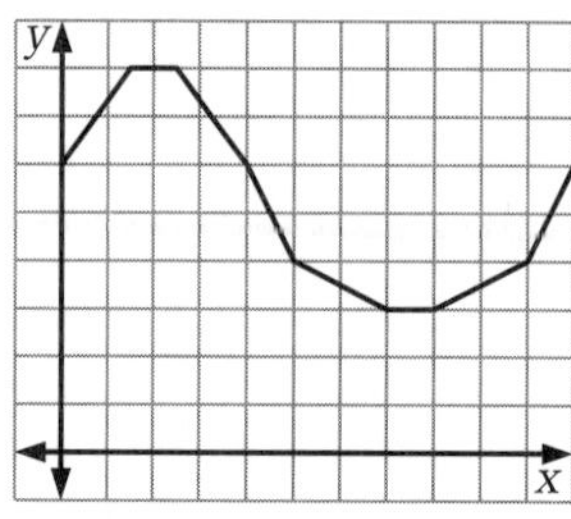

3.
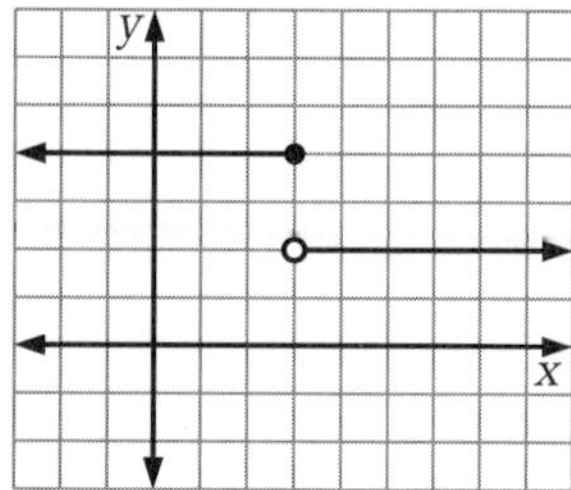

4.
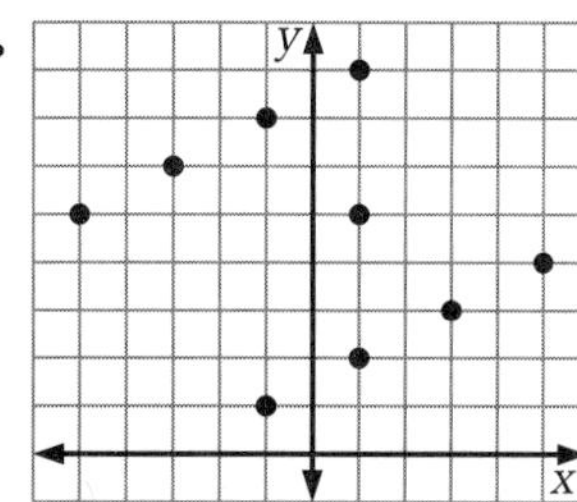

5.
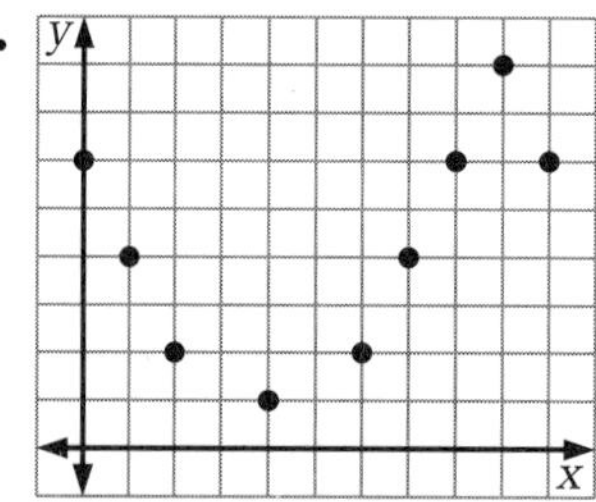

6.
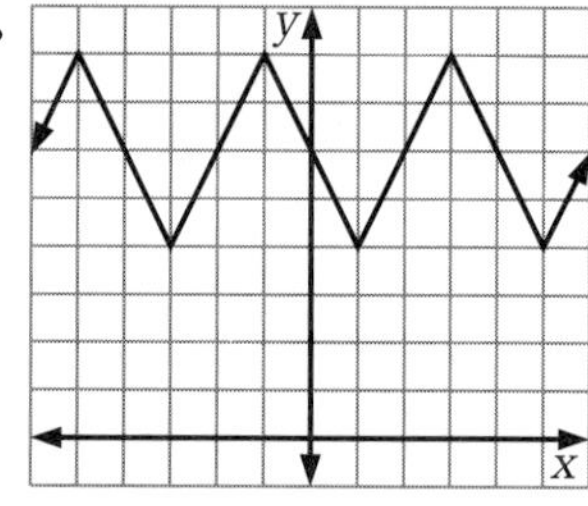

Graph each function.

7. Average Height (Girls)

Age	Height (in.)
1	29
2	33
3	36
4	39
5	41
6	44
7	47
8	50
9	52
10	54

8. Wind Chill (Temp. 35°F)

Wind Speed (mi/h)	Wind Chill Factor (°F)
5	33
10	22
15	16
20	12
25	8
30	6
35	4
40	3
45	2

9. Distance of Free Fall

Time (s)	Dist. (m)
0	0
1	4.9
2	19.6
3	44.1
4	78.4
5	122.6
6	176.5
7	240.2

10. Use the graph you drew in Exercise 7 to estimate the average height of a girl at $6\frac{1}{2}$ years of age.

11. Use the graph you drew in Exercise 9 to estimate the time required for a free-falling object to fall 120 m.

12. Use the graph you drew in Exercise 8 to estimate the windchill factor for a temperature of 35°F and a 50 mi/h wind.

13. ***Writing*** Some graphs of functions consist of dots. Others are lines or curves. How do you know whether or not to connect the dots when graphing a real-life function?

Name ______________________________ Date ______________

Practice 33

For use with Section 4-7

Write an equation to represent each function.

1.

x	y
–3	3
–2	2
–1	1
0	0
1	–1
2	–2
3	–3

2.

x	y
–3	0
–2	1
–1	2
0	3
1	4
2	5
3	6

3.

x	y
–3	–9
–2	–6
–1	–3
0	0
1	3
2	6
3	9

4.

x	y
–3	–8
–2	–7
–1	–6
0	–5
1	–4
2	–3
3	–2

In Exercises 5–19, (a) make up a table of values, using values from –3 to 3 for the control variable (use 0.5 and –0.5 instead of 0 in Exercises 17–19), and (b) graph each function.

5. $y = x + 1$

6. $y = x - 2$

7. $y = -x + 3$

8. $y = 2x$

9. $y = \frac{1}{2}x$

10. $y = -3x$

11. $y = -x^2$

12. $y = \frac{1}{4}x^2$

13. $y = 2x^2$

14. $y = -|x|$

15. $y = |x| + 1$

16. $y = \frac{1}{2}|x|$

17. $y = -\frac{1}{x}$

18. $y = \frac{6}{x}$

19. $y = -\frac{4}{x}$

Write each function as an equation. Then graph the function.

20. Suppose you drive a car at a steady speed of 50 mi/h. The distance (in miles) that you cover depends on the driving time (in hours).

21. The fare on city buses is being raised by $.25. The new fare depends on the old fare.

22. In Springfield, 40% of the money collected in taxes goes to support education. The money used for education depends on the money collected in taxes.

23. An amusement park has an admission charge of $2.00, and each ticket for a ride costs $.50. The total amount that a person spends at the amusement park depends on the number of tickets bought.

Name ______________________ Date ______________

Practice 34

Cumulative Practice through Unit 4

Simplify. Write each answer in scientific notation.

1. $3.2(4.5 \times 10^5)$ **2.** $(9.25 \times 10^3)(6.4 \times 10^4)$ **3.** $\frac{1.8 \times 10^{-3}}{3000}$

In Exercises 4–7, use the graph at the right, which shows the prices turkey farmers received for their turkeys at 10-year intervals from 1930 to 1990.

Average Turkey Price per Pound (received by farmers)

Cents: 0, 10, 20, 30, 40, 50
Year: 1930, 1950, 1970, 1990

4. In which year did farmers receive the highest price per pound for their turkeys?

5. In which year did farmers receive the lowest price per pound for their turkeys?

6. In which two 10-year spans did the prices increase most rapidly?

7. Does the graph show a steady increase in the prices turkey farmers received, a steady decrease in these prices, or neither?

The table at the right lists counts of a certain kind of bird at a wildlife preserve on successive days. Use the table for Exercises 8–10.

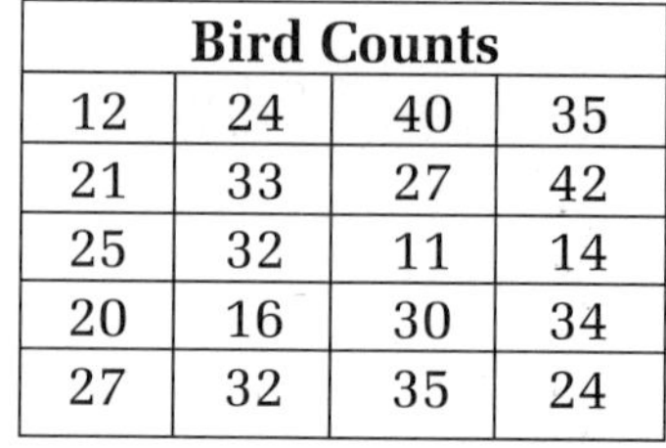

Bird Counts			
12	24	40	35
21	33	27	42
25	32	11	14
20	16	30	34
27	32	35	24

8. Make a stem-and-leaf plot using the data.

9. Find the median of the data.

10. Make a histogram from the data using the intervals 10–19, 20–29, 30–39, and 40–49.

The circle graph at the right compares audience share for four radio stations during a one-hour time period. Use this graph in Exercises 11–14.

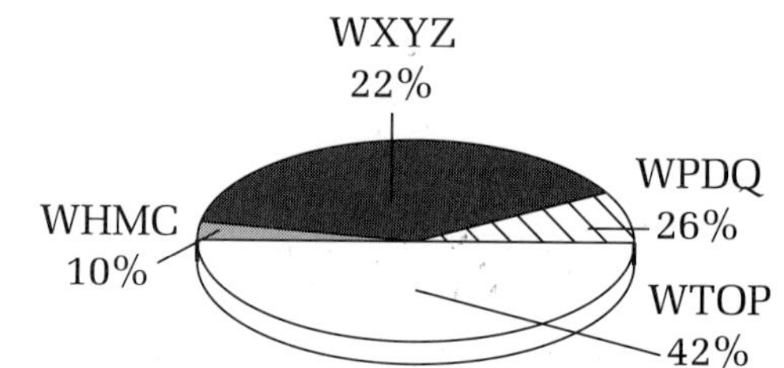

11. From the wedges in the graph, does it appear from the graph that WTOP has half of the audience during the time period?

12. Is it really true that WTOP has more than half of the audience?

13. Does WPDQ have one-fourth of the audience? Does this appear to be true from the graph? Why is this so?

14. Suppose one of the four radio stations made this graph to show prospective advertisers? Which station do you think it was?

Name ______________________ Date ______________

Practice 35

For use with Section 5-1

Model each situation using a spreadsheet or table and then solve.

1. Your summer job pays $4.50 per hour. How many hours of work will it take to earn a total of $35 for a pair of concert tickets?

2. An earthmoving company must move 80 tons of dirt from a construction site. Each of the company's trucks carries 14 tons. How many loads would one driver have to carry to do the job alone?

3. A lumber mill has 15 ft of a certain custom molding on hand. The mill can produce 18 ft of the molding per hour. How many hours will it take to fill an order for 175 ft?

4. David Jackson's job pays him $20,000 this year. Suppose that in every future year he works, his salary is 1.1 times what it was the year before. After how many years will his salary be over $32,000?

Model each situation using a graph and then solve.

5. A jetliner has completed 225 miles of a 3000-mile flight. At an airspeed of 475 mi/h, how long will it take the jetliner to reach its destination?

6. A package of tomato plant seeds states that about 85% of the seeds can be expected to sprout. Jo Stillwater wants to have 80 tomato plants. How many seeds should she plant?

Model each situation using an equation and then solve.

7. Emily Niquette pays a monthly charge of $3.40 for electricity and in addition there is a $.07 charge for each kilowatt-hour she uses. One month her bill was $12.50. How many kilowatt-hours did she use?

8. On May 5, there are 14 h 4 min of daylight in Denver, Colorado. The amount of daylight goes up by about 2 min each day. On what day in May should there be 14 h 36 min of daylight in Denver?

9. Goncalves Textiles pays an employee when the employee uses his or her own car for business. Each employee is entitled to $12.50 plus $1.80 for every mile driven. One employee is paid $228.50 for a business trip. How many miles did the employee drive?

10. ***Writing*** Describe as many situations as you can that could be modeled by the equation $7.5 = 1.5 + 0.25x$.

Name ______________________ Date ______________

Practice 36

For use with Section 5-2

Simplify.

1. $-(-4r)$ **2.** $-(5 - y)$ **3.** $-(10 - 2z)$

4. $6 - (-3p + 1)$ **5.** $x - (0.4 + 0.7x)$ **6.** $12 - (-m - 8)$

7. $a^2 - (5 - 9a^2)$ **8.** $3 + c - (4 + c)$ **9.** $3 - b - (b - 3)$

10. $n - 2(-n + 4)$ **11.** $6t - t^2 - 5(t - t^2)$ **12.** $10v - v(6 - 4v)$

Solve.

13. $9 - x = 16$ **14.** $-32 - n = -7$ **15.** $2z - 5 + z = 43$

16. $y + 17 - 4y = -4$ **17.** $-2d + 6 - 5d = 62$ **18.** $-(4 - t) = 15$

19. $-(7 + 6w) = -19$ **20.** $-(5 - 2g) = -11$ **21.** $4(8 - m) = 56$

22. $-7(5 - y) = 49$ **23.** $6 - (3 + 2n) = 25$ **24.** $5 - 2(a + 7) = 32$

25. $8 + 3(5 - b) = -10$ **26.** $k - 3(6 - k) = -14$ **27.** $6(3 - z) - 5z = -4$

28. $(5 + r) - (6 - r) = 13$ **29.** $-2(u - 5) - (u + 1) = -18$

Find the measure of each angle.

30.

$2x°$ $3(x - 5)°$

31.

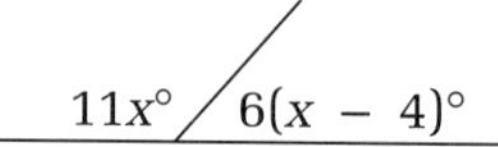

32.

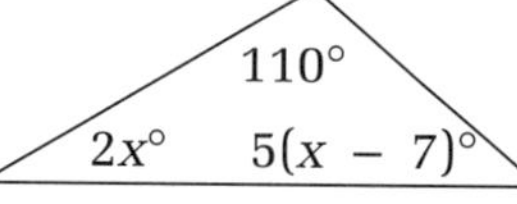

33. The sum of the measures of the angles of a convex polygon is 1980°. How many sides does the polygon have?

Lin Hsia plans to invest \$1400 in two stocks: Consolidated Industries (CI) and Amalgamated Manufacturing (AM).

34. Let x = the amount she invests in CI. Write an expression for the amount Lin has left to invest in AM.

35. Suppose that after 5 years Lin's CI stock does not change in value, but her AM stock triples, making her stocks worth \$3300. Write an equation that expresses this fact.

36. Find out how much she invested in each company by solving the equation you wrote in Exercise 35.

Name ______________________ Date ______________

Practice 37

For use with Section 5-3

Solve.

1. $3x = 4x - 5$

2. $-5t = t + 12$

3. $2w + 70 = -3w$

4. $4y + 33 = 15y$

5. $26 - 4a = 9a$

6. $-3n + 28 = -7n$

7. $2(b - 21) = -5b$

8. $-3(8 - c) = 7c$

9. $7(m - 56) = -m$

10. $-6(m + 5) = 9m$

11. $8x = -11(6 - x)$

12. $z = 5(12 + z)$

13. $0.5(102 - p) = 2.5p$

14. $0.3t = 0.8(t - 5)$

15. $5k = -2(21 + k)$

16. $-5 - d = 3(7 - d)$

17. $29 + q = -2(q - 13)$

18. $-2r - 3 = 7(11 - r)$

19. $4(n - 3) - 18 = -n$

20. $-6(8 - b) - 20 = 5b$

21. $-2(c + 7) - 30 = 9c$

Find x in each diagram.

22.
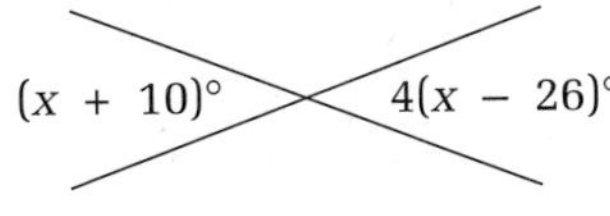

23.
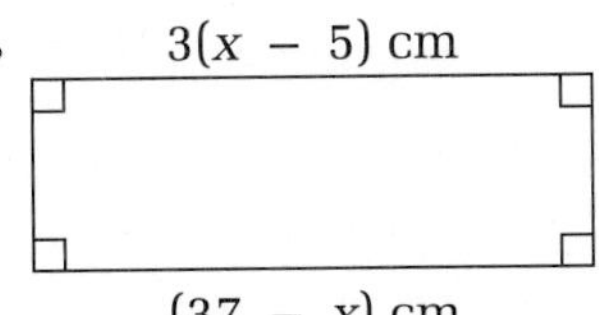

24.
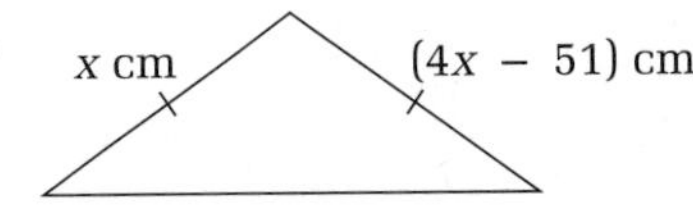

Marissa left her apartment at 7:00 A.M. riding her bike at 12 mi/h. At 7:30 A.M. Marissa's roommate Kim realized that Marissa had forgotten her lunch and set off after her, by the same route, riding her moped at 18 mi/h.

25. Let t = Marissa's travel time. Write an expression for Kim's travel time, using t. Write expressions for Marissa's distance and for Kim's distance, using t.

26. Write and solve an equation to find the time it took Kim to catch up to Marissa.

Chesterton's population is 37,500 and is growing by 650 each year. Melville has a population of 36,300 and is growing by 800 each year.

27. Write expressions for the populations after x years.

28. Write and solve an equation to determine how many years it will take before the two towns have the same population.

29. ***Writing*** Tell whether you think the expressions you wrote for Exercise 27 would be useful in predicting the populations of the towns a hundred years from now. Explain your thinking.

Name ______________________ Date ______________

Practice 38

For use with Section 5-4

Solve and graph each inequality.

1. $p + 3 < 5$ **2.** $c - 4 \geq 2$ **3.** $x - 1 > -6$

4. $7 - y \leq 2$ **5.** $-9 - q \geq -5$ **6.** $2 - v > -3$

7. $5w \geq -35$ **8.** $-3n > 9$ **9.** $-4k \leq 24$

10. $-12b < 0$ **11.** $0.27 < -0.06h$ **12.** $10d \leq -35$

13. $2u - 5 < 7$ **14.** $8 - 2r \geq 10$ **15.** $6t + 5 > -7$

16. $-3m + 22 > 4$ **17.** $9 \leq 24 - 5z$ **18.** $18 \leq -8 - 13a$

19. $2(x - 5) \leq -12$ **20.** $-4(7 - t) > -28$ **21.** $3 > -3(y + 7)$

22. $-15 \leq -3(8 + v)$ **23.** $6(w - 9) < -21$ **24.** $-10(5 - c) \leq 25$

25. Fashion Statement, Inc. makes men's shirts for department stores. A store needs at least 525 shirts. The company has 84 shirts in its stock. Write and solve an inequality to find the number of shirts the company will have to make to fill the store's order.

26. An elevator has an inspection certificate stating that the maximum weight the elevator can carry is 2100 lb. Suppose each person who takes the elevator weighs 140 lb. Write and solve an inequality for the number of persons the elevator can carry.

27. Miguel Santos saves \$65 a week out of his salary toward a vacation trip. Suppose the trip will cost at least \$1430. Write and solve an inequality to find the number of weeks it will take him to pay for his vacation trip.

28. Dugungi's hardware store has 17 pitchforks in its inventory. The store manager estimates that the store will need over 65 pitchforks for the coming growing season. Pitchforks are packed 4 to a box. Write and solve an inequality to find the number of boxes of pitchforks Dugungi's should order.

29. Mei Ling Won wants to keep her local telephone bill under \$20. The phone company charges a base rate of \$5.60 each month and \$.24 for each message unit used. Write and solve an inequality to find how many message units she can use.

30. A supermarket manager wants to price a box of cereal. During a sale in which each box is marked \$1.50 off, the manager wants 5 boxes to sell for less than 3 boxes did before the sale. Write and solve an inequality to find the price the supermarket should charge for a box of cereal.

Name ______________________________ Date ______________

Practice 39

For use with Section 5-5

Solve each equation for the variable indicated.

1. $C = 2\pi r$ for r

2. $V = \pi r^2 h$ for h

3. $T = kPV$ for P

4. $E = k + p$ for p

5. $y = mx + b$ for b

6. $E = I^2 R$ for R

7. $ax + by = c$ for x

8. $v = s + at$ for t

9. $w = 3m - 4k$ for k

10. $s = \frac{u}{1 - r}$ for r

11. $I = p(1 + r)$ for r

12. $m = \frac{360}{n}$ for n

For Exercises 13 and 14, suppose there is an 8% sales tax on all items purchased at a craft supplies store.

13. Write a formula to show the total amount T, including tax, that you would pay for items at the store that cost c dollars altogether.

14. Brian Chung wants to spend \$81, including tax, for a gift certificate. What amount will the gift certificate show?

For Exercises 15–17, suppose Felicia has saved \$140 and plans to save an additional \$15 each week out of the salary she makes at her part-time job.

15. Write a formula to show the total amount d that she has saved after w weeks.

16. Rewrite the formula you found in Exercise 15 to show the number of weeks w it will take Felicia to save d dollars.

17. Use the formula you found in Exercise 16 to calculate how many weeks it will take Felicia to save \$410 to buy a guitar.

For Exercises 18 and 19, suppose Takeisha has made 34 free throws so far this season in basketball. She has made 75% of her free-throw shots.

18. Suppose she continues to hit 75% of her free-throw shots. Write a formula to show the total number of free throws f that Takeisha can expect to have made after her next s shots.

19. Use the formula you found in Exercise 18 to find how many more shots Takeisha needs to take if she wants to equal the league record of 55.

Name ______________________ Date ______________

Practice 40

For use with Section 5-6

Solve.

1. $-6x = 15$

2. $\frac{3}{4}w = -24$

3. $-\frac{2}{3}k = -18$

4. $14 - \frac{3}{5}y - 1$

5. $-\frac{5}{6}p + 2 = -23$

6. $8 = -\frac{3}{7}c - \frac{1}{7}$

Solve each equation for the indicated variable.

7. $A = \frac{1}{2}bh$ for b

8. $V = \frac{1}{3}b^2h$ for h

9. $p = \frac{1}{2}mv^2$ for m

10. $V = \frac{1}{6}lwh$ for w

11. $A = \frac{2}{5}k$ for k

12. $m = -\frac{3}{4}v$ for v

13. $y = -\frac{2}{3}x + b$ for x

14. $A = \frac{1}{2}(a + b)h$ for a

15. $g = \frac{v^2}{2h}$ for h

Roberto and two roommates ordered take-out shrimp, and the three agreed to split the cost (c) equally. Let s = Roberto's share of the cost.

16. Write an equation that describes this situation.

17. Rewrite the formula to solve for c.

18. Suppose Roberto's share was \$2.63. Find the total cost of the shrimp.

Carlotta Mendez overhauled her tractor and mowed two of her five equal-sized fields. Overhauling the tractor took her 1.5 h. Let t = the time it takes her to mow all five fields, and let s = the time for the work she has already done.

19. Write an equation that describes this situation.

20. Rewrite the equation to solve for t.

21. Suppose the work she has already done took Carlotta 6.5 h. How long does it take her to mow all five fields?

22. ***Open-ended*** On a calculator, enter any number other than 0 or 1. Press the reciprocal key. Press the reciprocal key again. What do you notice? Try this with other numbers. What can you say in general about pressing the reciprocal key twice? Try starting with the number $\frac{\sqrt{5} + 1}{2}$. What is unusual about the reciprocal of this number and the number itself?

Name ______________________ Date ______________

Practice 41

For use with Section 5-7

Find the area of each figure.

1.

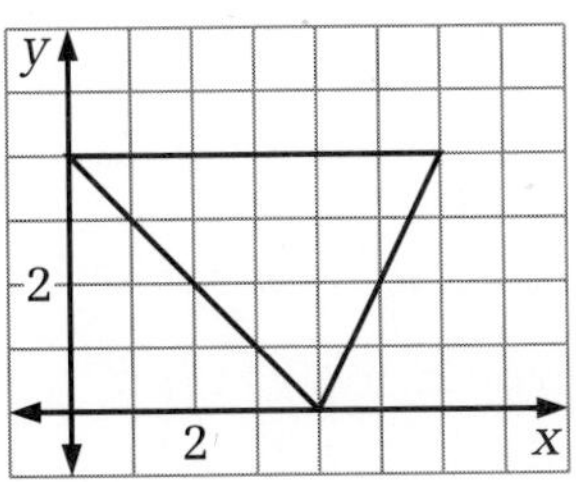

2.

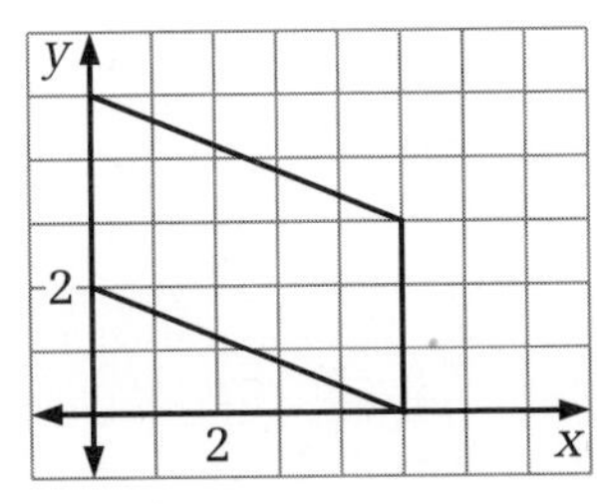

3.

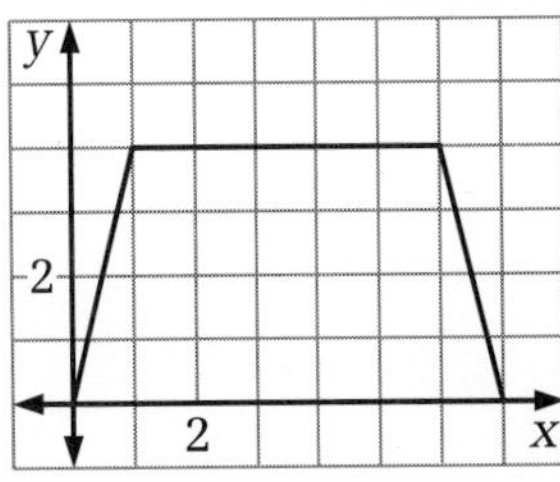

4.

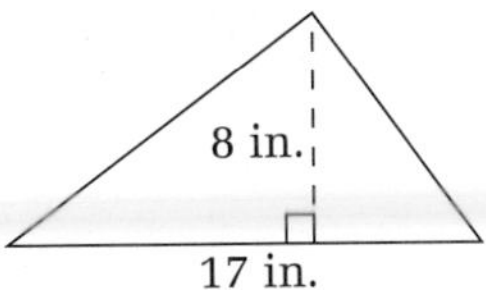

5.

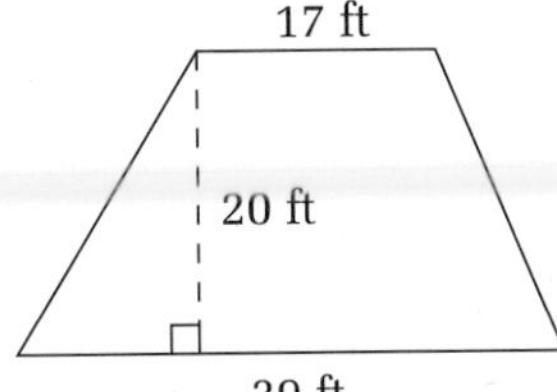

6.

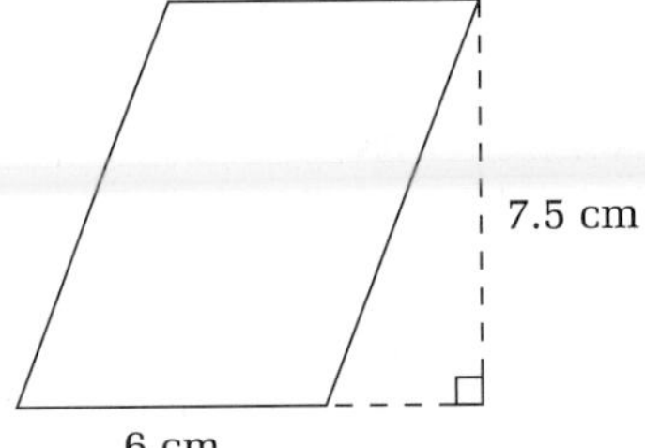

Find the area of a parallelogram having the given dimensions.

7. Base 15.8 cm; height 6.5 cm

8. Base 3.5 in.; height 6.8 in.

9. Find the base of a parallelogram having area 25.6 cm^2 and height 8 cm.

Each entry in the following tables gives information about a different trapezoid. Find x for each trapezoid.

	Base 1	Base 2	Height	Area
10.	14	18	x	80
12.	17	x	8	168

	Base 1	Base 2	Height	Area
11.	27	35	x	248
13.	x	15	6	102

14. One side of a parallelogram has length 10 in. With this side as base, the height of the parallelogram is 9 in. Another side of the parallelogram has length 15 in. What is the height of the parallelogram using this other side as the base?

15. A parallelogram has a base of $3(n - 4)$ in. The height of the parallelogram is 5 in. and its area is $7n$ in.^{2}. Find n.

16. A trapezoid has bases of length $(3x - 2)$ cm and $(4x + 1)$ cm. The height of the trapezoid is 5 cm, and its area is 120 cm^2. Find x.

Name ______________________ Date ______________

Practice 42

For use with Section 5-8

Solve each system of equations.

1. $y = 3x$
$2x + y = 5$

2. $7a - b = 32$
$b = 3a$

3. $m = -5n$
$m + 2n = 18$

4. $p = 2q + 1$
$3p - q = -12$

5. $v = 4u - 3$
$u - v = 27$

6. $3d - 5e = 30$
$d = 2e + 7$

7. $w = 5 - 3z$
$-4w + 2z = 50$

8. $8x - 3y = 49$
$y = 2x - 5$

9. $10c - 7d = -9$
$d = 3c + 6$

Rewrite one of the equations in each system to get one of the variables alone on one side of the equation. Then solve the system of equations.

10. $2x + y = 12$
$3x - 4y = 7$

11. $5c - 2d = -11$
$2c + d = 1$

12. $-3j + k = -7$
$2j - 3k = 7$

Find *x* and *y* in each diagram, using a system of equations.

13.

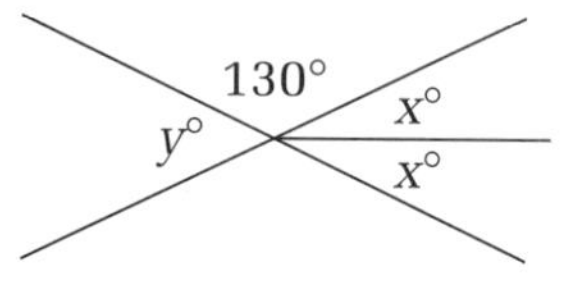

14.

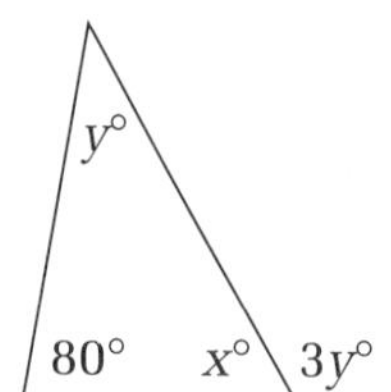

15.

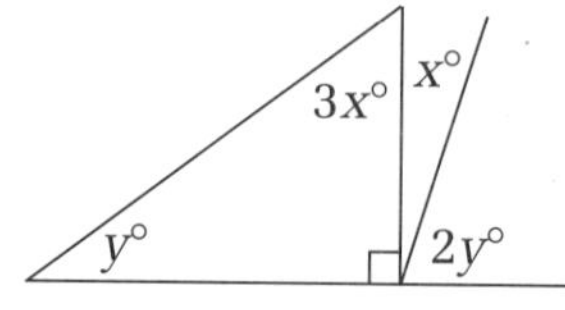

16. One angle of a triangle is 4 times as large as another angle of the same triangle. The third angle of the triangle has measure 60°. What are the measures of the other two angles of the triangle?

17. One acute angle of a right triangle is 5 times as large as the other. What are the measures of the two acute angles of the triangle?

18. The width of a rectangle is 3 in. less than its length. The perimeter is 24 in. Find the length and width of the rectangle.

19. In isosceles triangle *ABC*, each of the base angles is twice as large as the third angle. What are the measures of the three angles of the triangle?

20. ***Open-ended*** What happens when you try to solve the system

$$y = 3x$$
$$6x - 2y = 5 \quad ?$$

Suppose the number 5 in the second equation is changed to 0. What happens when you try to solve the new system? Make up some other systems like these two.

Name ______________________ Date ______________

Practice 43

Cumulative Practice through Unit 5

Make a box-and-whisker plot of the set of data.

1. Passengers entering a public transit system station per hour (weekday): 50, 165, 272, 441, 324, 266, 295, 195, 180, 220, 233, 310, 470, 368, 310, 275, 163, 152, 85, 70

Find the area of each polygon.

2. 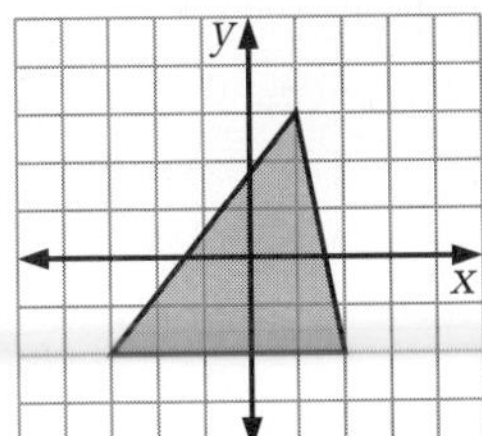

3. 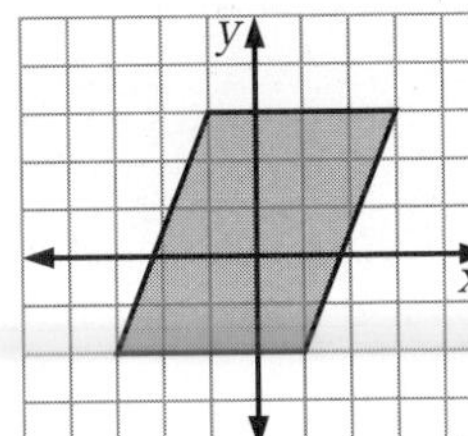

4. 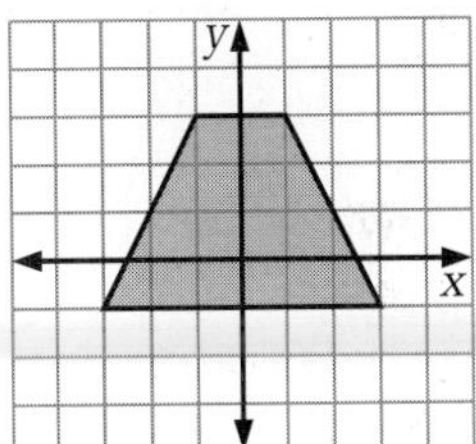

In a laboratory experiment, plants were given a certain number of hours of light per day, and their heights were measured.

Hours of light (h)	1	2	2	4	4	6	6	8	8	10
Height of plant (cm)	10	22	16	24	30	28	35	44	32	36

5. Make a scatter plot for the data in the table. Tell whether there is a positive correlation, a negative correlation, or no correlation.

Solve.

6. $15 - 2c = -7$

7. $-5 + 0.5b = 12$

8. $-4(2 - x) = 28$

Solve and graph each inequality.

9. $5x + 3 < -2$

10. $24 \geq -3(x + 2)$

11. $5x \leq 7x - 8$

Write an equation to represent each function. Explain your variables.

12. Kameisha made 48 oatmeal cookies for a party. She estimates that each guest will eat 3 cookies. The number of cookies left after the party depends on the number of guests.

13. An empty elevator cab weighs 500 lb. Suppose each person in the cab weighs 160 lb. The total weight of the elevator cab depends on the number of people in the cab.

Name ______________________ Date ______________

Practice 44

For use with Section 6-1

Express each ratio as a fraction in simplest form.

1. 11 : 55 **2.** 175 : 50 **3.** 12 to 18 **4.** 14 to 35

5. 3 min : 2 h **6.** 9 in. : 2 ft **7.** 63¢ : $9 **8.** 40 s : 2 min

Give the unit price of each item.

9. 8 pears cost $1.20 **10.** 3 rolls of paper towels cost $1.29

11. 4 tires cost $236 **12.** 12 ball-point pens cost $2.76

13. On a certain day of stock market trading, losing stocks outnumbered gaining stocks by a ratio of 7 to 3. What percent of all stocks gained in price on that day?

14. The number of miles a car can go on one gallon of fuel (mpg) is called its fuel economy. What is the fuel economy of a car that goes 224 miles on 8 gallons of fuel?

15. A photographic enlargement made from a negative measuring 24 mm by 36 mm is to have the same width to length ratio as the negative. Which of these sizes are possible for the enlargement? (There may be more than one.)

a. 8 in. by 10 in. **b.** 16 in. by 20 in. **c.** 6 in. by 9 in. **d.** 10 in. by 15 in.

16. A television news program contains 18 minutes of news and 12 minutes of commercials. What percent of program time is devoted to news?

The ratio of the volume inside one of a car's cylinders when the piston is down to the volume inside the cylinder when the piston is up is called the *compression ratio* of the engine. Find each compression ratio.

17. Down: 56 cm^3 Up: 7 cm^3 **18.** Down: 63 cm^3 Up: 9 cm^3

19. A salad dressing company found that the ratio of buyers who preferred its onion flavor to buyers who preferred its salsa flavor was 7 : 5. The company plans to produce 1,800,000 bottles of salad dressing next year. How many should be onion flavor?

20. ***Writing*** Starting with the third number, each number in the sequence 1, 1, 2, 3, 5, 8, 13, 21, 34, 55, ... is the sum of the two numbers just before it. (So the number after 55 will be 89.) Use a calculator to investigate the ratios of two numbers next to each other, such as 2 : 3, 8 : 13, and so on. What do you notice about the ratios?

Name ______________________ Date ______________

Practice 45

For use with Section 6-2

A spinner with the numbers 1 through 12 is spun. Find each probability.

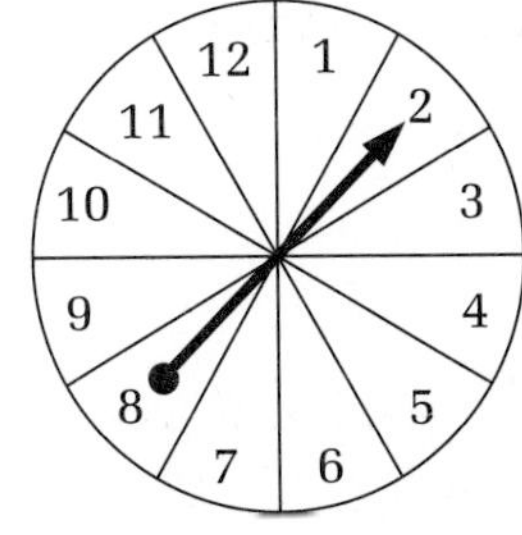

1. $P(7)$ **2.** $P(5 \text{ or } 6)$ **3.** $P(\text{odd number})$

4. $P(\text{multiple of three})$ **5.** $P(\text{even number})$ **6.** $P(13)$

A compact disc player randomly chooses a track to play out of the 18 tracks on a disc. Find the probability that the chosen track is of each kind.

7. track 6 **8.** before track 5 **9.** after track 9

Tags containing the 9 letters of the word ACOUSTICS are placed in a hat and a tag is selected at random. Find each probability.

10. $P(\text{C})$ **11.** $P(\text{A or S})$ **12.** $P(\text{vowel})$

13. $P(\text{consonant})$ **14.** $P(\text{letter after W})$ **15.** $P(\text{letter before V})$

Exercises 16–18 use the table at the right, which shows the number of vehicles passing a certain intersection in an hour. Find the probability that a vehicle passing the intersection is of each type.

	Cars	Trucks	Vans
Pre-1988	28	14	4
Post-1988	49	7	10

16. a truck **17.** a pre-1988 vehicle **18.** a post-1988 car

Use the following information for Exercises 19–21. Fred bought 5 tickets out of 100 sold on the first day of a charity raffle.

19. What was the probability of his winning the prize at that point?

20. Another 140 tickets were sold on the second and final day of the raffle. Suppose Fred did not buy any more tickets. What was the probability of his winning?

21. How many of the 140 tickets sold on the second day would Fred have had to buy in order to keep the probability of his winning the same as it was after the first day?

22. At Emma's school, the probability of having a locker on the 3rd-floor is $\frac{1}{3}$ and of having one on the 2nd-floor is $\frac{1}{2}$. All 1740 lockers are on the first three floors of the building. How many lockers are on the 1st floor?

Name ______________________ Date ____________

Practice 46

For use with Section 6-3

Solve each proportion.

1. $\frac{5}{4} = \frac{t}{36}$
2. $\frac{w}{45} = \frac{4}{9}$
3. $\frac{15}{32} = \frac{x}{96}$
4. $\frac{12}{0.12} = \frac{u}{27}$
5. $\frac{75}{z} = \frac{57}{19}$
6. $\frac{1.25}{y} = \frac{3.6}{144}$
7. $\frac{28}{48} = \frac{35}{n}$
8. $\frac{84}{q} = \frac{6}{5}$
9. $\frac{6}{1.5} = \frac{18}{z}$
10. $\frac{1000}{19} = \frac{j}{1.9}$
11. $\frac{125}{s} = \frac{25}{16}$
12. $\frac{280}{56} = \frac{h}{15}$
13. $\frac{a}{0.56} = \frac{48}{0.128}$
14. $\frac{12}{26} = \frac{18}{k}$
15. $\frac{15}{2000} = \frac{m}{3200}$
16. $\frac{7.5}{r} = \frac{13}{78}$
17. Using the numbers x, 8, 12, 15, write four proportions that each have the solution $x = 10$.

In Exercises 18–21, solve the proportion

$$\frac{x}{12} = \frac{p}{60},$$

using each of the given values for *p*.

18. $p = 5$
19. $p = 35$
20. $p = 65$
21. $p = 170$
22. In one month Margarethe earned \$540 at her part-time job, and \$81 was withheld for federal income tax. Suppose she earns \$620 next month. How much will be withheld for federal income tax?
23. A television rating service found that out of a sample of 100 households, 35 were watching Town Talk during its time slot. Suppose there are 210,000 households in a marketing region. How many of them would you expect to be watching Town Talk?
24. José Balboa left his office at 12:00 noon, and by 3:00 P.M. he had driven 126 of the 189 miles between his office and the office of a client. If he continues driving at the same speed, at what time could he expect to arrive at the client's office?
25. A 3 lb bag of lawn seed covers 5000 ft^2. Lawn seed comes in 6 lb bags costing \$7.50 and 3 lb bags costing \$4.50. What is the smallest amount it would cost to cover a 24,000 ft^2 area with lawn seed?
26. ***Writing*** The speed of a computer's processor is measured in millions of cycles (operations) per second, or *megaherz*. If you were using a computer with a 4.77 megaherz processor for your work and you switched to one with a 25 megaherz processor, how would it affect the time it took you to do your job? Explain.

Name ______________________ Date ______________

Practice 47

For use with Section 6-4

1. In a capture-recapture study, a biologist tagged and released 300 deer. A month later she captured 50 deer, 12 of which had tags. About how many deer were in the population?

2. Suppose the margin for error in Exercise 1 was ±2%. Give an interval for the population.

3. In a semiconductor company's quality control test, a machine found that 12 out of a sample of 300 computer chips were defective. How many of the 4200 such chips that the company makes each month would you expect to be defective?

4. If the margin for error in Exercise 3 was ±1%, give an interval for the number of defective chips produced each month.

For Exercises 5–9, use the graph at the right, showing the weekly mileages of bicycle riders. The graph is based on a sample of 200 responses to a helmet maker's registration questionnaire. Suppose the helmet maker sells 48,000 helmets each year. How many are sold to riders who ride each weekly mileage?

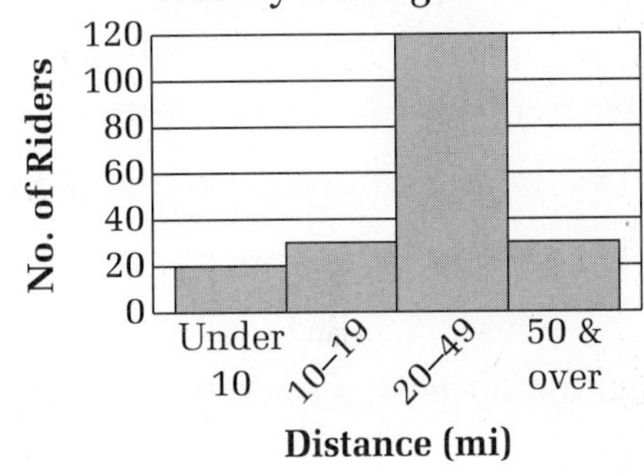

5. Less than 10 miles

6. 10 to 19 miles

7. 20 to 49 miles

8. 50 or more miles

9. How many of the helmets sold each year go to riders who ride less than 20 mi per week?

For Exercises 10–13, use the table showing voter preference of a sample of the voting-age population in a district. The voting-age population is 65,000.

	Estrada	Venzon	Undecided
Registered	36	42	18
Unregistered	21	12	31

10. About how many people have not yet registered?

11. About how many registered voters intend to vote for Estrada? How many of the registered voters intend to vote for Venzon?

12. Of all the voters in the population, how many intend to vote for Estrada? How many intend to vote for Venzon? Would a registration drive be a good idea for Estrada supporters?

13. ***Writing*** Discuss ways the undecided vote may affect the election.

Name ______________________ Date ____________

Practice 48

For use with Section 6-5

In the diagram, *ABCD* ~ *PQRS*. Find each measure.

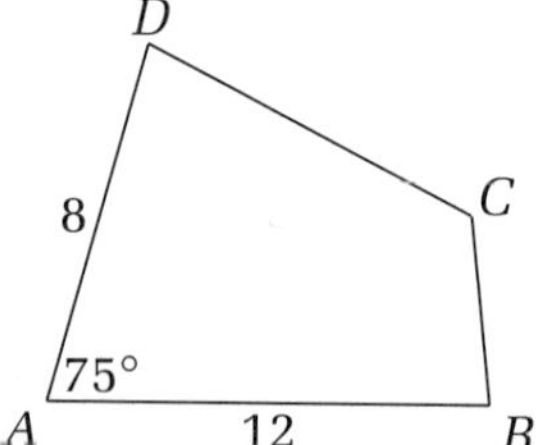

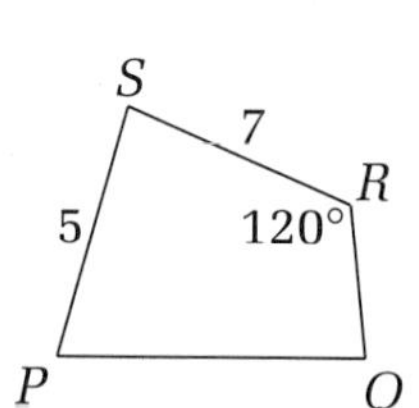

1. $\angle P$
2. $\angle C$
3. PQ
4. CD

For Exercises 5–8, refer to the diagram at the right.

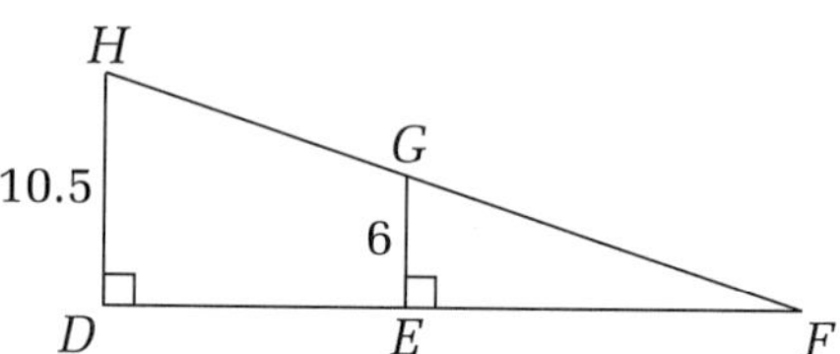

5. In the diagram, is triangle *FDH* similar to triangle *FEG*? Explain your answer.
6. If $EF = 8$, find DF.
7. If $FH = 21$, find FG.
8. If $DF = 17.5$, find EF.

A scale drawing of a proposed recreation center has a scale of 1 in. : 20 ft. Find the actual measurement corresponding to each measurement in the drawing.

9. the length of a basketball court: 4.5 in.
10. the length of a wrestling room: 2.6 in.
11. the width of a hockey rink: 4.25 in.
12. the height of a ceiling: 1.4 in.

On a map with a scale of $\frac{1}{2}$ in. : 10 mi, find the length on the map corresponding to each actual length.

13. 60 mi
14. 150 mi
15. 85 mi
16. 64 mi
17. An illustration of a microorganism in a biology book has a scale of 200 : 1. That is, each measurement in the illustration is 200 times as large as the actual measurement. What is the width of the actual microorganism if the width of the illustration is 8 cm?
18. At 3:00 P.M. the shadow of a 4 ft pole is 7 ft long. At the same time the shadow of a tree is 56 ft long. How tall is the tree?
19. Northport and Southport are 120 mi apart. If you want to draw a map on which the two cities are 8 in. apart, what should the scale of the map be?
20. ***Open-ended*** Suppose you wanted to build a scale model of your school building. Find out the actual height, length, and width of the building, and propose a scale that will allow the model to fit on the top of a table. Calculate the length, width, and height of your model. Construct the model out of cardboard or construction paper, if you can.

Name ______________________ Date ______________

Practice 49

For use with Section 6-6

Tell whether each diagram shows a dilation, a rotation or a translation.

1.

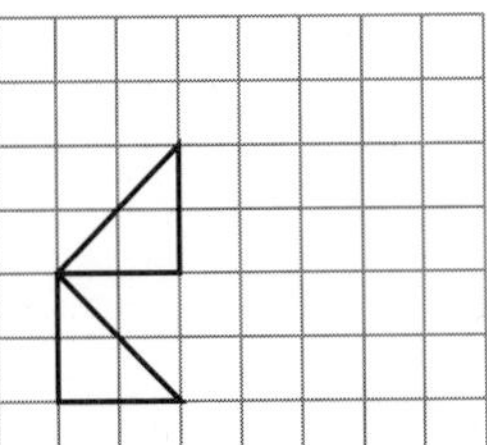

2.

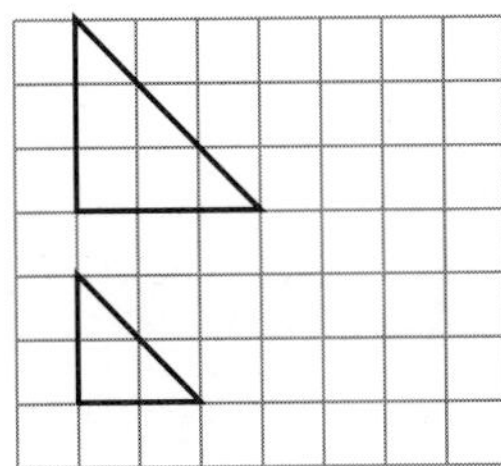

3.

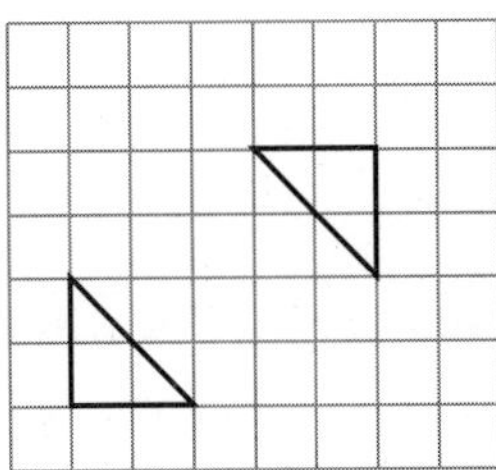

In each dilation, the smaller figure is the original figure. For each, find

a. **the center of the dilation**

b. **the scale factor**

4.

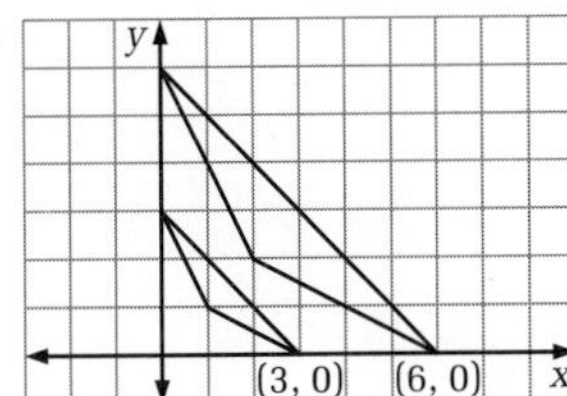

5.

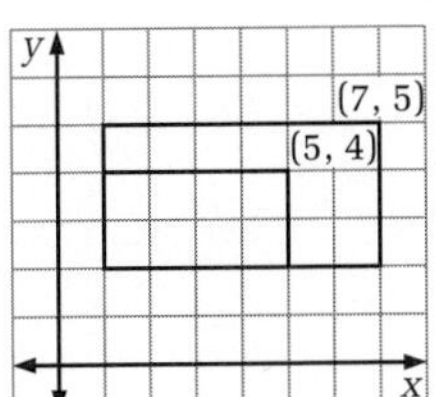

6.

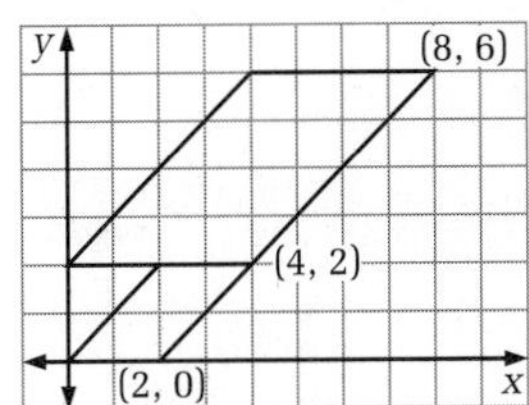

Draw a dilation of the polygon with the given vertices, using the given center of dilation and the given scale factor.

7. $A(0, 0)$, $B(1, 2)$, $C(-1, 2)$; center $A(0, 0)$; scale factor 3

8. $A(2, 1)$, $B(3, 3)$, $C(1, 4)$; center $P(-1, 2)$; scale factor 2

9. $A(4, 0)$, $B(8, 0)$, $C(9, 4)$, $D(1, 4)$ center $P(-1, 0)$; scale factor $\frac{1}{2}$

10. $A(3, 0)$, $B(0, 3)$, $C(-3, 0)$, $D(0, -3)$; center $P(9, 6)$; scale factor $\frac{2}{3}$

11. ***Writing*** Suppose $\triangle KLM$ is a dilation of $\triangle ABC$ with center P and scale factor 5. Suppose also that $\triangle XYZ$ is a dilation of $\triangle ABC$ with center P and scale factor 3. Is it possible that $\triangle KLM$ is a dilation of $\triangle XYZ$? Explain your thinking.

Name ______________________ Date ______________

Practice 50

For use with Section 6-7

Use a calculator to find each value as a decimal rounded to hundredths.

1. sin 48° **2.** cos 76° **3.** cos 56° **4.** sin 21°

5. cos 9° **6.** sin 63° **7.** cos 18° **8.** sin 67°

Express each ratio as a decimal rounded to hundredths.

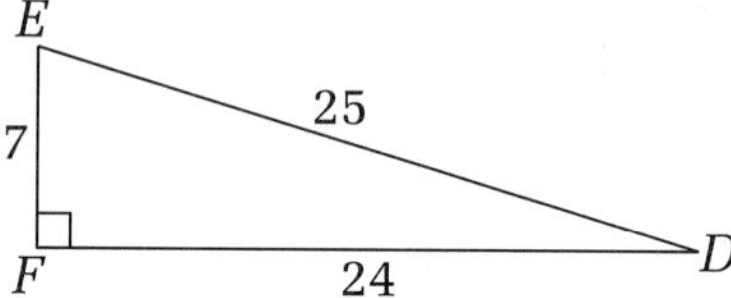

9. sin E **10.** cos E

11. sin D **12.** cos D

For each set of data about right triangle ABC,

a. **Write an equation, involving sine or cosine, that you would use to find the value of x, using the given measures.**

b. **Use your equation to find the value of x to the nearest tenth.**

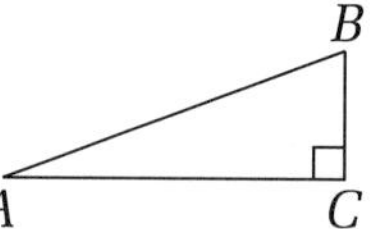

13. $\angle A = 38°$; $AB = 2.6$; $BC = x$ **14.** $\angle B = 63°$; $AB = 5.5$; $BC = x$

15. $\angle B = 72°$; $BC = 4.2$; $AB = x$ **16.** $\angle A = 14°$; $BC = 2.3$; $AB = x$

17. $\angle B = 54°$; $AC = 5.5$; $AB = x$ **18.** $\angle A = 25°$; $AB = 8.3$; $BC = x$

19. A support wire for a telephone pole must make an angle of 78° with the level ground and reach to a point on the pole 27 ft above the ground. How long should the wire be, to the nearest tenth of a foot?

20. The diagonal of a rectangular computer chip is 54.0 mm and makes an angle of 23° with one edge of the chip. Find the length and width of the chip, to the nearest 0.1 mm.

21. Refer to the diagram below. At high tide, a 40-ft gangplank makes an angle of 77° with the pier. At low tide this angle is 65°. To the nearest tenth of a foot, how far does the water fall between high and low tides?

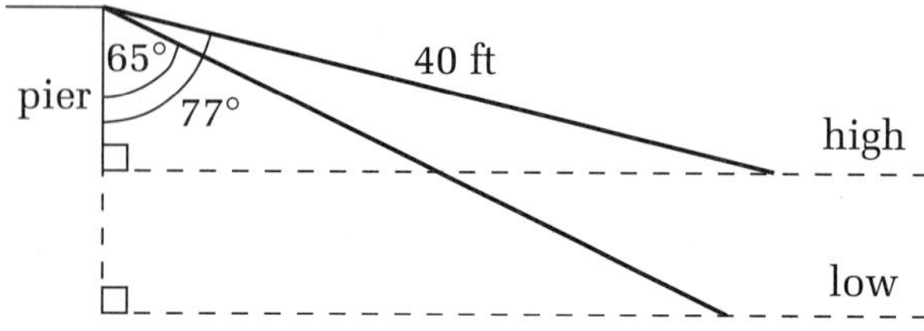

Name ______________________ Date ______________

Practice 51

Cumulative Practice through Unit 6

What type of graph is a good choice for displaying each data set: a *bar graph*, a *histogram*, a *circle graph*, a *line graph*, a *stem-and-leaf plot*, or a *box-and-whisker plot*?

1. The changes in the consumer price index between 1970 and 1990.

2. The percents of the different gases that make up our atmosphere.

3. The average number of movies attended per person per month by age group (under 20, 20–29, 30–39, and so on), from among a sample of 1000 persons.

4. The distribution of the ages of major-league baseball players, showing the median age and the range within which the middle 50% of all ages falls.

5. The numbers of students in your class choosing each of the colors red, orange, yellow, green, blue, or violet as their favorite color.

Solve.

6. $\frac{n}{3} - 5 = 8$

7. $9 - 3.2y = -55$

8. $41 = 13 - 2.5x - 4.5x$

Solve each equation for the indicated variable.

9. $3x - 6y = 15$ for y

10. $y = -\frac{1}{4}x + 8$ for x

11. $x - \frac{3}{5}y = \frac{1}{5}$ for y

12. The measures of two angles of a triangle are equal. The third angle of the triangle has measure 34°. What is the measure of the two angles of equal measure?

13. Two angles are supplementary. One angle is 5 times as large as the other. Find the measures of the two angles.

Use the part of a spreadsheet at the right for Exercises 14–19. Name the contents of each cell.

	A	B	C	D
1	1985	$25	$80	31.25%
2	1987	$32	$86	37.21%
3	1989	$50	$125	40%
4	1991	$62	$220	28.18%

14. B4

15. D2

16. A3

Tell which cell contains each item.

17. $125

18. 31.25%

19. 1991

Find the coordinates of the point (–1, 3) after each translation.

20. 4 units to the left and 6 units up

21. 5 units to the right and 4 units down

Name ______________________ Date ______________

Practice 52

For use with Section 7-1

For each direct variation equation:

a. **Rewrite the equation so that it does not have a fraction in it.**

b. **Find the value of a when $b = 5$.**

c. **Find the value of b when $a = 24$.**

1. $\frac{a}{b} = 36$ **2.** $\frac{a}{b} = 1.6$ **3.** $\frac{a}{b} = 4.8$ **4.** $\frac{a}{b} = 720$

For Exercises 5–7, find each tangent ratio.

5. $\tan \angle A$

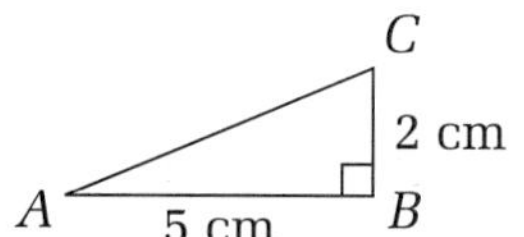

6. $\tan \angle R$

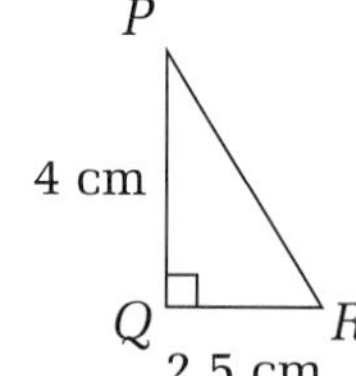

7. $\tan \angle H$

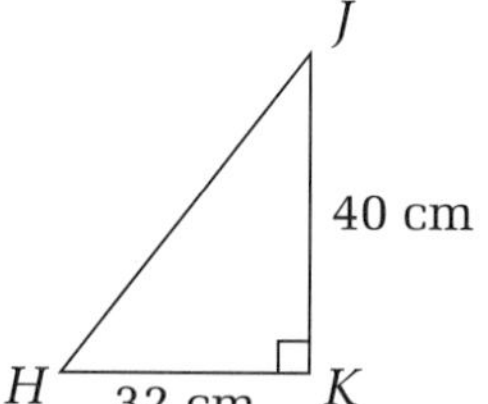

Find each value to the nearest hundredth, using a calculator.

8. $\tan 38°$ **9.** $\tan 54°$ **10.** $\tan 15°$ **11.** $\tan 87°$

For Exercises 12–17, use the diagram at the right. For each set of data, express the tangent of the given angle as a ratio of the lengths of two sides of triangle ABC. Find the length of the missing side to the nearest 0.1 cm.

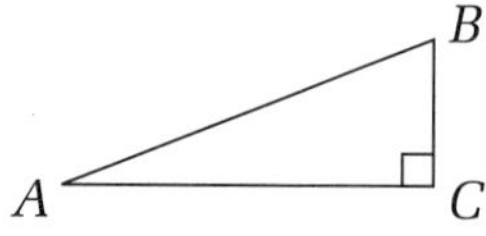

12. $\angle A = 34°$; $AC = 8$ cm; $BC = \underline{?}$

13. $\angle A = 22°$; $AC = 75$ cm; $BC = \underline{?}$

14. $\angle A = 18°$; $BC = 9$ cm; $AC = \underline{?}$

15. $\angle B = 57°$; $BC = 50$ cm; $AC = \underline{?}$

16. $\angle B = 73°$; $BC = 62$ cm; $AC = \underline{?}$

17. $\angle B = 61°$; $AC = 3.6$ cm; $BC = \underline{?}$

For Exercises 18 and 19, use the diagram at the right. A lamppost $\overline{EC}$ casts a shadow $\overline{AC}$. A 30-cm ruler $\overline{DB}$ has been moved from A so that its shadow falls just within the shadow of the lamppost.

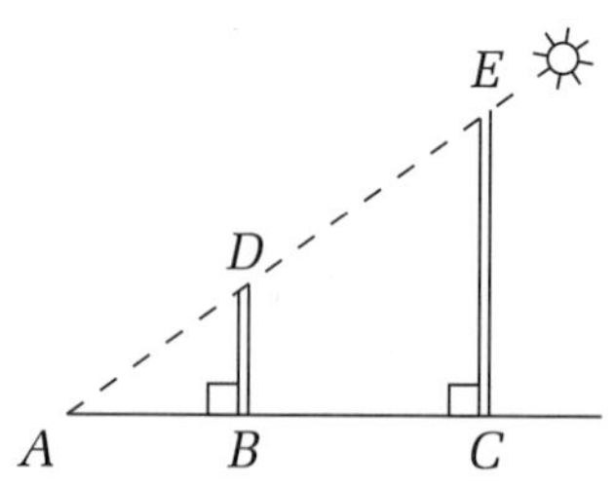

18. Suppose the length of the ruler's shadow is 42 cm. What is the slope of the imaginary line $\overline{AE}$?

19. Suppose the lamppost's shadow is 15 m long. How tall is the lamppost?

Name ______________________ Date ______________

Practice 53

For use with Section 7-2

For Exercises 1–6, decide whether direct variation is a good model for the data in each table. If it is, write an equation that includes the variation constant.

1.

x	y
3	4.5
4	6
5	7.5
10	15

2.

x	y
15	6
20	8
28	11.2
36	14.4

3.

x	y
1	3
2	6
4	18
8	66

4.

x	y
4.5	10.5
15	35
21	49
102	238

5.

x	y
7	17.5
20	30.5
15.5	26
19.5	30

6.

x	y
5	18
15	54
17.5	63
21.5	77.4

For each direct variation relationship, find the missing value.

7. $\frac{a}{b} = 2.4$; $b = 35$; $a =$ __?__

8. $\frac{p}{q} = 0.6$; $p = 33$; $q =$ __?__

9. $\frac{c}{d} = 2.2$; $c = 18.7$; $d =$ __?__

10. $\frac{v}{w} = 16.8$; $w = 3.5$; $v =$ __?__

For Exercises 11–14, use the table at the right, which shows the results of an experiment in re-introducing a certain type of plant into a region.

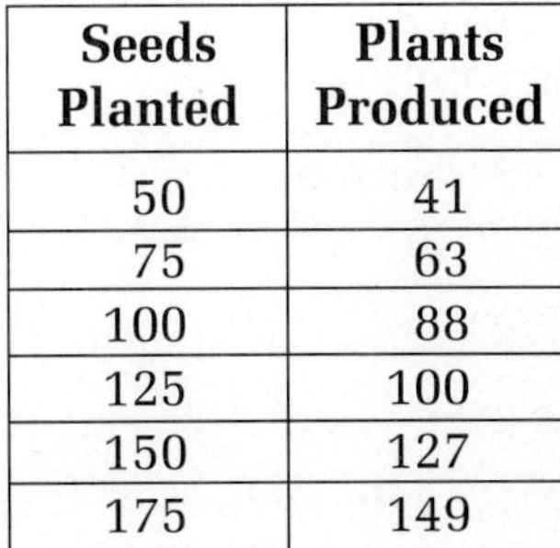

Seeds Planted	Plants Produced
50	41
75	63
100	88
125	100
150	127
175	149

11. Do these data seem to show direct variation? If so, write an equation to model the situation.

12. Plot these data on a graph and draw a fitted line.

13. Find the slope of the line you have drawn.

14. About how many seeds would have to be planted to produce 136 plants?

For Exercises 15 and 16, use the graph at the right.

Weight of Panes of Glass

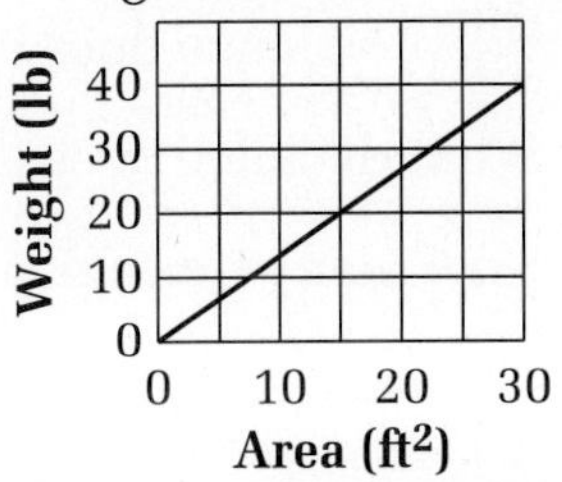

15. Estimate the variation constant.

16. Estimate the weight of a pane of glass whose area is 25 ft^2.

Name ______________________ Date ______________

Practice 54

For use with Section 7-3

Find the circumference of each circle.

1.
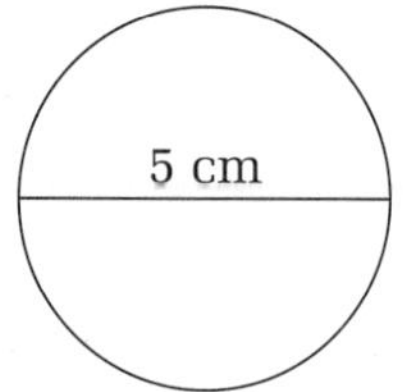

2.
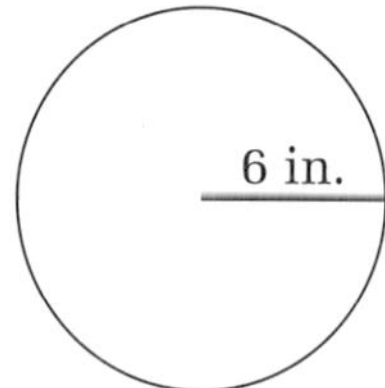

3.
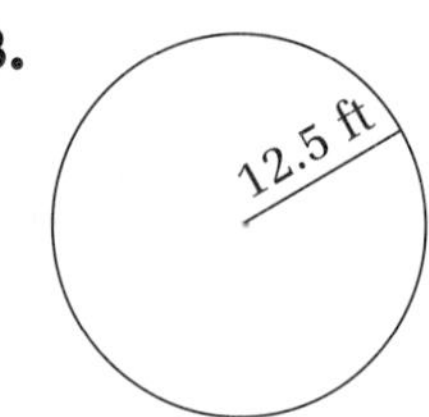

4.
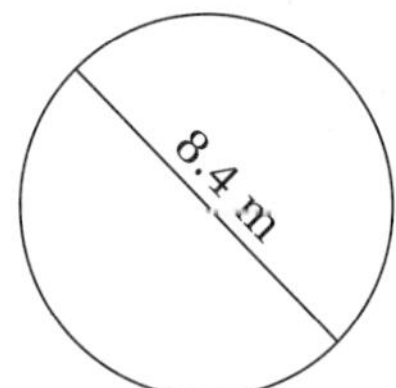

5. diameter = 14 m **6.** radius = 10 cm **7.** radius = 3.4 ft **8.** diameter = 17.5 m

Find each arc length.

9.
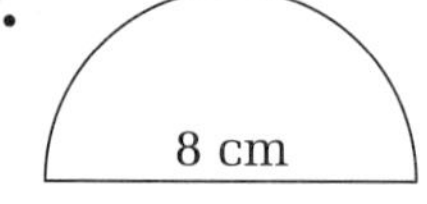

10.
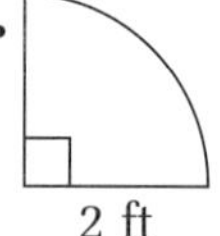

11.
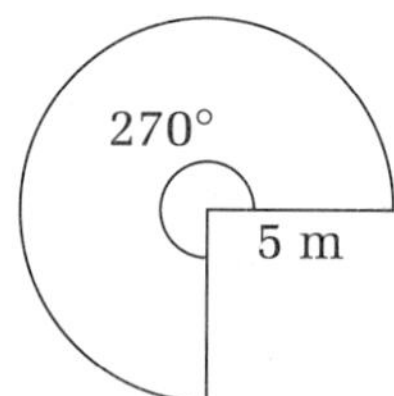

12.
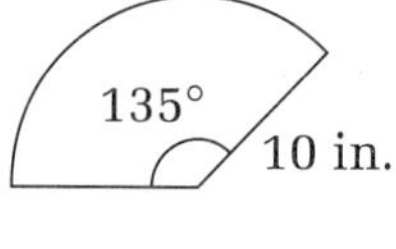

Find the length of the arc with each central angle and each radius.

13. central angle = 40°; radius = 12 cm

14. central angle = 36°; radius = 15 in.

15. central angle = 210°; radius = 30 ft

16. central angle = 315°; radius = 24 cm

A regular octagon is drawn inside a circle of radius 14 cm. Its vertices are on the circle.

17. Suppose a radius is drawn to each vertex of the octagon. What is the smallest central angle between two radii?

18. Find the length of the arc connecting two consecutive vertices.

A bicycle wheel has a radius of 35 cm. Each time the wheel makes one complete turn, the bicycle goes a distance equal to the circumference of the wheel.

19. What distance does the wheel go in one turn?

20. What distance does the wheel go in kilometers in 2000 turns?

21. How many times does the wheel turn in a trip of 15 km?

Name ________________________ Date ____________

Practice 55

For use with Section 7-4

Write an equation of the form $y = kx$ to describe each line.

1. 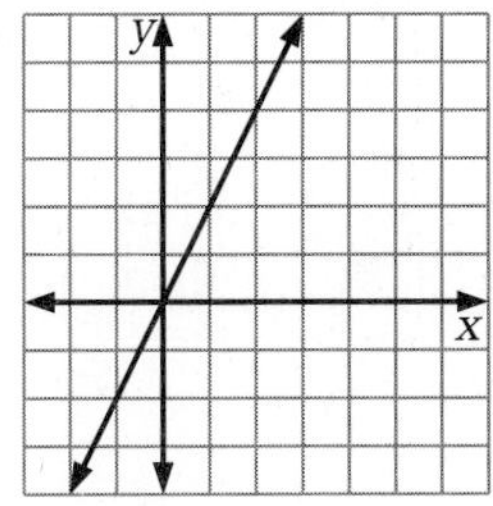

2. 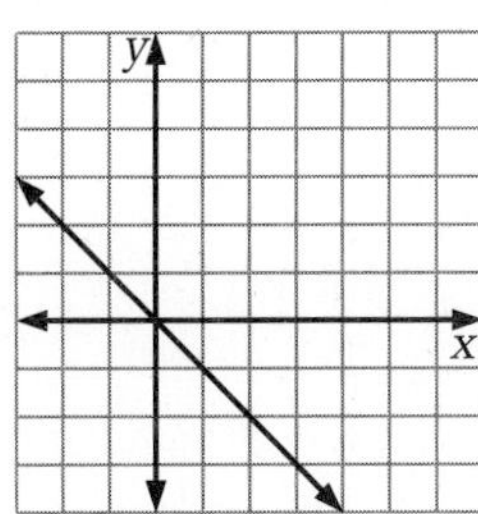

3. 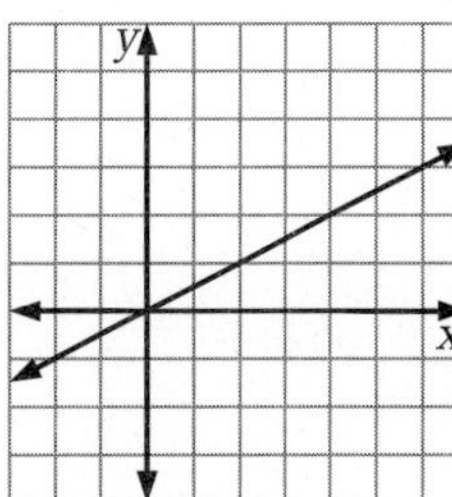

4. 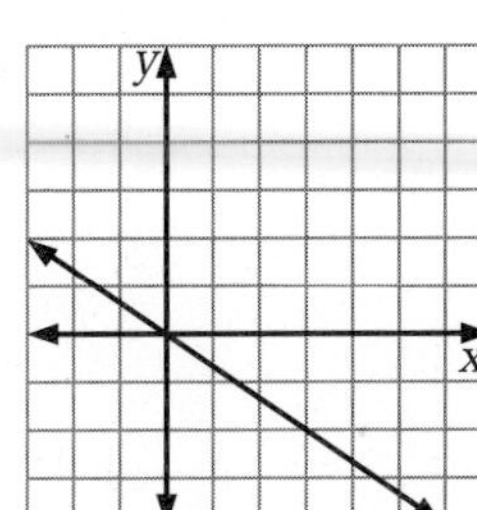

5. 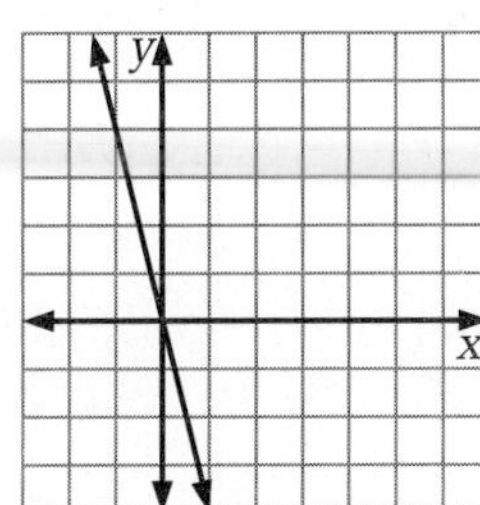

6. 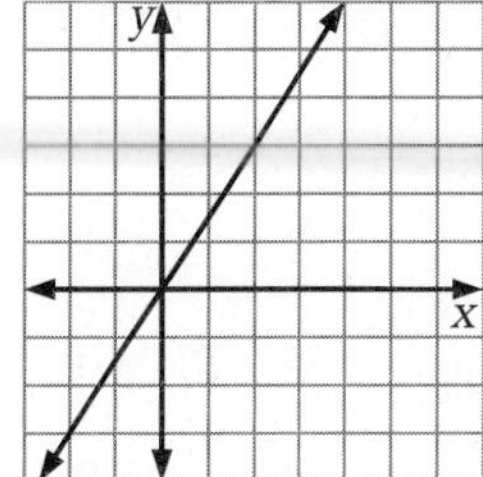

Graph each equation.

7. $y = -2x$

8. $y = \frac{2}{3}x$

9. $y = -1.5x$

10. $y = 4x$

11. $y = 3x$

12. $y = -\frac{4}{3}x$

13. $y = -0.25x$

14. $y = \frac{1}{5}x$

The rise and run from (0, 0) to another point are given. Plot the other point using the directions below. Then draw the line, and find its slope.

15. rise = 4, run = 5

16. rise = −4, run = 6

17. rise = 3, run = −2

18. The wavelength of a clarinet note varies directly with the length of the air column that produces the note. A note with a wavelength of 7.5 ft is produced by an air column 22.5 in. long. How long an air column is needed to produce a wavelength of 4.75 ft? What wavelength is produced by an air column 9.5 in. long?

19. ***Open-ended*** Suppose the number of students in your school started to increase. Give some examples of quantities that might vary directly with the number of students. Estimate the variation constant for each quantity, and write an equation of each variation.

Name ______________________ Date ______________

Practice 56

For use with Section 7-5

For Exercises 1–6, each expression shows the units of a conversion problem. Use dimensional analysis to find the unit(s) of the answer.

1. $\frac{\text{mi}}{\text{h}} \times \text{h} = \underline{\ ?\ }$

2. $\frac{\text{mi}}{\text{min}} \times \frac{\text{min}}{\text{h}} = \underline{\ ?\ }$

3. $\frac{\text{ft}}{\text{s}} \times \frac{\text{s}}{\text{min}} = \underline{\ ?\ }$

4. $\frac{\text{in.}^2}{\text{ft}^2} \times \frac{\text{ft}^2}{\text{yd}^2} = \underline{\ ?\ }$

5. $\frac{\text{mm}}{\text{in.}} \times \frac{\text{in.}}{\text{ft}} \times \frac{\text{ft}}{\text{yd}} = \underline{\ ?\ }$

6. $\frac{\text{cm}^3}{\text{L}} \times \frac{\text{L}}{\text{qt}} \times \frac{\text{qt}}{\text{gal}} = \underline{\ ?\ }$

For Exercises 7–10, identify the control variable and the dependent variable. Express the variation constant as a rate.

7. The weight of a quantity of water varies directly with its volume. 2 ft^3 of water weighs 125 lb.

8. The price of an amount of sliced turkey at the delicatessen varies directly with its weight. 1.5 lb of sliced turkey costs $7.47.

9. The diameter of a tree trunk varies directly with the age of the tree. A 45-year-old tree has a trunk diameter of 18 in.

10. The number of words Julio can type on his word processor varies directly with time. In 17.5 min he typed 250 words.

11. How many cubic centimeters are there in 25 in.^3? ($1 \text{ in.}^3 = 16.4 \text{ cm}^3$)

12. Earth travels at 66,636 mi/h in its orbit. How many feet per second is this? (1 mile = 5280 ft)

Sonya bought 8.5 gal of gasoline for $11.38. She then drove her car 161 mi and used 7 gal of gasoline.

13. What was the cost of a gallon of gasoline? How much would 11 gal cost?

14. How many gallons would it take to go 120 mi?

15. How much does it cost Sonya, in gasoline alone, to drive one mile?

16. ***Open-ended*** Invent your own unit of length and a conversion factor to a standard unit of length. Then make up a table listing the conversion factors from your unit into other standard units of length, both metric and U.S. customary units. List as many as you can.

Name ______________________ Date ______________

Practice 57

For use with Section 7-6

For Exercises 1–6, find the unknown measurement for each circle.

1. radius = 12 in.
area = ?

2. radius = 28 m
area = ?

3. diameter = 13.9 mm
area = ?

4. area = 43 cm^2
radius = ?

5. area = 89 $in.^2$
radius = ?

6. area = 53 ft^2
diameter = ?

Find the area of each circle in a coordinate plane.

7. With center at (3, 4) and passing through the point (3, –2)

8. With the points (–1, 5) and (6, 5) at opposite ends of a diameter

Find the area of each sector.

9.

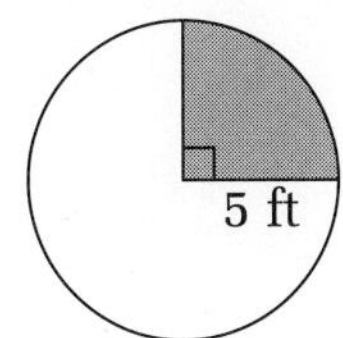

10.

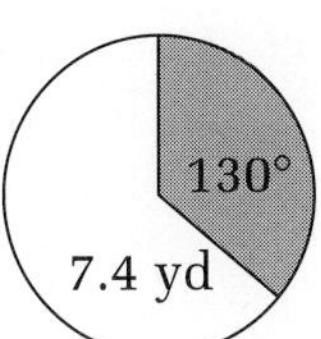

11.

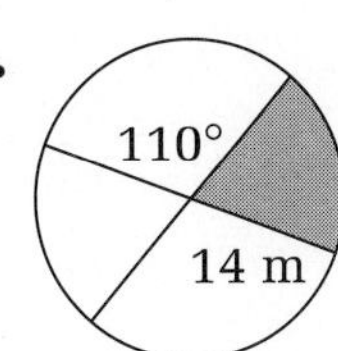

12.

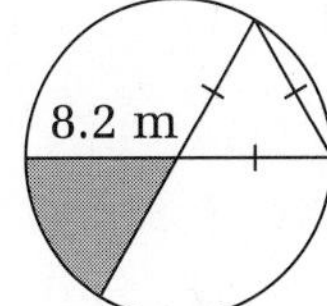

Find the area of each circle.

13.

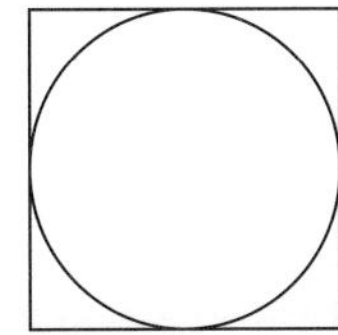

Perimeter of square = 144 ft

14.

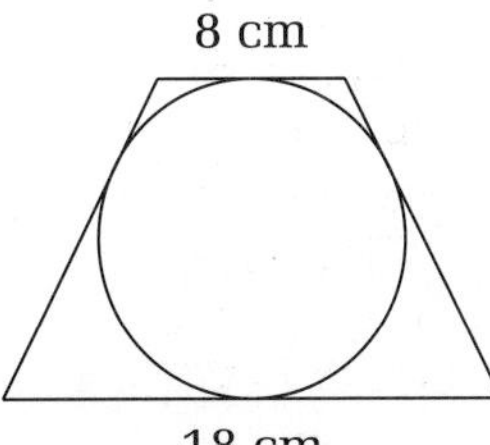

Area of trapezoid = 156 cm^2

15.

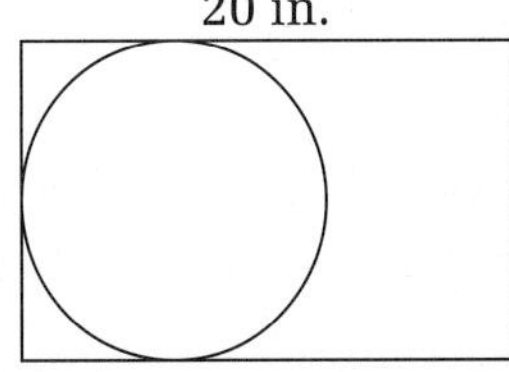

Area of rectangle = 268 $in.^2$

For Exercises 16 and 17, use the circle graph at the right, which shows a manufacturer's costs.

16. The *Salaries* sector is 42% of the whole circle. What is the central angle of this sector?

17. Suppose the radius of the graph is 3 cm. What is the area of the salaries sector?

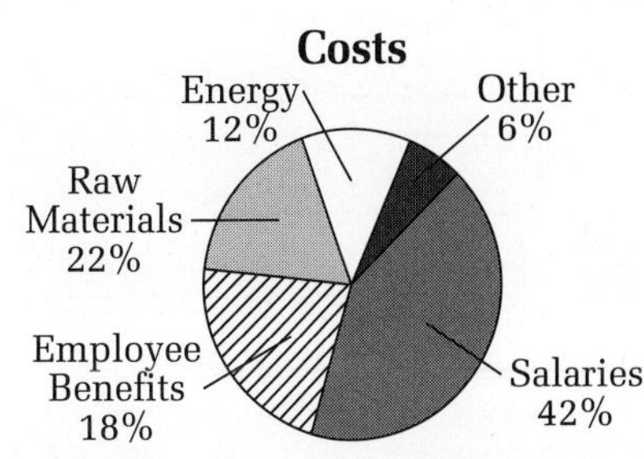

Name ______________________ Date ____________

Practice 58

Cumulative Practice through Unit 7

Tell whether each figure has rotational symmetry. If it does, describe the symmetry.

1. 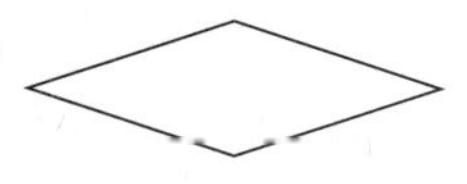

2. 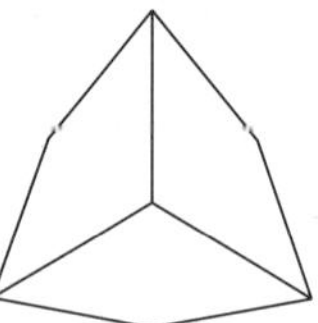

3. 

4. 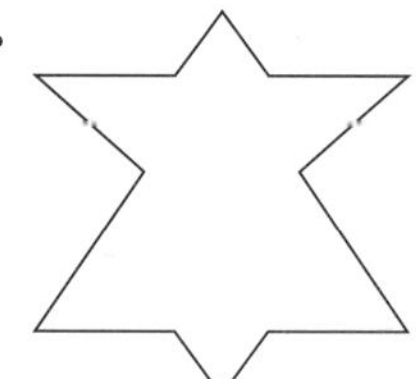

Model each situation using an equation and then solve.

5. Consuela would like to score the same number of points in her next 5 basketball games. So far she has scored 46 points. How many points must she score in each game in order to tie the league record of 101 points?

6. In a heat-loss survey of Victor Tan's house, the area of one wall was listed as 400 ft^2. There are 4 identical windows in the wall, and the siding area (not including the windows) was listed as 340 ft^2. What is the area of each window?

Solve each equation for the variable indicated.

7. $ax - by = c$ for b

8. $A = \frac{1}{3}\pi r^2 h$ for h

9. $2l + 2w = p$ for w

For Exercises 10–15, players may spin the wheel only once. Find the theoretical probability of each outcome.

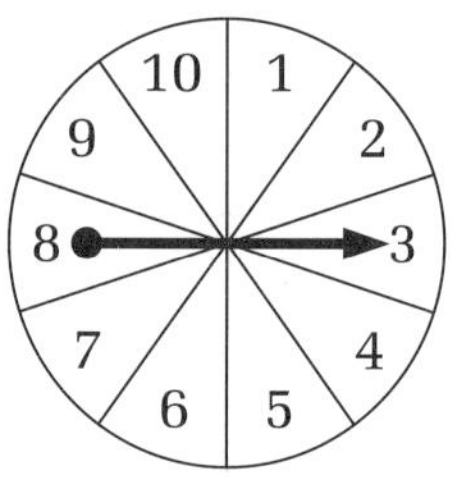

10. 7

11. an even number

12. 2, 3, or 9

13. 9 or 10

14. 3, 4, 5, or 6

15. 13

For Exercises 16–18, the smaller figure is the original figure. State the coordinates of the center of dilation and find the scale factor.

16. 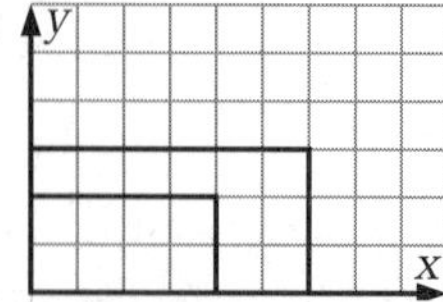

17. 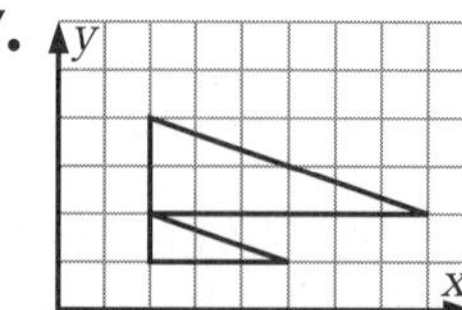

18. 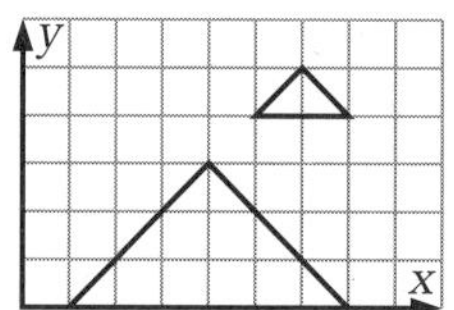

19. A map has a scale of 0.5 in. : 40 mi. Eastville and Westville are connected by a straight road and are 100 mi apart. How far apart are they on the map?

Name ______________________________ Date ______________

Practice 59

For use with Section 8-1

Without graphing, find the slope and the vertical intercept of the line modeled by each equation.

1. $y = 9x + 5$ **2.** $y = -8x + 7$ **3.** $y = 11 - 4.6x$

4. $y = x + 15$ **5.** $y = -2 + 12x$ **6.** $y = -17x$

Graph each equation.

7. $y = x - 1$ **8.** $y = -x + 3$ **9.** $y = 0.5x - 3$

10. $y = -3x + 2$ **11.** $y = -0.2x + 4$ **12.** $y = 4 - \frac{1}{2}x$

For Exercises 13–15, find the slope and vertical intercept of each line. Write an equation of each line.

13.

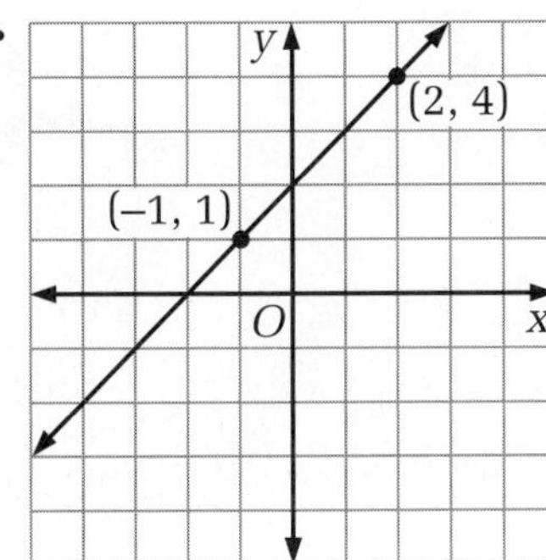

14.

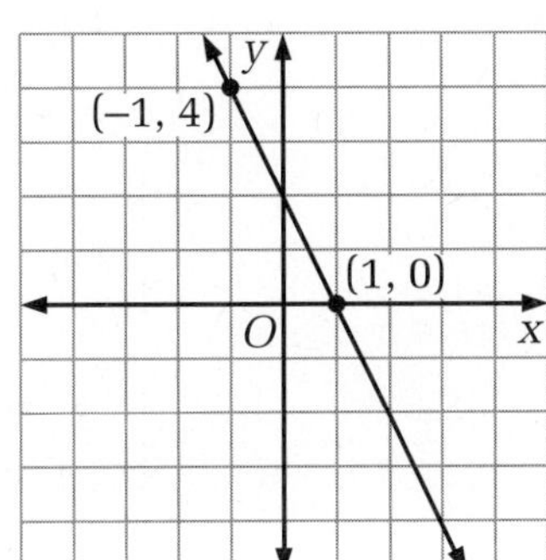

15.

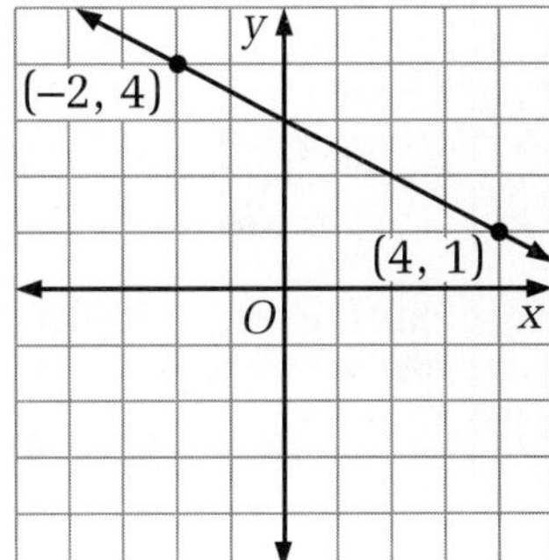

Model each situation with an equation.

16. Jing walked toward his apartment at 3 mi/h from a point 5 mi from the apartment. (control variable: time; dependent variable: Jing's distance from home)

17. A garage charges $14 for an oil change plus $1.50 for each quart of new oil. (control variable: amount of new oil; dependent variable: cost of oil change)

18. The temperature of a laboratory sample of liquid oxygen is at –210°C, and it is rising at 7°C each minute. (control variable: time; dependent variable: temperature)

19. ***Writing*** How are linear functions and direct variations related? Explain how the graphs of the two types of functions are alike and how they are different.

Name ______________________________ Date ______________

Practice 60

For use with Section 8-2

Find three solutions of each equation.

1. $2x + y = 7$

2. $x - y = 1$

3. $3x - 2y = 6$

4. $-5x - y = 10$

5. $\frac{1}{2}x + 3y = 9$

6. $\frac{1}{3}x - 3y = 15$

Rewrite each equation in slope-intercept form.

7. $4x + y = 13$

8. $\frac{1}{2}x + y = 25$

9. $5x - y = -9$

10. $3x + \frac{1}{3}y = 5$

11. $-9x - 4y = 7$

12. $\frac{1}{2}x - 3y = 12$

Find the intercepts of the graph of each equation.

13. $x + 3y = -3$

14. $4x - 3y = 18$

15. $-2x + 7y = -28$

16. $-\frac{1}{2}x - 2y = 5$

17. $\frac{1}{3}x + \frac{1}{2}y = 6$

18. $0.6x + 1.5y = 9$

Graph each group of equations on one set of axes.

19. $x + 3y = -3$; $x + 3y = 0$; $x + 3y = 3$

20. $3x - 2y = 6$; $-3x + 2y = 4$; $6x - 4y = 4$

For Exercises 21–23, write an equation relating each group of variables.

21. An isosceles triangle has a perimeter of 25 cm. Relate the length x of the two congruent sides and the length of the third side y.

22. In basketball, a field goal counts 2 points, a long field goal counts 3 points, and a free throw counts 1 point. In one game, Indrani scored 14 points. Relate the number of field goals g, the number of long field goals l, and the number of free throws t she made.

23. At the Smart Shop, a shirt sells for $28 and each shirt costs the store $16 at wholesale. In one month, the store made a net profit of $236 just on the new shirts it ordered that month. Relate the number of shirts s that the store sold and the number of shirts b that it bought wholesale that month.

Name ______________________ Date ______________

Practice 61

For use with Section 8-3

Find the slope of each line and write an equation for each line.

1.
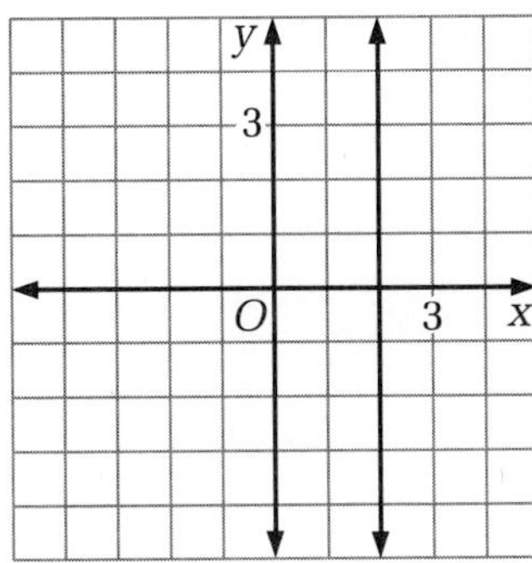

2.
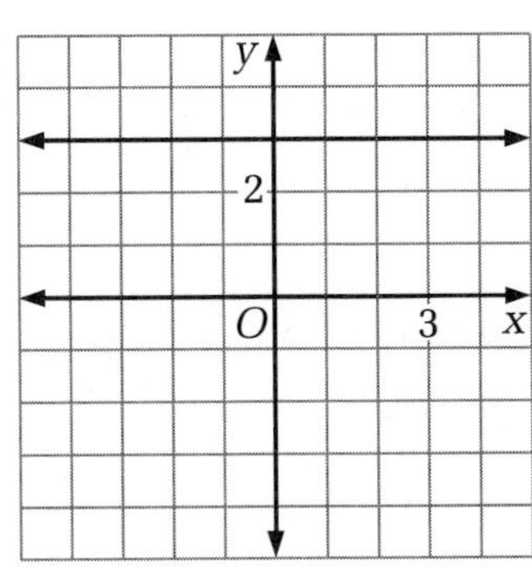

3.
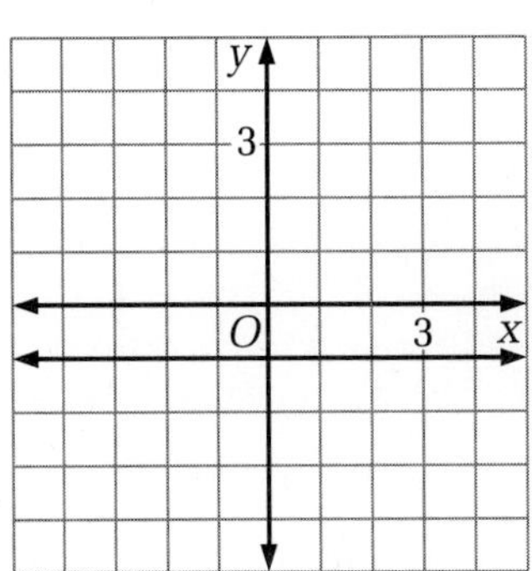

Graph each equation and find the slope of each line.

4. $y = -2$ **5.** $x = 3$ **6.** $y = 4$ **7.** $x = -1$

8. $x = -4$ **9.** $y = -3$ **10.** $x = 1.5$ **11.** $y = 2.5$

For Exercises 12–16, write an equation for each line.

12. the line through the points (6, –3) and (6, 5)

13. the line with slope 0 through the point (–2, 7)

14. the line with undefined slope through the point (8, –6)

15. the horizontal line through the point (1, 9)

16. the vertical line through the point (–5, –3)

17. What is an equation of the *x*-axis? What is its slope?

18. What is an equation of the *y*-axis? What is its slope?

Tell whether a good model for each situation would be a line with 0 slope, a line with undefined slope, or neither.

19. The distance (*y*) of a parked car from its destination after a length of time (*x*).

20. The points (*x*, *y*) on a flagpole, where *y* is the height of the point above the ground and *x* is its distance from the side of a certain building nearby.

21. The distance (*y*) of a jogger from her starting point after running for a length of time (*x*) at a constant speed.

Name ______________________________ Date ______________

Practice 62

For use with Section 8-4

Write an equation for the line that has each slope and each vertical intercept.

1. slope = 5; intercept = –1

2. slope = –2; intercept = 1

3. slope = 0.5; intercept = 3

4. slope = $\frac{2}{3}$; intercept = –4

5. slope = –6; intercept = 0

6. slope = $-\frac{1}{3}$; intercept = $\frac{4}{3}$

Write an equation for the line that has each slope and has each point on it.

7. slope = 2; (–1, 5) on line

8. slope = –3; (2, –1) on line

9. slope = –4; (–3, 9) on line

10. slope = $\frac{1}{2}$; (2, –7) on line

11. slope = $-\frac{3}{4}$; (–6, 2) on line

12. slope = $-\frac{3}{2}$; (5, –4) on line

Write an equation for the line that has each pair of points on it.

13. (2, 5), (6, 13)

14. (–1, 4), (1, 10)

15. (3, 6), (–5, –2)

16. (–1, 3), (5, 0)

17. (–7, –2), (5, –6)

18. (1, 0.8), (5, –4)

Find an equation of the line with each pair of intercepts.

19. vertical: 3; horizontal: 2

20. vertical: –5; horizontal: 10

21. A long-distance phone call costs $1.60 for the first minute and a fixed charge for each minute after that. A 7-minute call costs $2.92. Write an equation for the cost of a call as a function of time after the first minute.

22. A computer repair shop charges $25 to test an out-of-order computer plus an hourly charge for actual repairs. The shop charged a customer $92.50 for a job that took 1.5 h. Write an equation for the cost of a repair as a function of time.

23. ***Open-ended*** Estimate how far your school building is from your home. Then time your trip home. Assume that you travel at a constant speed, and write an equation for your distance from home as a function of time during your trip.

Name ______________________ Date ______________

Practice 63

For use with Section 8-5

For Exercises 1–3, estimate the solution of each system of equations from the graph. Then use substitution to find the exact solution.

1.

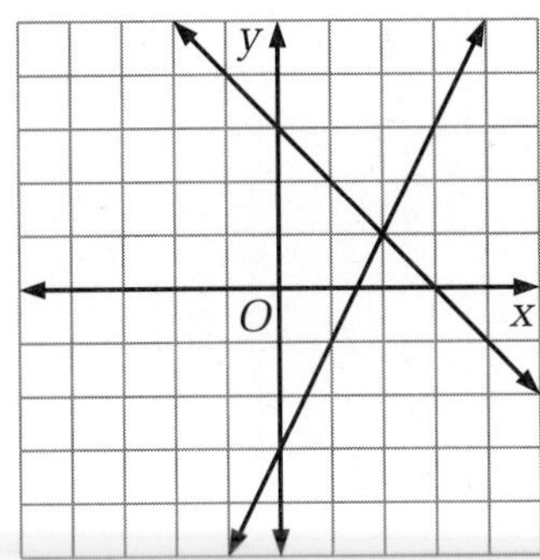

$y = -x + 3$

$y = 2x - 3$

2.

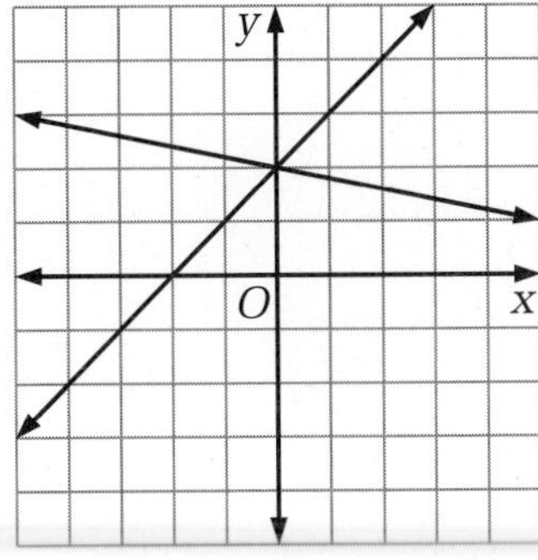

$y = -\frac{1}{5}x + 2$

$y = x + 2$

3.

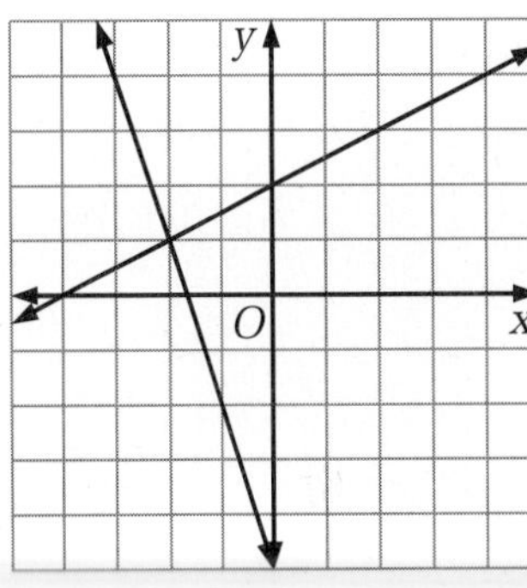

$y = -3x - 5$

$y = \frac{1}{2}x + 2$

Graph each system of equations. Estimate the solution of the system or write no solution.

4. $y = 2x + 1$
$y = 2x - 1$

5. $y = -x + 3$
$y = 3x - 1$

6. $y = -2x + 4$
$y = \frac{1}{3}x - 3$

Without graphing, tell whether each system of equations has a solution or no solution.

7. $y = -6x + 2$
$y = -6x - 1$

8. $y = -2x + 5$
$y = -x + 5$

9. $y = 7x - 2$
$y = -7x + 2$

For Exercises 10–12, rewrite each equation in slope-intercept form. Then tell whether each system of equations has a solution or no solution.

10. $3x - y = 2$
$6x - 2y = 2$

11. $6x + 2y = 1$
$9x - 3y = 2$

12. $4x - 10y = 5$
$-2x + 5y = 5$

13. Carlos was climbing a mountain that Vijay was descending when they met. Carlos had left at 8 A.M. from an altitude of 3350 ft and gained 100 ft/h. Vijay had left at 8 A.M. from an altitude of 4850 ft and had lost 150 ft/h. What time did Carlos and Vijay meet? At what altitude?

Name ______________________________ Date ____________

Practice 64

For use with Section 8-6

Fill in the blank with one of the signs: >, <, ≥, or ≤.

1.

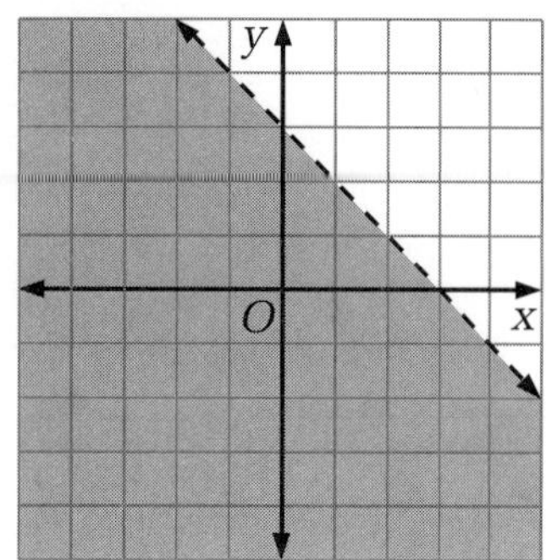

$y \underline{\ ?\ } -x + 3$

2.

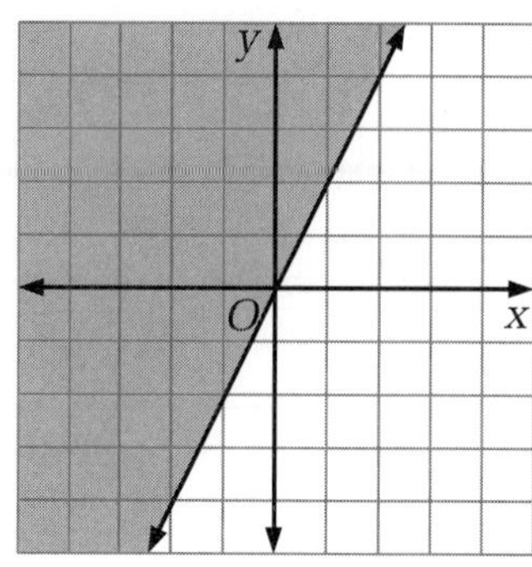

$y \underline{\ ?\ } 2x$

3.

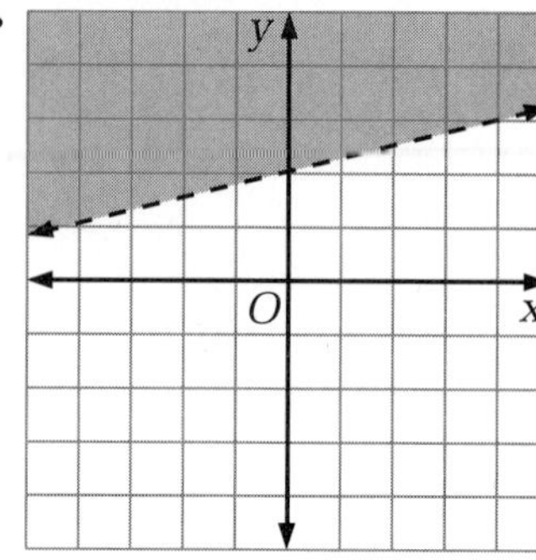

$y \underline{\ ?\ } \frac{1}{4}x + 2$

Tell whether each point is a solution of each inequality.

4. $(3, -1)$; $y > x - 2$

5. $(1, 0)$; $y \le 5x - 3$

6. $(2, -3)$; $y < -2x + 4$

7. $(5, -3)$; $y \ge -2x + 8$

8. $(-4, -5)$; $y > 2x + 1$

9. $(-1, 6)$; $y \le -5x + 1$

Graph each inequality.

10. $y > 4x$

11. $y \le x + 1$

12. $y > -x - 4$

13. $y < -\frac{1}{2}x + 3$

14. $y \ge 2x + 2$

15. $y \le -3x + 1$

16. $x - 3y < 6$

17. $2x + 0.5y \ge 1$

18. $3x - 2y > 4$

The ticket machine for the rapid transit train gives change if you put in too much money. Juan's trip costs $1.25, and he has only dimes and quarters.

19. Suppose Juan puts x dimes and y quarters into the machine. Write a linear combination that expresses the value of the money he puts in.

20. Write an inequality that relates the number of dimes and the number of quarters he must put into the machine in order to buy the ticket he wants. Graph the inequality.

21. Dynell plans to go at least 6 miles in a charity walkathon, walking part of the way and jogging the rest. She walks at 3 mi/h and jogs at 9 mi/h. Write an inequality that models the situation. Graph the inequality.

Name ______________________ Date ______________

Practice 65

For use with Section 8-7

For Exercises 1–6, tell whether each ordered pair is a solution of each system. Write yes or no.

1. $(1, 2)$; $y \geq 1$
$x < 5$

2 $(-3, 2)$; $y > x + 1$
$y \leq -x - 1$

3. $(5, -2)$; $y \geq 2x - 9$
$y < x - 5$

4. $(-1, -4)$; $x + 2y < -5$
$x - y \geq 4$

5. $(0, 5)$; $5x + 2y > 7$
$-3x - y < -5$

6. $(-1, 6)$; $5x + 2y \geq 1$
$-7x - y < 2$

Fill in each blank with one of the signs: >, <, ≥, or ≤.

7.

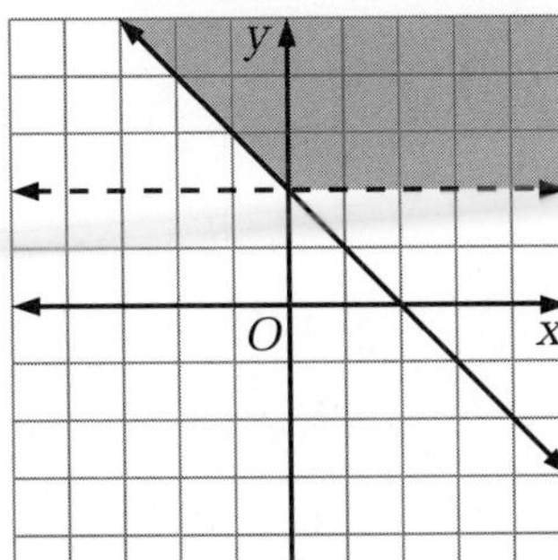

y __?__ $-x + 2$

y __?__ 2

8.

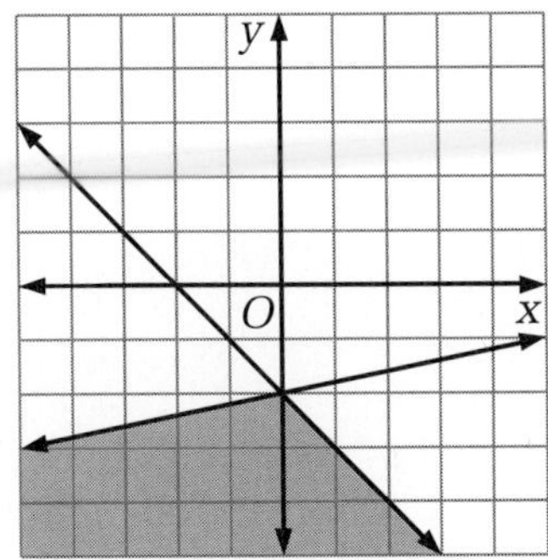

y __?__ $\frac{1}{5}x - 2$

y __?__ $-x - 2$

9.

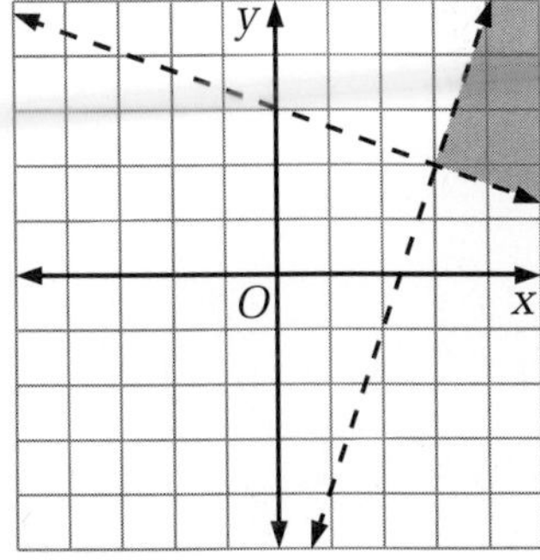

y __?__ $-\frac{1}{3}x - 3$

y __?__ $3x - 7$

For Exercises 10–18, graph each system of inequalities.

10. $x > -1$
$y \geq 2$

11. $y \leq -x$
$x > -3$

12. $x < y$
$y \leq 2$

13. $y > -x - 3$
$y \leq x + 3$

14. $y \leq 2x - 1$
$y > -3x + 2$

15. $y \leq -2x + 2$
$y \leq x - 4$

16. $x + y \leq 2$
$x + y > 1$

17. $y > -\frac{1}{2}x - 1$
$2x - y \leq -3$

18. $2x - y < 4$
$2x + y < 4$

19. Tito Fernandez needs to mix crushed stone and mortar to make a concrete mix to pave his walk. For structural stability he needs to use at least as much mortar as stone, and he wants to end up with at least 40 lb of mix. Write and graph a system of inequalities to model this situation. What combination of mortar and stone will use the smallest amount of mortar?

Name ______________________ Date ____________

Practice 66

Cumulative Practice through Unit 8

Find the area of each figure.

1.

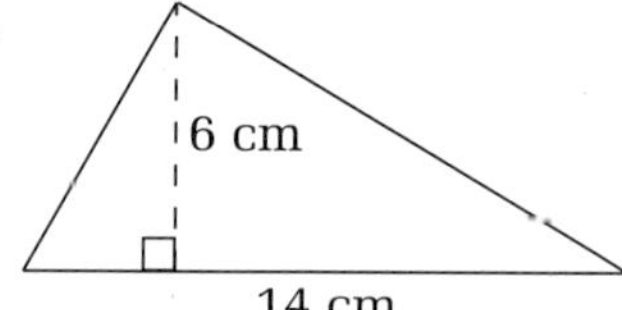

2.

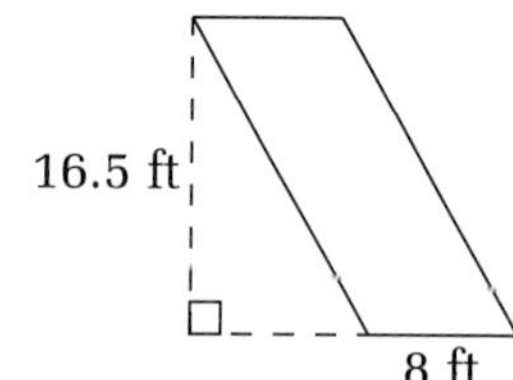

3.

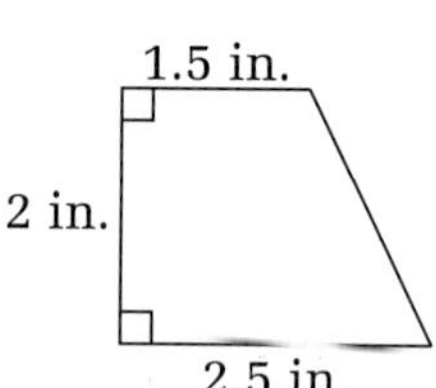

Tell whether each graph represents a function.

4.

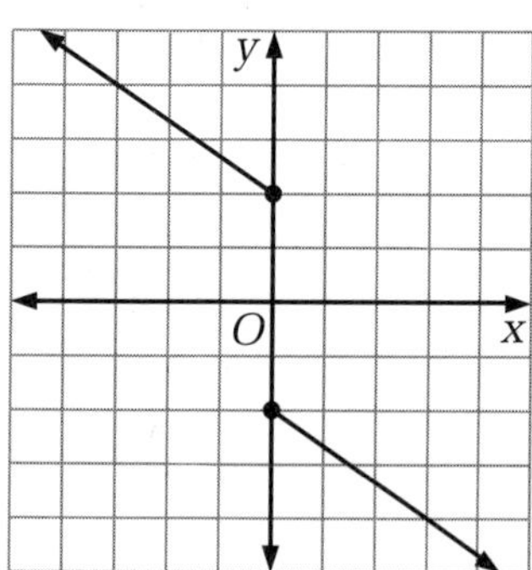

5.

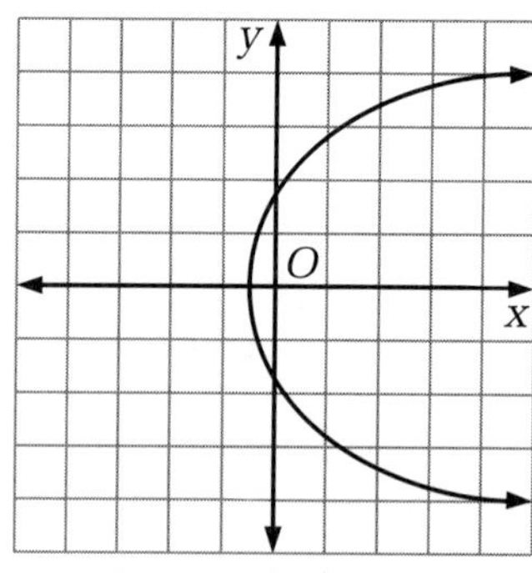

6.

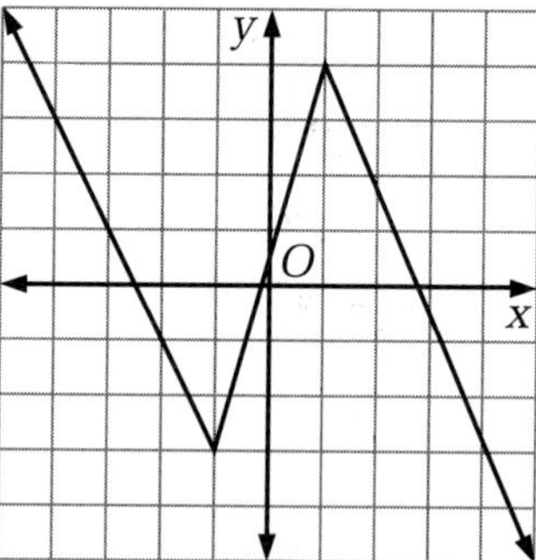

7. Felicia had run 6 mi of a marathon, with 20 mi to go, when she stopped for water. What is the ratio of the distance she had already run to the whole distance of the race?

For Exercises 8–10, each expression shows the units of a conversion problem. Use dimensional analysis to find the unit(s) of the answer.

8. $\frac{\text{cents}}{\text{mi}} \times \frac{\text{mi}}{\text{h}} = \underline{\ ?\ }$

9. $\frac{\text{lb}}{\text{in.}^2} \times \frac{\text{in.}^2}{\text{ft}^2} = \underline{\ ?\ }$

10. $\frac{\text{mi}}{\text{h}} \times \frac{\text{h}}{\text{s}} \times \frac{\text{ft}}{\text{mi}} = \underline{\ ?\ }$

For Exercises 11–13, use the following information. Express answers in scientific notation. The distance from the planet Venus to the sun is about 6.7×10^7 mi. Venus travels around the sun in a nearly circular orbit in 225 Earth days.

11. How far does Venus travel in 225 Earth days? How far does Venus travel in one Earth day?

12. Find the length of an arc of Venus's orbit with a central angle of 90°.

13. About how many Earth days does it take Venus to travel 1.31×10^8 mi?

Name ______________________ Date ____________

Practice 67

For use with Section 9-1

Find the missing length in each right triangle.

1.

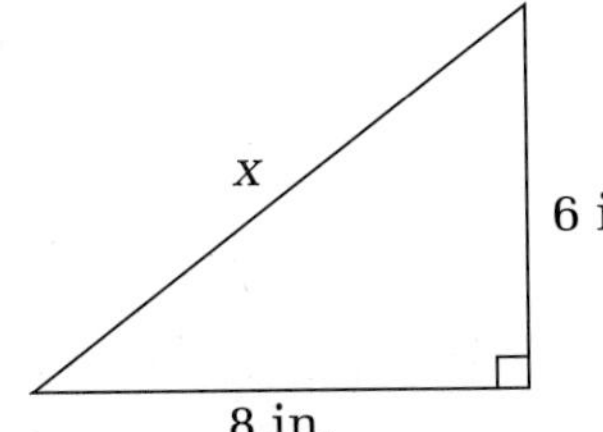

2.

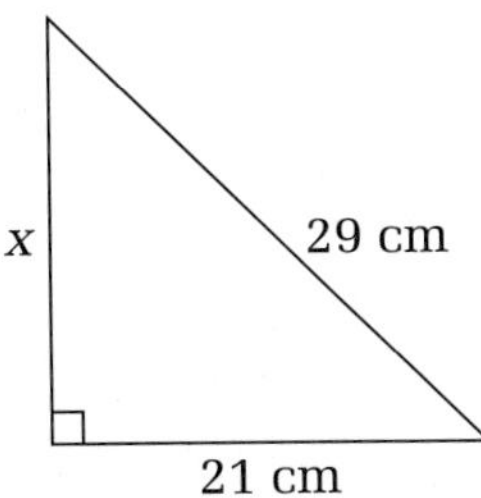

3.

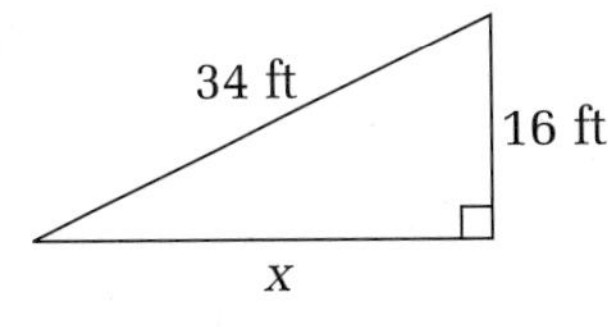

A right triangle has legs of length a and b and hypotenuse of length c. Find each missing length.

4. $a = 12$, $c = 20$, $b =$? **5.** $a = 14$, $b = 48$, $c =$? **6.** $b = 9$, $c = 41$, $a =$?

7. $a = 39$, $c = 89$, $b =$? **8.** $b = 2.4$, $c = 4$, $a =$? **9.** $a = 4.2$, $b = 14.4$, $c =$?

Find the value of x in each triangle, then use the value you found to find y.

10.

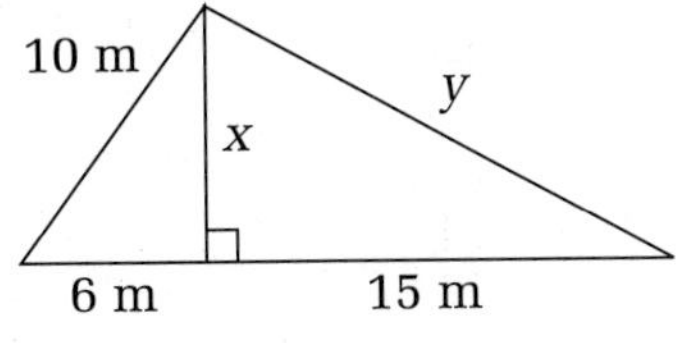

11.

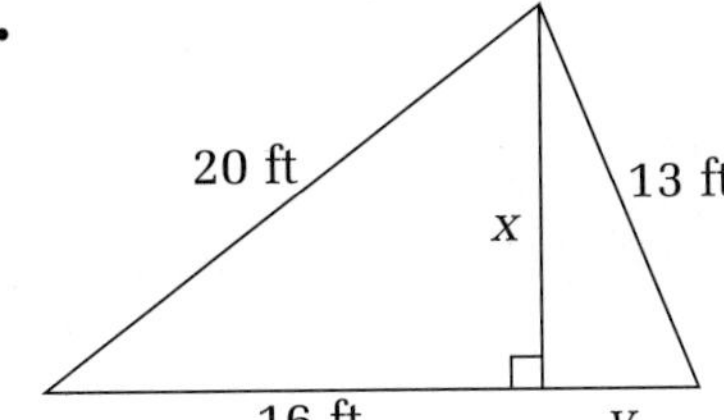

12.

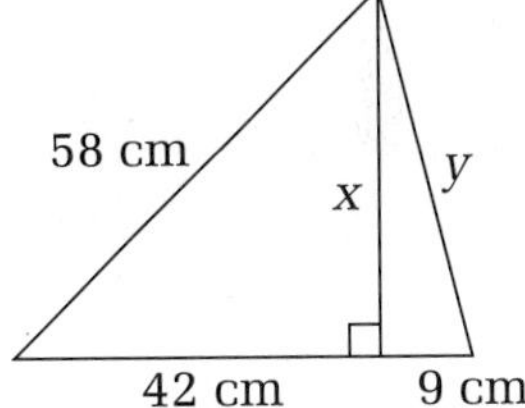

Tell whether each person is using inductive or deductive reasoning.

13. Domingo measures the angles made by the diagonals of several rhombuses. He conjectures that the diagonals of a rhombus will always be perpendicular.

14. Vida's favorite major-league baseball player had 17 home runs as of yesterday. This morning he has 18. Vida concludes that the player played in yesterday's game.

15. ***Writing*** Suppose you substitute 1, 2, 3, and so on, for n in the expression $n^2 - n + 11$. Marta says that you always get a *prime number* (a number greater than 1 that has no whole number divisors except itself and 1). Is she right? Is she using inductive or deductive reasoning? Is this type of reasoning always correct? Explain.

Name ______________________ Date ____________

Practice 68

For use with Section 9-2

Simplify.

1. $\sqrt{40}$
2. $\sqrt{75}$
3. $\sqrt{80}$
4. $\sqrt{108}$
5. $\sqrt{150}$
6. $\sqrt{98}$
7. $\sqrt{700}$
8. $\sqrt{60}$
9. $\sqrt{450}$
10. $\sqrt{245}$
11. $\sqrt{128}$
12. $\sqrt{242}$
13. $2\sqrt{27}$
14. $5\sqrt{32}$
15. $3\sqrt{175}$
16. $4\sqrt{63}$
17. $6\sqrt{125}$
18. $2\sqrt{54}$
19. $7\sqrt{192}$
20. $10\sqrt{162}$
21. $(\sqrt{8})^2$
22. $\sqrt{10} \cdot \sqrt{10}$
23. $\sqrt{6} \cdot \sqrt{2}$
24. $\sqrt{13^2}$
25. $\sqrt{3} \cdot \sqrt{15}$
26. $\sqrt{6} \cdot \sqrt{14}$
27. $\sqrt{5} \cdot \sqrt{30}$
28. $\sqrt{21} \cdot \sqrt{35}$
29. $4\sqrt{8} \cdot 3\sqrt{2}$
30. $10\sqrt{6} \cdot 9\sqrt{6}$
31. $7\sqrt{15} \cdot 2\sqrt{5}$
32. $8\sqrt{7} \cdot 5\sqrt{14}$

Solve for *x*.

33. $x^2 = 44$
34. $x^2 = 27$
35. $x^2 = 96$
36. $3x^2 = 150$
37. $5x^2 = 90$
38. $2x^2 = 360$
39. $3y^2 = x^2$
40. $x^2 = 6a^2 + 6a^2$
41. $x^2 = 10k^2 - k^2$
42. $(3b)^2 + (4b)^2 = x^2$
43. $x^2 = (4m)^2 - (2m)^2$
44. $x^2 + c^2 = 19c^2$
45. A square has a perimeter of $12a$. Write an expression for the length of the diagonal of the square, in terms of a, in simplified radical form.
46. A rectangle has length $3b$ and width $6b$. Write an expression for the length of the diagonal of the rectangle, in terms of b, in simplified radical form.

Use triangle *PQR* for Exercises 47 and 48. This triangle is "half" of an equilateral triangle.

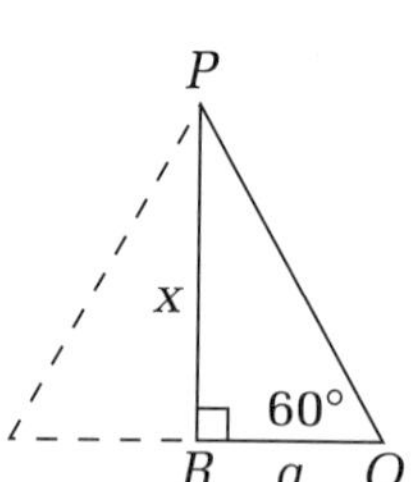

47. Write an expression, in terms of a, for the hypotenuse $\overline{PQ}$ of triangle PQR.
48. Using the Pythagorean theorem, write an equation that relates x and a. Solve the equation for x in simplified radical form.

Name ______________________ Date ____________

Practice 69

For use with Section 9-3

Solve.

1. $(x - 1)(x - 2) = 0$

2. $n(n - 5) = 0$

3. $3k^2 = 0$

4. $(a + 1)(a - 1) = 0$

5. $(y - 3)(y + 2) = 0$

6. $2w(w - 4) = 0$

7. $3t(t + 6) = 0$

8. $7b(b - 9) = 0$

9. $-5c(c - 8) = 0$

10. $z(2z - 7) = 0$

11. $6m(3m + 4) = 0$

12. $-3v(4v - 18) = 0$

In Exercises 13–24, the lengths of the sides of a triangle are given. Is the triangle a right triangle?

13. 2 m, 3 m, 4 m

14. 20 mm, 21 mm, 29 mm

15. 4 yd, 5 yd, 6 yd

16. 8 in., 15 in., 17 in.

17. 4 ft, 7 ft, 8 ft

18. 5 cm, 5 cm, 7 cm

19. 3 m, 5 m, 6 m

20. 9 yd, 40 yd, 41 yd

21. 5 m, 10 m, 15 m

22. 2.5 cm, 6 cm, 6.5 cm

23. 2.1 in., 2.8 in., 3.5 in.

24. 3.3 m, 3.5 m, 4.8 m

Tell whether each statement is *true* or *false*. If it is false, give a counterexample.

25. If you swim, you will get wet.

26. If $x^2 > 16$, then $x > 4$.

27. If you cannot see your shadow, the sun has set.

28. If an animal is a bird, then it can fly.

29. If quadrilateral *ABCD* is a square, then it is a rectangle.

30. If two sides of a quadilateral are parallel, then it is a parallelogram.

For Exercises 31–36, write the converse of the statement and tell whether the converse is *true* or *false*. If it is false, give a counterexample.

31. If y is even, then y^2 is even.

32. If it is raining, then the ground is wet.

33. If $a > 0$, then $a^2 > 0$.

34. If you are at school, it is not July 4.

35. If $x = 0$, then $xy = 0$.

36. $x < 7$ if $x < 5$.

37. ***Open-ended*** Draw several triangles with sides a, b, and c, such that $c^2 > a^2 + b^2$. What can you say about the angle opposite side c? Draw some triangles in which $c^2 < a^2 + b^2$. What seems to be true now about the angle opposite side c?

Name ______________________________ Date ______________

Practice 70

For use with Section 9-4

Find the probability that a dart landing inside each shape lands in the shaded region.

1. 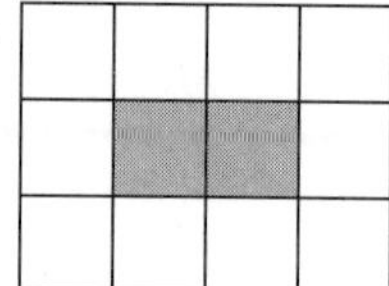

2. 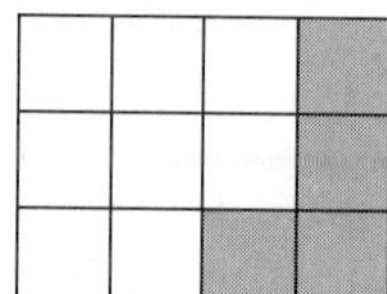

3. 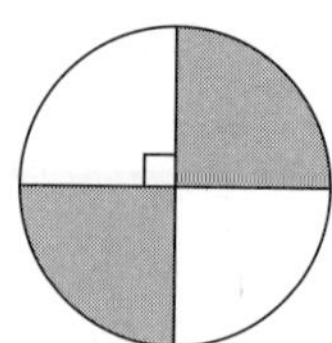

4. 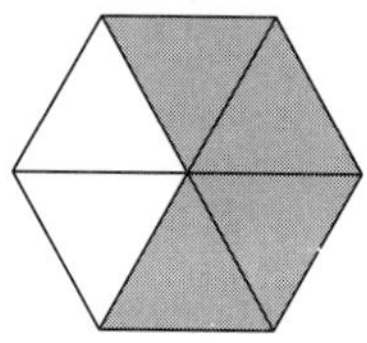

(regular hexagon)

5. 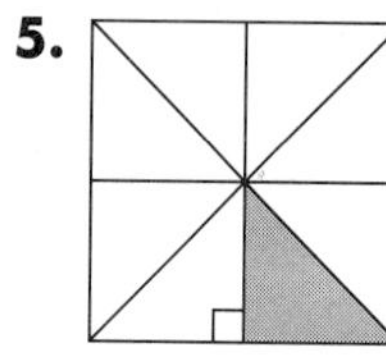

(square)

6. 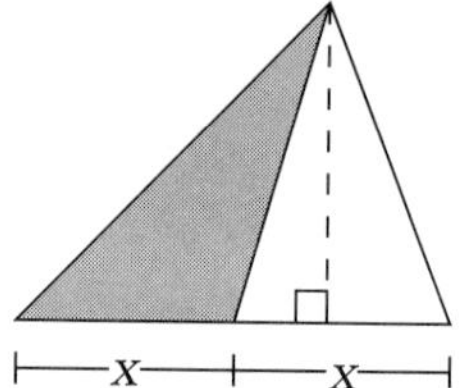

7. During each cycle, a traffic light turns green for cars in one direction for 30 s. It is green for cars in the other direction for 25 s. The *WALK* sign is then on for 20 s. Find the probability that when you arrive at the intersection on foot, you can cross without waiting.

8. A television news program has 18 min of news and 12 min of commercials. Suppose you tune in at a random time during the program. What is the probability that a commercial will be in progress?

9. A circular target that has a diameter of 48 in. has a bull's-eye with a diameter of 8 in. What is the probability that an arrow hitting the target will land in the bull's-eye?

10. A running track is as shown. Suppose you run at a constant speed around the track. At a random time, what is the probability that you are on one of the straightaways?

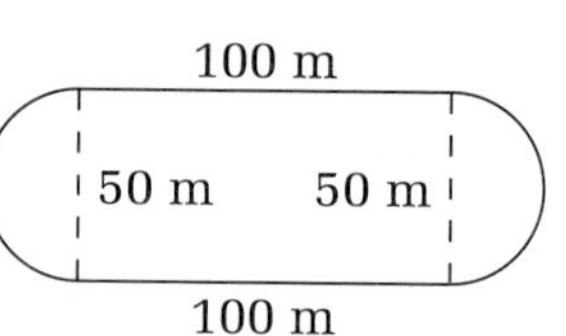

A circular target has a sector marked off and shaded. Find the angle the shaded sector should have so that a dart hitting the target has each probability of landing in the sector.

11. $\frac{1}{3}$

12. $\frac{3}{5}$

13. $\frac{5}{6}$

14. $\frac{2}{9}$

15. ***Writing*** The group Endangered Species performed for 12 min at some point during a 2-hour rock concert. Suppose you taped 1 h of the concert. Write a full explanation of how you could find the probability that you taped all of the group's performance.

Name ______________________ Date ______________

Practice 71

For use with Section 9-5

Find the surface area of each prism.

1. 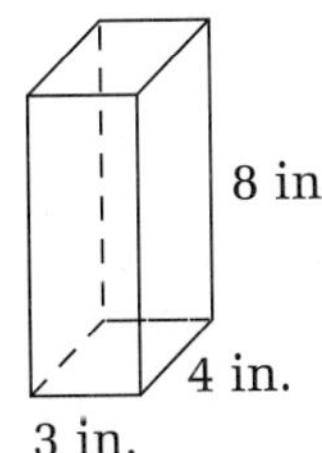

2. 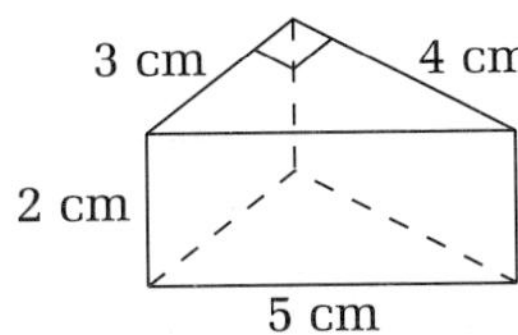

3. 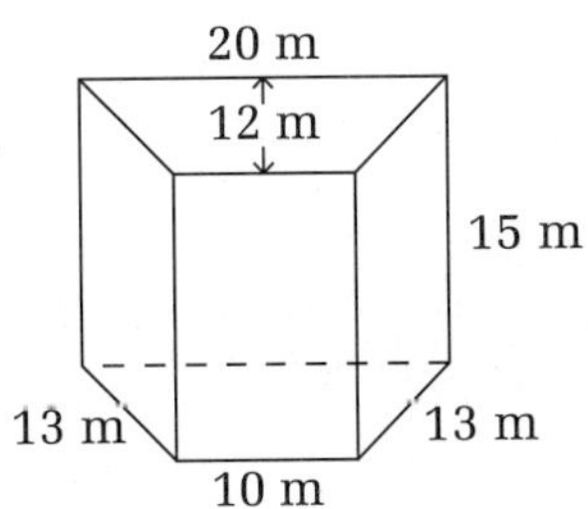

Find the surface area of each cylinder or half cylinder.

4. 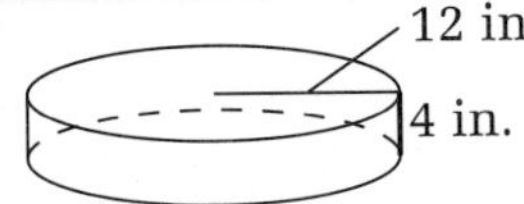

5. 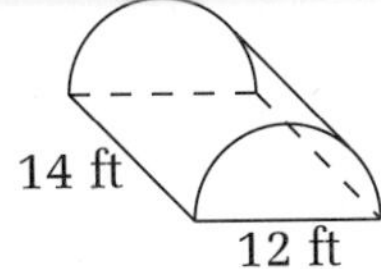

6. 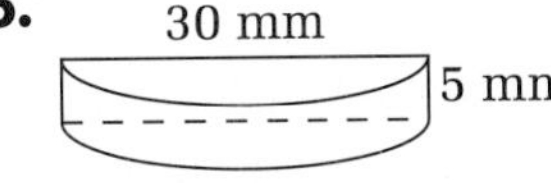

Find the surface area of the regular square pyramid having each set of measurements.

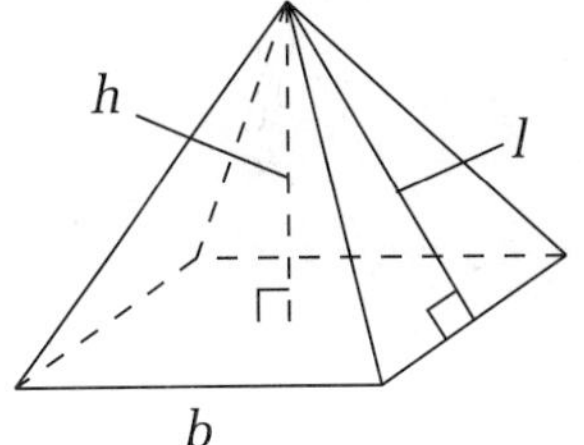

7. $b = 10; h = 12$

8. $b = 16; h = 6$

9. $b = 48; h = 7$

10. $l = 29; h = 21$

11. $l = 17; h = 8$

12. $l = 26; h = 24$

13. A jewelry manufacturer wants to plate an old coin with silver to make a piece of jewelry. The coin has a thickness of 2 mm and is 25 mm in diameter. How many square millimeters must be plated. Answer to the nearest 10 square millimeters.

14. A prism has bases that are congruent equilateral triangles with sides of length 6 cm. The height of the prism is 8 cm. Find its surface area, to the nearest square centimeter.

15. A block of cheese has the shape of a quarter of a cylinder. The bases are quarter circles of radius 5 in. and the height of the block is 6 in. How many square inches must be covered if you wish to coat the outer surface of the block with wax?

16. The bases of a prism are trapezoids with parallel sides of length 10 in. and 22 in. Each of the nonparallel sides of the bases has length 10 in. The height of the prism is 11 in. Sketch one base of the prism and use the Pythagorean theorem to find the height of the trapezoid. Then find the surface area of the prism.

Name ______________________ Date ______________

Practice 72

For use with Section 9-6

For Exercises 1–6, use the space figures below.

A.

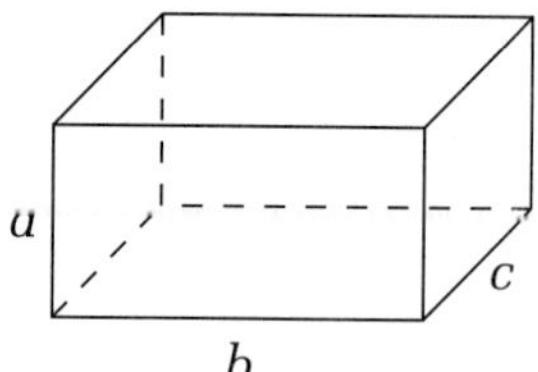

B.

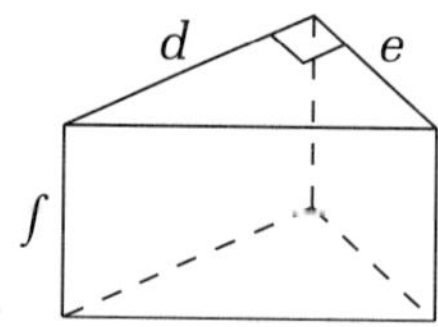

C.

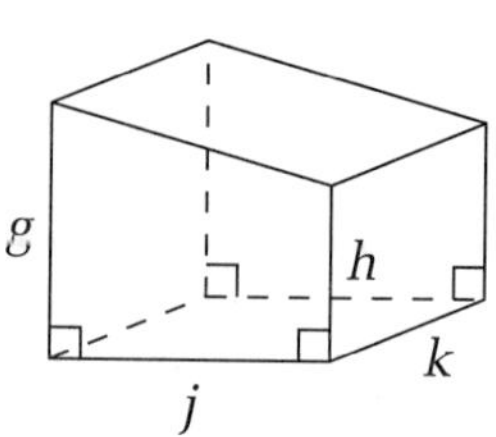

Find the volume of each figure with each set of measurements.

1. Use Fig. A: $a = 8$ in.; $b = 10$ in.; $c = 12$ in.

2. Use Fig. B: $d = 11$ cm; $e = 8$ cm; $f = 14$ cm

3. Use Fig. C: $g = 15$ m; $h = 13$ m; $j = 8$ m; $k = 10$ m

Find the missing dimension.

4. Use Fig. A: $a = 12$ mm; $b = 15$ mm; volume $= 2340$ mm^3; $c =$ __?__

5. Use Fig. B: $d = 8$ in.; $e = 10$ in.; volume $= 440$ in.^{3}; $f =$ __?__

6. Use Fig. C: $g = 17$ cm; $h = 7$ cm; $j = 5$ cm; volume $= 1020$ cm^3; $k =$ __?__

Find the volume of each space figure. Answer to the nearest tenth.

7.

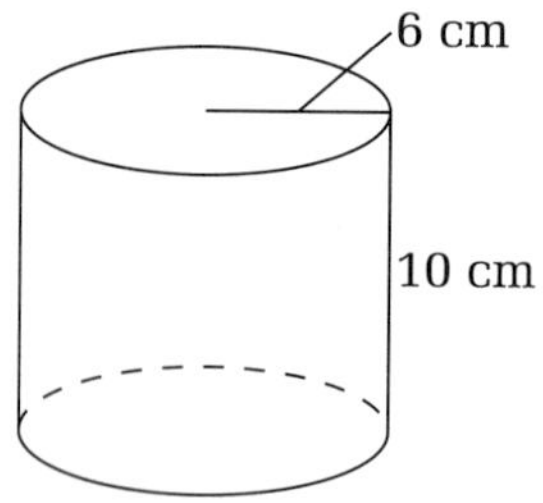

8.

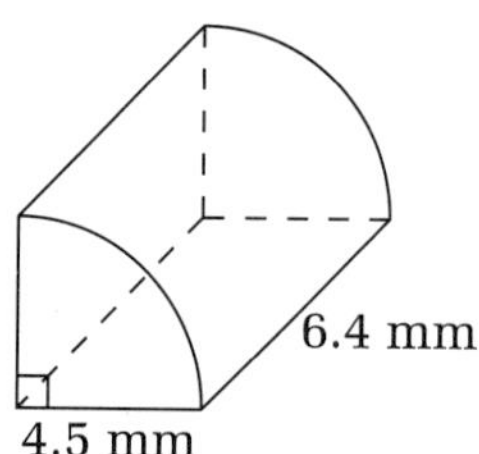

9.

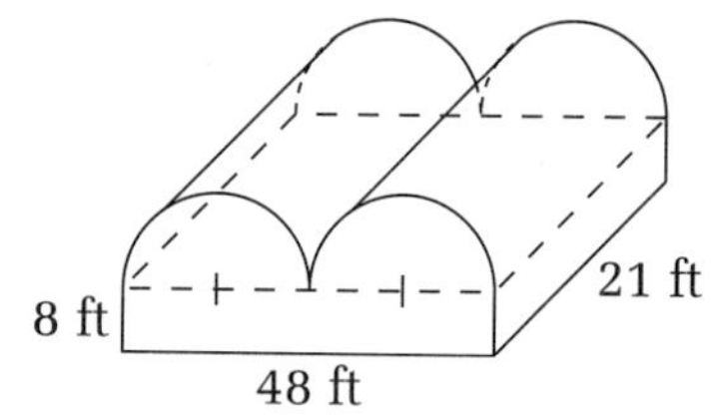

10. Andreas has an aquarium with a rectangular base 40 cm × 25 cm. He wants to put in the aquarium a decorative rock in the shape of a cylinder 3 cm tall and having circular bases of radius 8 cm. Suppose he does so. By how much will the water level in the aquarium rise?

11. ***Open-ended*** Design your own candy in the shape of a prism, using for a base rectangles, triangles, trapezoids, parallelograms and/or sectors of circles. Find the volume of your candy.

Name ______________________ Date ______________

Practice 73

For use with Section 9-7

Find the volume of each space figure.

1.

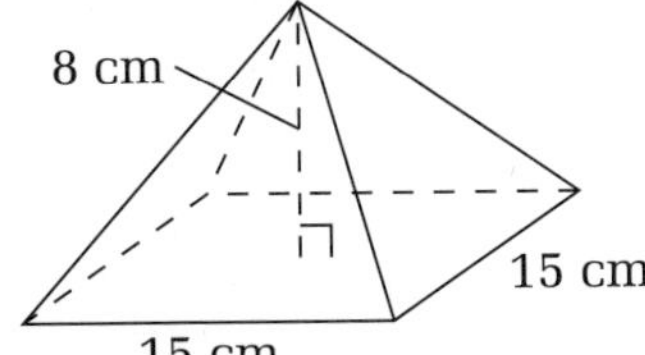

2.

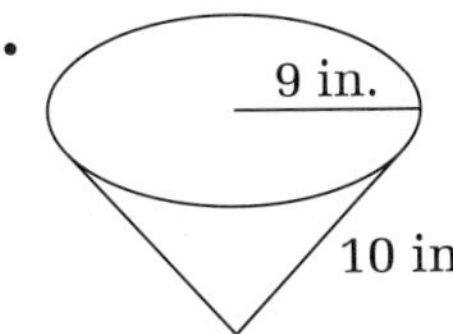

3.

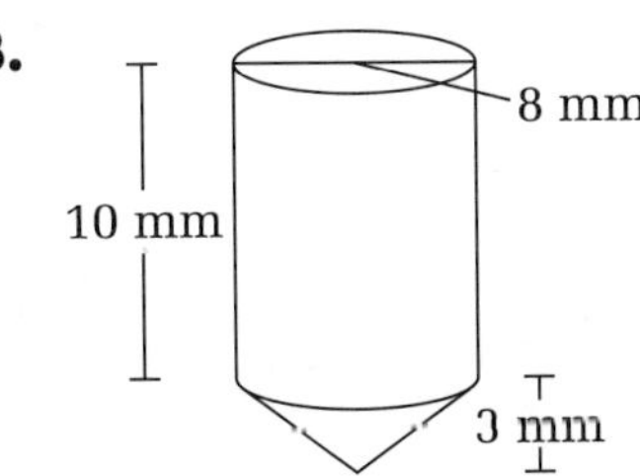

For Exercises 4–9, use the regular square pyramid at the right. Find the volume of the pyramid, using each set of measurements.

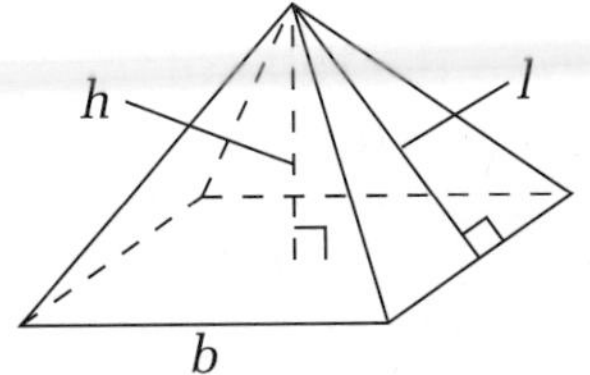

4. $b = 42$ in.; $h = 28$ in. **5.** $b = 25$ cm; $h = 15$ cm

6. $b = 12$ m; $l = 13$ m **7.** $b = 24$ ft; $l = 30$ ft

8. $h = 11$ cm; $l = 61$ cm **9.** $h = 48$ in.; $l = 73$ in.

10. A cone has a slant height of 25 cm and a height of 7 cm. Find the volume of the cone.

11. The slant height of a cone is 26 in. and the diameter of its base is 20 in. Find the volume of the cone, to the nearest cubic inch.

12. At a soft-ice-cream stand, the waffle cones for ice cream cones come in two sizes. The smaller size has a radius of 1.5 in. and a height of 4 in. The larger size has a radius of 2 in. and a height of 6 in. Suppose each cone were filled with ice cream and leveled at the top. Find the ratio of the larger volume of ice cream to the smaller.

13. A tent manufacturer wants to build a tent in the shape of a square pyramid with a base 8 ft on each side. The tent should have a volume of at least 108 ft^3. To the nearest foot, what is the smallest height such a tent can have?

14. A popcorn container has the shape shown at the right. The measures shown are approximate. Find the volume of the container. (*Hint:* Think about the difference between the volumes of two cones.)

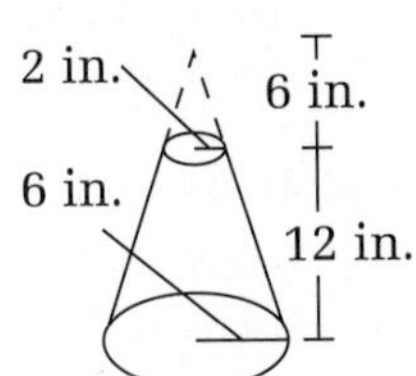

15. Draw a cone and a regular square pyramid with the same height. Suppose the diameter of the base of the cone is the same as the length of a side of the base of the pyramid. Find the ratio of the volume of the cone to the volume of the pyramid.

Name ______________________ Date ____________

Practice 74

For use with Section 9-8

In Exercises 1–4, for each ratio of the lengths of corresponding sides of two similar figures, find the ratio of their areas.

1. 3 : 4 **2.** 5 : 7 **3.** 3 : 8 **4.** $\frac{1}{13}$

In Exercises 5–8, for each ratio of the lengths of corresponding sides of two similar space figures, find the ratio of their volumes.

5. 6 : 4 **6.** 3 : 10 **7.** 5 : 12 **8.** $\frac{2}{5}$

Find the ratio of the areas of each pair of similar figures. Then find the missing area.

9.

3 cm

Area = 18 cm^2

8 cm

Area = ?

10.

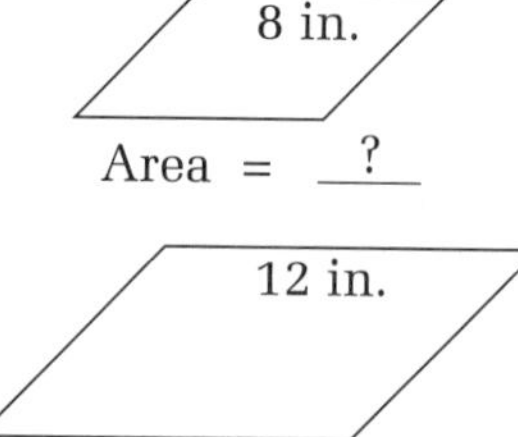

11.

5 ft

Area = 20 ft^2

9 ft

Area = ?

For Exercises 12–14, use the similar pyramids at the right. Find each missing measurement using the given measurements.

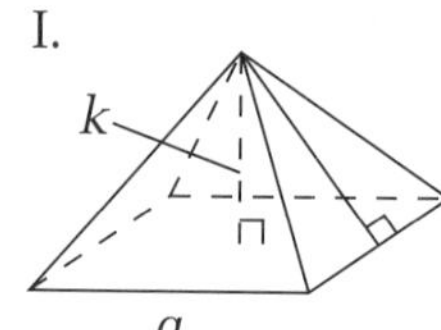

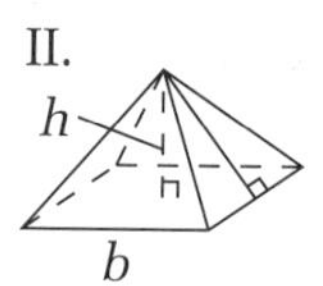

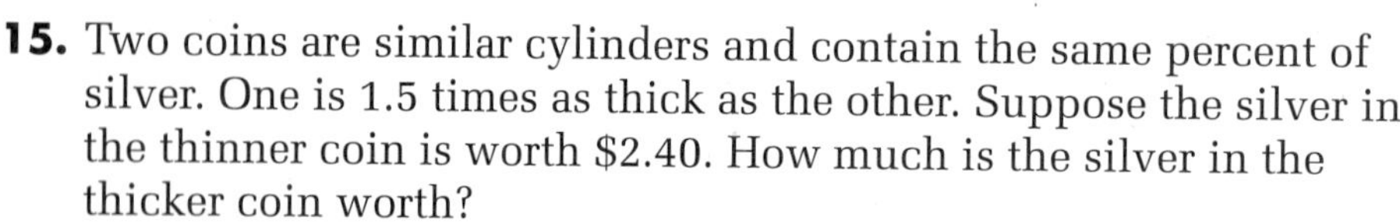

12. a = 15 cm; b = 10 cm; Volume II = 8 cm^3; Volume I = ?

13. h = 4 ft; Volume I = 54 ft^3; Volume II = 16 ft^3; k = ?

14. k = 15 mm; h = 6 mm; Volume I = 62.5 mm^3; Volume II = ?

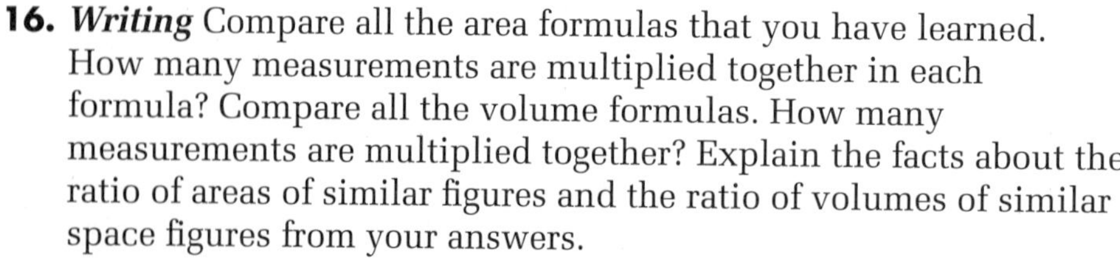

15. Two coins are similar cylinders and contain the same percent of silver. One is 1.5 times as thick as the other. Suppose the silver in the thinner coin is worth $2.40. How much is the silver in the thicker coin worth?

16. ***Writing*** Compare all the area formulas that you have learned. How many measurements are multiplied together in each formula? Compare all the volume formulas. How many measurements are multiplied together? Explain the facts about the ratio of areas of similar figures and the ratio of volumes of similar space figures from your answers.

Name ______________________ Date ____________

Practice 75

Cumulative Practice through Unit 9

Without graphing, find the slope and the vertical intercept of the line modeled by each equation.

1. $y = 4x + 9$ **2.** $y = 7 - 2.5x$ **3.** $y = -0.5x$

In Exercises 4–7, write an equation for each line.

4. The slope is –3 and the vertical intercept is 8.

5. The slope is $\frac{3}{2}$ and the point (4, 7) is on the line.

6. The vertical intercept is 2 and the horizontal intercept is 5.

7. The points (–1, 6) and (3, 8) are on the line.

Graph each inequality.

8. $y \geq -x + 3$ **9.** $y < \frac{1}{3}x - 2$ **10.** $2x + y \leq 5$

Find the area of each sector.

11. 9 cm

12.

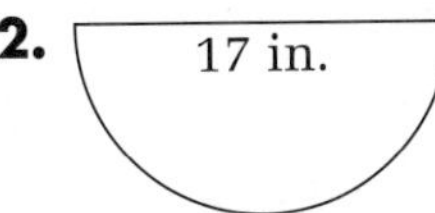

13.

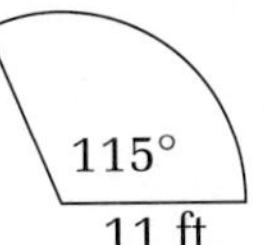

14. A sign for Monoco gas stations is to have the name MONOCO inside a rectangle that measures 3.5 ft by 10 ft. The rectangle is to be inside a circle. What is the smallest diameter the circle can have?

15. A spaghetti sauce can has a height of 10.5 cm. It has circular bases of diameter 7.2 cm. Find the surface area of the can, to the nearest square centimeter.

16. Find the volume of the can in Exercise 15, to the nearest tenth of a cubic centimeter.

17. A spinner dial has congruent sectors numbered from 1 to 12. What is the probability of spinning a number less than 7?

18. Pisces Rent-a-Car charges $250 for a one-week rental plus $.20 per mile. CPS Rent-a-Car charges $190 for a one-week rental plus $.35 per mile. For how many miles would the two companies charge the same amount?

Name ______________________ Date ____________

Practice 76

For use with Section 10-1

In Exercises 1–6, tell whether each transformation is a reflection. If it is, draw the line of reflection.

1. p q

2. “ ”

3.

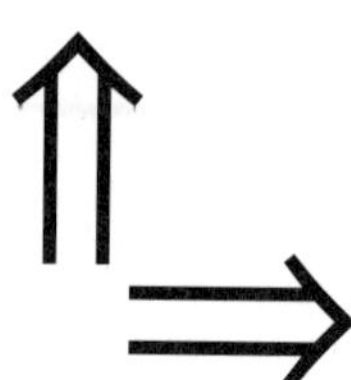

4.

U

5. C c

6.

M

Each diagram below shows a figure and its image.

I.

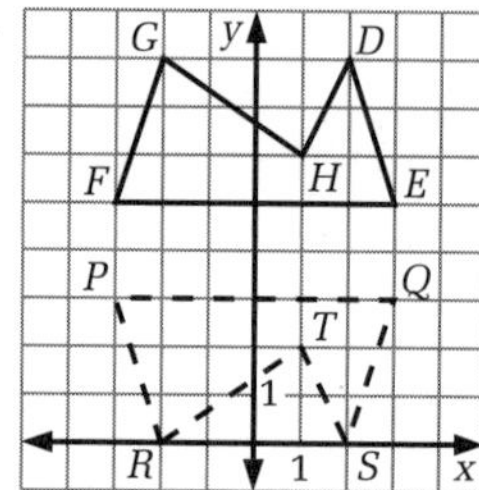

II.

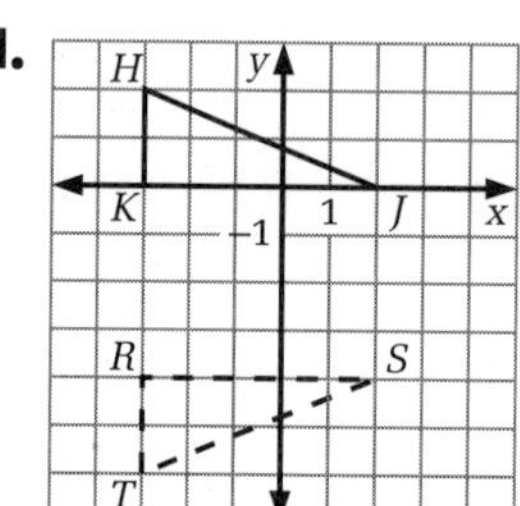

III.

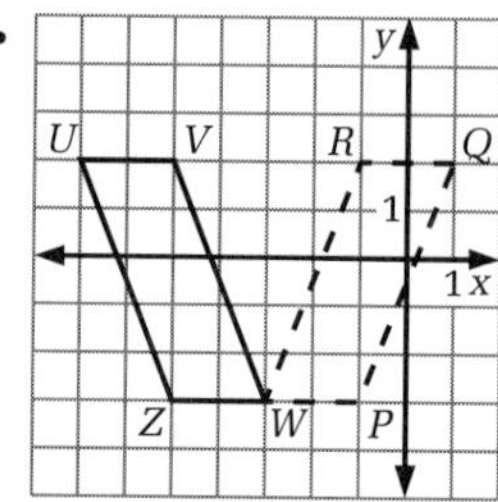

Write an equation of each line of reflection.

7. Diagram I

8. Diagram II

9. Diagram III

In each diagram, tell the image of each point.

10. For I: *D, E, F, G, H*

11. For II: *H, J, K*

12. For III: *U, V, W, Z*

For each ordered pair (x, y), tell the image of the point under each reflection. Give an equation of the line of reflection.

13. $(x, y) \rightarrow (x, -y)$: (3, 2), (1, −1)

14. $(x, y) \rightarrow (-x, y)$: (−5, 1), (3, 4)

15. $(x, y) \rightarrow (-y, -x)$: (4, −3), (5, 1)

16. $(x, y) \rightarrow (x, 6 - y)$: (2, 5), (−1, 4)

17. ***Open-ended*** Look in magazines for ads that picture an object and its reflection. For each ad, trace the object and its reflection and draw the line of reflection.

Name ______________________ Date ______________

Practice 77

For use with Section 10-2

In Exercises 1–3, match each function with its graph.

1. $y = x^2 - 2$

2. $y = (x - 2)^2$

3. $y = (x + 2)^2$

A.

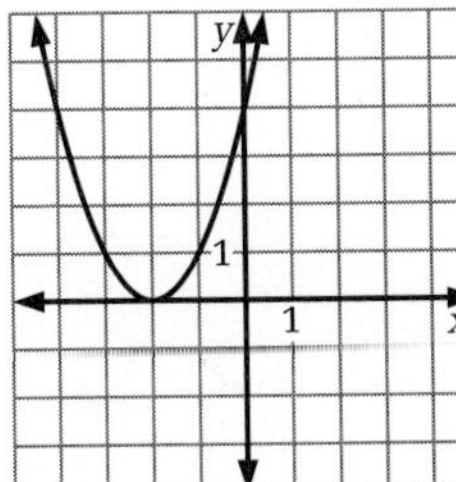

B.

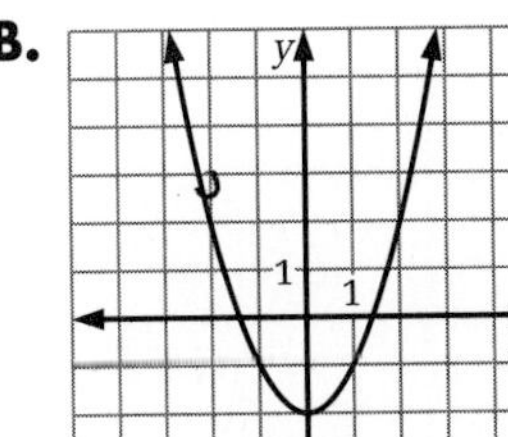

C.

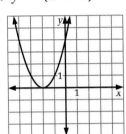

In Exercises 4–9, describe in words the translation of the graph of $y = x^2$ that produces the graph of each equation.

4. $y = (x - 3)^2$

5. $y = x^2 + 4$

6. $y = x^2 - 1$

7. $y = (x + 5)^2$

8. $y = (x - 6)^2$

9. $y = x^2 + 7$

Tell how to translate the graph of $y = x^2$ or $y = -x^2$ in order to produce the graph of each function.

10. $y = -x^2 - 2$

11. $y = x^2 + 5$

12. $y = -x^2 + 3$

13. $y = -(x - 1)^2$

14. $y = -x^2 - 6$

15. $y = -(x + 1)^2$

16. $y = (x - 4)^2$

17. $y = (x - 2)^2 + 1$

18. $y = (x + 5)^2 - 3$

For the graph of each function, find an equation of the line of symmetry and the coordinates of the vertex.

19. $y = x^2 - 5$

20. $y = (x + 1)^2$

21. $y = (x - 10)^2$

22. $y = -(x - 8)^2$

23. $y = -x^2 + 11$

24. $y = x^2 - 7$

Find a function whose graph fits each description and has the same shape as the graph of $y = x^2$.

25. vertex at the point (3, 0)

26. translation of $y = x^2$ up 5 units

27. translation of $y = -x^2$ left 6 units

28. vertex at the point (–9, 0)

Name ______________________ Date ______________

Practice 78

For use with Section 10-3

Match each equation with its graph.

1. $y = (x - 2)(x - 4)$ **2.** $y = (x - 3)(x + 1)$ **3.** $y = -x(x - 4)$

A. 

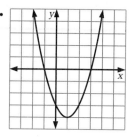

B. 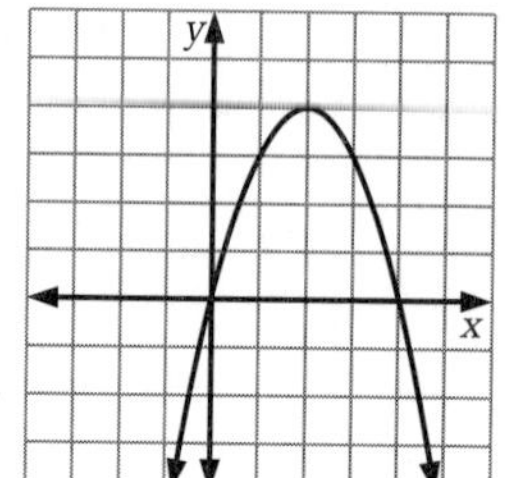

C. 

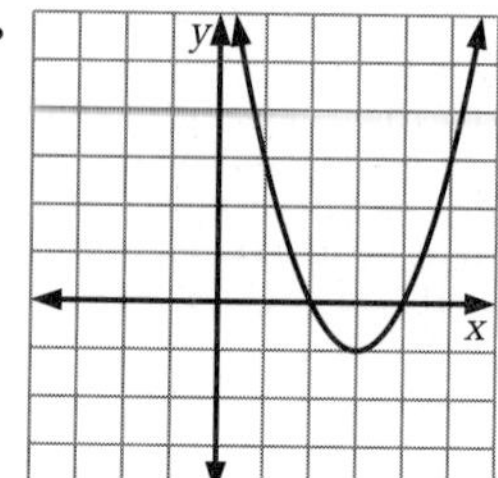

Graph each parabola.

4. $y = x(x - 4)$ **5.** $y = x(x + 2)$ **6.** $y -x(x + 4)$

7. $y = (x - 1)(x + 1)$ **8.** $y = (x - 2)(2 - x)$ **9.** $y = (x - 1)(x + 3)$

10. $y = (x + 2)(4 - x)$ **11.** $y = (x - 1)(3 - x)$ **12.** $y = (2x - 6)(x + 1)$

Find the x-intercepts and y-intercept of the graph of each equation.

13. $y = x(x - 3)$ **14.** $y = -x(x + 7)$ **15.** $y = (x - 1)(x - 6)$

16. $y = (x + 4)(x - 11)$ **17.** $y = (3x - 1)(x + 4)$ **18.** $y = (2 - x)(4x + 3)$

Dinah Johnson, an economist for a cable TV company, graphed the relationship between total monthly revenue (y) and proposed increase (x) in the monthly fee. The fee is now \$8.00 and revenue is \$128,000.

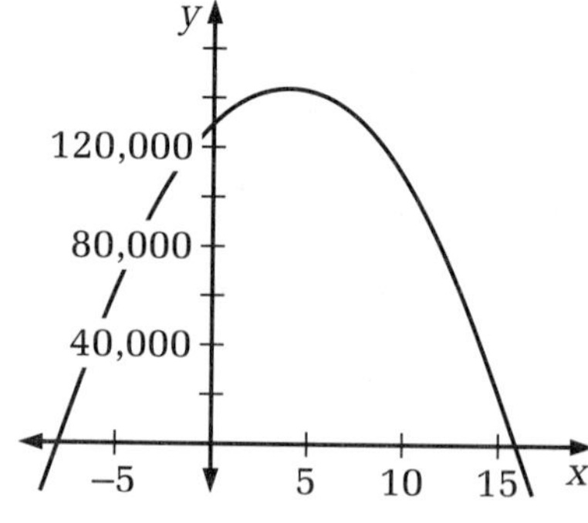

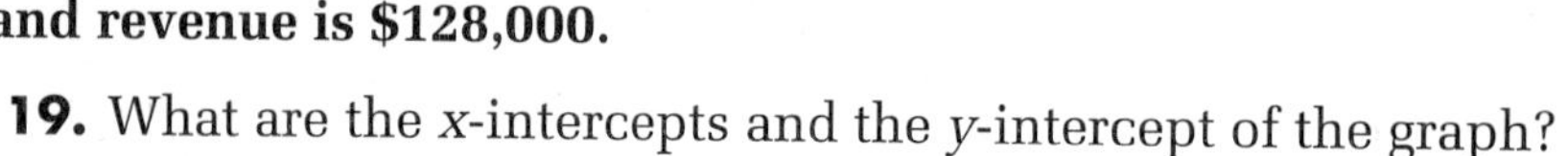

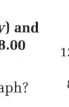

19. What are the x-intercepts and the y-intercept of the graph?

20. What fee increase will maximize revenue?

21. Which equation could represent the graph?

a. $y = (16{,}000 + 1000x)(8 + x)$

b. $y = (16{,}000 + 1000x)(8 - x)$

c. $y = (16{,}000 - 1000x)(8 + x)$

d. $y = (16{,}000 - 1000x)(8 - x)$

22. ***Writing*** The two factors in the answer for Exercise 21 represent proposed fee and audience size. Describe how one of these quantities affects the other.

Name ______________________ Date ______________

Practice 79

For use with Section 10-4

Simplify.

1. $a^3 \cdot a^2$
2. $n^4 \cdot n^3$
3. $x^2 \cdot x^6$
4. $b^6 \cdot b^2 \cdot b$
5. $r^4 \cdot r^2 \cdot r^3$
6. $5c^3 \cdot c^5$
7. $6p^8 \cdot 4p^3$
8. $-10z^6 \cdot 3z^4$
9. $(8k^7)(-3k^3)$
10. $(-7x^6)(2x^3)$
11. $(11y)(-4y^5)$
12. $(-n^7)(-6n^8)$
13. $x^3y \cdot x^7y^2$
14. $(a^4b^3)(-a^6b^5)$
15. $(-m^4n^2)(mn^6)$
16. $(-5u^2v^3)(4uv^2)$
17. $3xy^2 \cdot 8xy^4$
18. $(-3j^3k)(-5j^2k^2)$

Simplify.

19. $(x^4)^3$
20. $(y^2)^5$
21. $(c^3)^2$
22. $(2n)^5$
23. $(-2k)^4$
24. $(-3r)^3$
25. $(xy^2)^5$
26. $(-m^5n)^2$
27. $(-a^2b^3)^3$
28. $(-2r^2s)^4$
29. $(4uv^5)^3$
30. $(-2x^2y^3)^7$
31. $a^5(3a^3)^2$
32. $(-2a^4)(2a^2)^5$
33. $(4n)(-2n^3)^4$
34. Write an expression in simplified form for the area of the square at the right.
35. Write an expression in simplified form for the volume of the cube at the right.

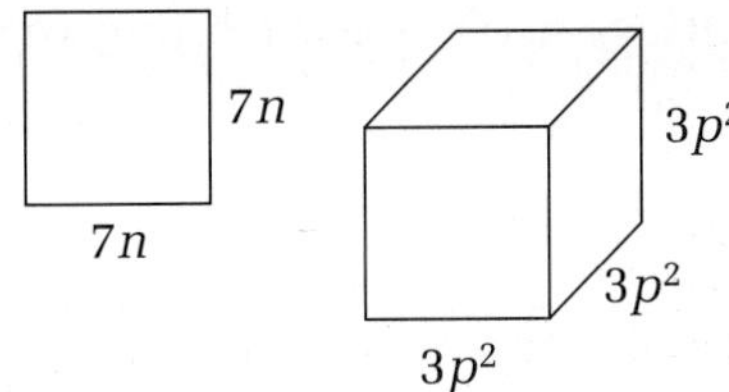

Insert parentheses in the expression on the left side of each equation to make a true statement.

36. $3c^2d^4 = 81c^8d^4$
37. $2x^3y^5 = 8x^3y^5$
38. $3a^2b^4 = 3a^8b^4$

Name ______________________ Date ____________

Practice 80

For use with Section 10-5

Expand each expression.

1. $x(x + 5)$
2. $x(x - 12)$
3. $-x(x - 3)$
4. $2x(x - 10)$
5. $-6x(x + 7)$
6. $9x(2 - x)$
7. $3x(4x + 5)$
8. $7x(8 - 3x)$
9. $-2x(4x - 11)$
10. $5x^2(x + 3)$
11. $-4x^2(5 - 6x)$
12. $-5x(x^3 + 2)$

For Exercises 13–24,

a. **factor one side of each equation completely.**

b. **find the x-intercepts and y-intercept of the graph of each equation.**

13. $y = x^2 + 3x$
14. $y = x^2 - 15x$
15. $y = x^2 + x$
16. $y = -x^2 - 6x$
17. $y = -x^2 + 7x$
18. $y = x - 4x^2$
19. $y = 2x^2 + 5x$
20. $y = -8x^2 + x$
21. $y = 10x^2 - 3x$
22. $y = 3x^2 - 6x$
23. $y = 5x^2 + 20x$
24. $y = -2x^2 + 2x$

A maker of medical supplies wants to design an adhesive bandage with a square pad in the center, as shown at the right.

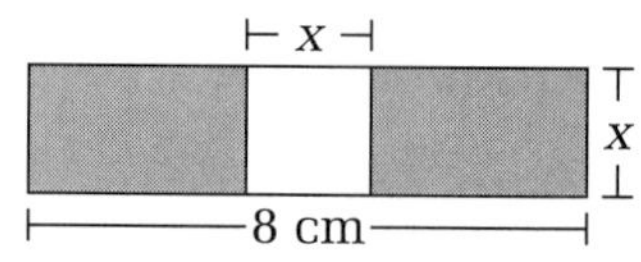

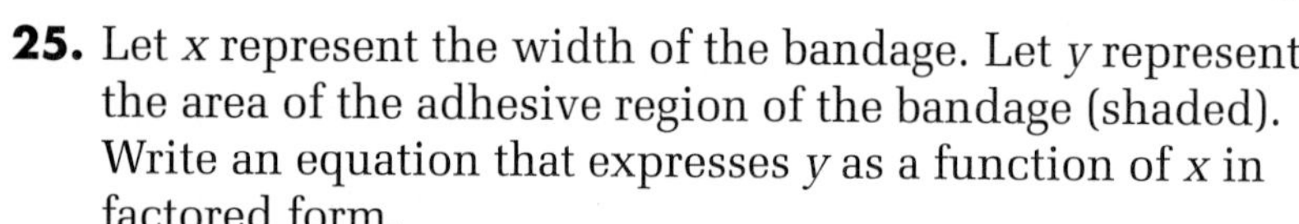

25. Let x represent the width of the bandage. Let y represent the area of the adhesive region of the bandage (shaded). Write an equation that expresses y as a function of x in factored form.

26. Find the x-intercepts for your equation. Use the x-intercepts to help you graph the equation you found in Exercise 25.

Yoshi is going to build a fence for a rectangular garden that will be alongside a brick wall at the back of his property. He has 120 ft of fencing. He will use the brick wall for one side of the garden. Refer to the diagram to answer Exercises 27 and 28.

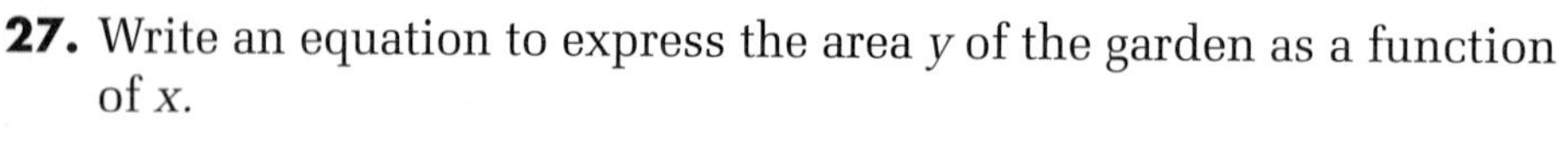

27. Write an equation to express the area y of the garden as a function of x.

28. Find the maximum area possible for the garden.

Name ______________________ Date ______________

Practice 81

For use with Section 10-6

Expand each product.

1. $(x + 1)(x + 4)$

2. $(x + 3)(x + 5)$

3. $(x - 2)(x + 2)$

4. $(x - 6)(x + 1)$

5. $(-x + 8)(x - 3)$

6. $(x - 7)(x + 9)$

7. $(x - 3)(x + 3)$

8. $(x - 6)(x - 6)$

9. $(-x - 8)(x - 5)$

10. $(x - 11)(x + 7)$

11. $(-x + 12)(x - 4)$

12. $(x - 9)(x - 4)$

13. $(5 - x)(2 + x)$

14. $(7 - x)(3 - x)$

15. $(x + 8)(2 - x)$

16. $(2x - 1)(x + 5)$

17. $(-3x + 2)(x + 6)$

18. $(3x - 4)(2x + 1)$

19. $(5x - 3)(4x - 1)$

20. $(8x + 3)(2x - 5)$

21. $(4x - 3)(-7x + 2)$

Match each equation with its graph.

22. $y = x^2 - 4$

23. $y = x^2 - 2x - 3$

24. $y = x^2 - 4x$

A.

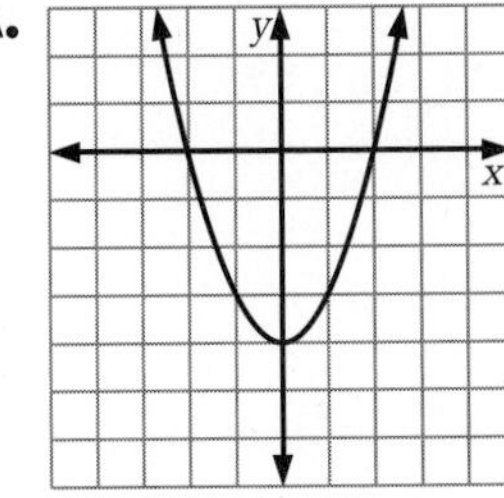

B.

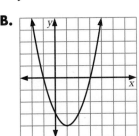

C.

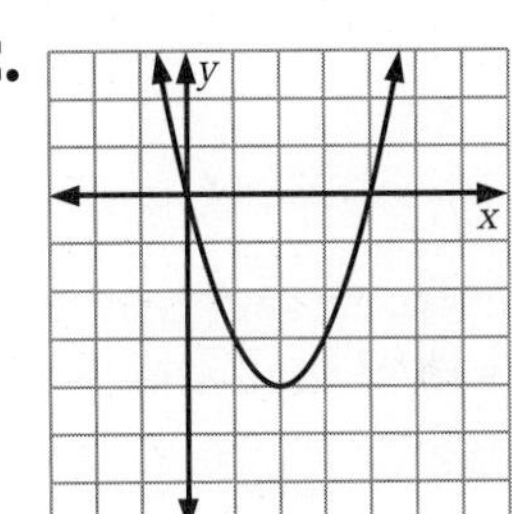

Without graphing, find each feature of the graph of each equation.

a. **the equation of the line of symmetry**

b. **the coordinates of the vertex**

c. **the *y*-intercept**

25. $y = x^2 - 6x - 5$

26. $y = x^2 + 4x + 7$

27. $y = x^2 - 8x + 12$

28. $y = -x^2 - 10x - 24$

29. $y = x^2 - 2x$

30. $y = -x^2 + 6x + 16$

31. $y = 2x^2 + 8x + 10$

32. $y = -3x^2 - 18x - 5$

33. $y = 6x^2 - 12x - 10$

34. $y = -2x^2 + 16x + 3$

35. $y = 5x^2 + 40x - 6$

36. $y = 4x^2 - 24x + 13$

37. ***Writing*** Suppose you examined a small piece of a parabola under a microscope. It would be nearly a straight line segment. Describe how the slope of such line segments would change as you made your way along the parabola.

Name ______________________ Date ____________

Practice 82

For use with Section 10-7

Factor each trinomial.

1. $x^2 + 3x + 2$
2. $x^2 + 7x + 10$
3. $x^2 + 8x + 12$
4. $x^2 - 11x + 18$
5. $x^2 - 10x + 24$
6. $x^2 + 9x + 14$
7. $x^2 - 9x + 20$
8. $x^2 - x - 6$
9. $x^2 - 2x - 15$
10. $x^2 + 3x - 10$
11. $x^2 + 8x + 15$
12. $x^2 - 5x - 6$
13. $x^2 + 4x - 21$
14. $x^2 - 12x + 27$
15. $x^2 - 3x - 40$
16. $x^2 - 5x - 24$
17. $x^2 + 7x - 18$
18. $x^2 - 11x + 28$

Factor each trinomial that can be factored using integers, or write *unfactorable*.

19. $x^2 - 6x + 8$
20. $x^2 - x + 12$
21. $x^2 + 5x - 4$
22. $x^2 - 9x + 20$
23. $x^2 + 3x - 18$
24. $x^2 - 6x + 16$
25. $x^2 + 10x - 24$
26. $x^2 + 10x + 24$
27. $x^2 - 4x + 12$

For Exercises 28–33, use the line of symmetry, the vertex, and the intercepts to sketch the graph of each equation.

28. $y = x^2 - 3x - 4$
29. $y = x^2 + x - 6$
30. $y = x^2 - 5x + 6$
31. $y = x^2 + 2x - 8$
32. $y = x^2 - 6x + 8$
33. $y = x^2 + 8x + 12$

34. The Chens enlarged their square kitchen by a whole number of feet in each direction. Margaret Chen said to her husband, "Suppose the length of each side of our old kitchen was x ft. Then our new kitchen has an area equal to $x^2 + 11x + 30$ square feet." By how many feet did the Chens enlarge their kitchen in each direction?

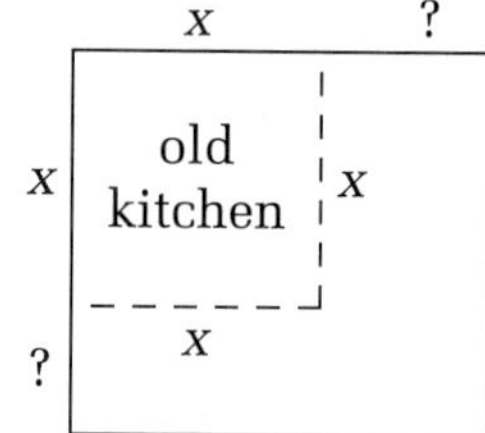

35. Lynn launched a model rocket straight up. The initial velocity of the rocket when it left the ground was 160 ft/s. The height h of the rocket t seconds after launch is given by the formula $h = 160t - 16t^2$. How many seconds will it take the rocket to hit the ground?

Name ______________________ Date ______________

Practice 83

For use with Section 10-8

For Exercises 1–7, use the graphs below.

A. $y = x^2 - x - 6$

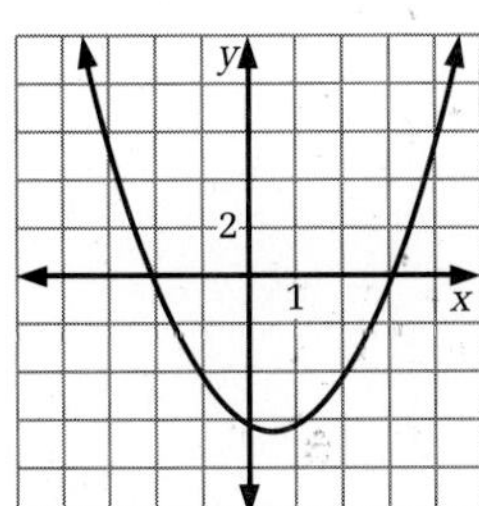

B. $y = x^2 - 5x + 6$

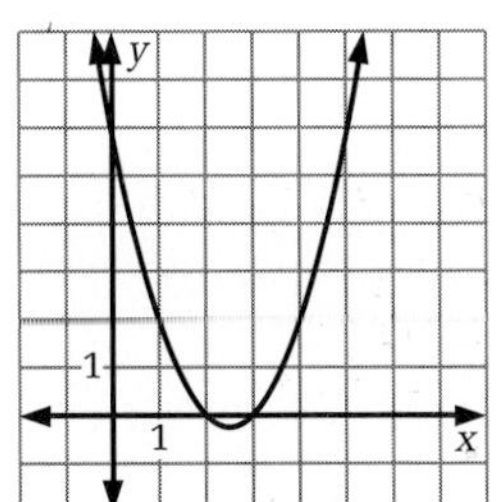

C. $y = x^2 + 6x + 5$

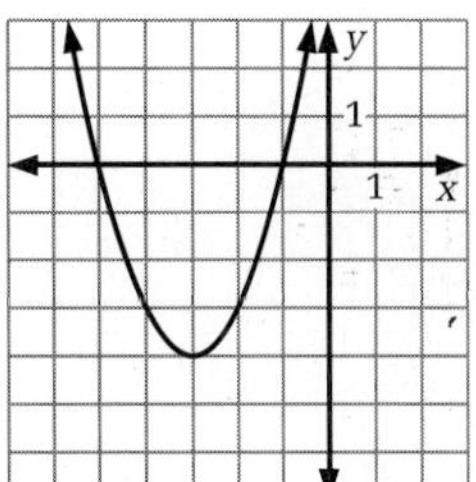

Use Graph A:

1. What are the x-intercepts of the graph?
2. What are the solutions of the equation $x^2 - x - 6 = 0$?

Use Graph B:

3. What are the x-intercepts of the graph?
4. What are the solutions of the equation $x^2 - 5x + 6 = 0$?

Use Graph C:

5. What are the x-intercepts of the graph?
6. What are the solutions of the equation $x^2 + 6x + 5 = 0$?
7. What are the solutions of the equation $x^2 + 6x + 5 = -3$?

Solve each quadratic equation by graphing.

8. $x^2 - 3x + 2 = 0$
9. $x^2 - 3x - 4 = 0$
10. $x^2 - 9 = 0$
11. $2x^2 - x = 3$
12. $3x^2 + x = 4$
13. $2x^2 - 7x = -3$

Solve each quadratic equation by using the quadratic formula. Round answers to the nearest hundredth.

14. $x^2 - 4x + 1 = 0$
15. $x^2 + 3x - 1 = 0$
16. $2x^2 - 5x + 2 = 0$
17. $2x^2 + 3x + 1 = 0$
18. $3x^2 - 5x - 2 = 0$
19. $2x^2 - 9x + 7 = 0$
20. $-2x^2 + 11x = 5$
21. $1 = 3x^2 + 3x$
22. $1.4x^2 + 3x + 4 = 6$
23. The height y (in feet) of a baseball thrown from the outfield is $y = -0.0016x^2 + 0.4x + 5$, where x is the horizontal distance (in feet) that the ball has traveled from its starting point. How far will a throw travel horizontally that is caught at a height of 5 ft?

Name ______________________ Date ______________

Practice 84

Cumulative Practice through Unit 10

Find the intercepts of the graph of each equation.

1. $-2x + 6y = 6$

2. $0.4x - 0.6y = 3$

3. $-\frac{1}{2}x - \frac{1}{3}y = 5$

Graph each system of inequalities.

4. $x - y \geq 3$
$y > -2$

5. $y < 2x - 1$
$x \leq 1$

6. $3x + 2y \leq 6$
$y \geq x - 2$

Simplify.

7. $(\sqrt{10})^2$

8. $\sqrt{8} \bullet \sqrt{18}$

9. $3\sqrt{14} \bullet \sqrt{7}$

10. $4\sqrt{50} \bullet 2\sqrt{6}$

11. $x^3 \bullet x^2$

12. $p^2q \bullet pq^4$

13. $4y^5 \bullet 3y^3$

14. $(2a^2)^5$

15. Write the converse of the statement "If n is even, then $6n$ is even." Tell whether the converse is *true* or *false*. If it is false, give a counterexample.

16. At a school fund-raising carnival, the target for a beanbag toss is a circle of diameter 10 in. The circle is inside a square that measures 22 in. on each side. Suppose a beanbag falls inside the square. What is the probability that it will hit the target?

Without graphing, find the equation of the line of symmetry, the coordinates of the vertex, and the *y*-intercept of the graph of each equation.

17. $y = x^2 - 6x + 2$

18. $y = x^2 + 2x - 5$

19. $y = x^2 - 12x$

20. A 32-foot ladder leaning against the side of a building makes an angle of 70° with the ground. How high up on the wall of the building will the ladder reach?

Each diagram shows a figure and a reflection image of the figure. Write an equation of the line of reflection.

21.

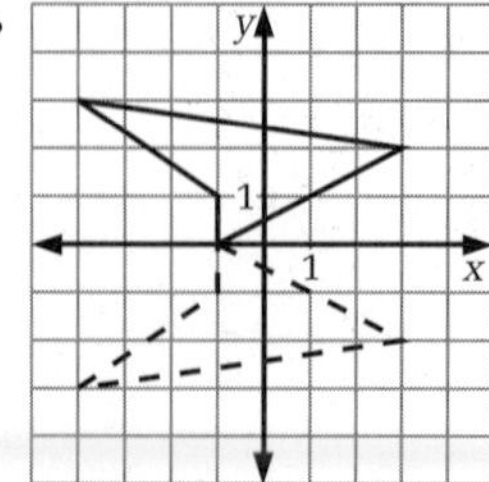

22.

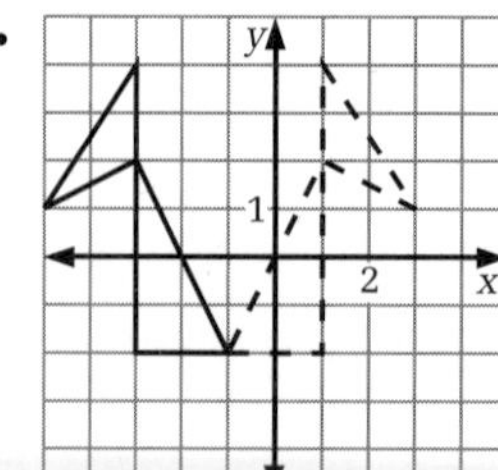

23.

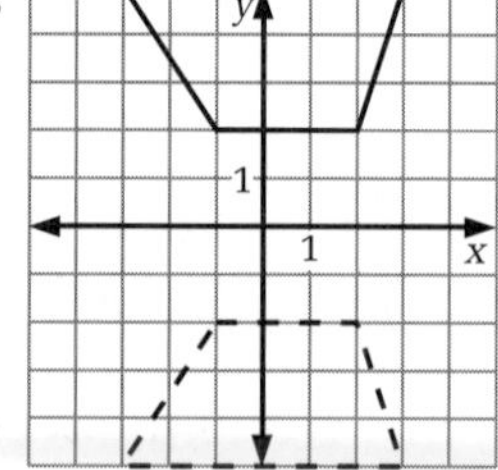

Name ______________ Date ______________

Practice 1

For use with Section 1-1

For Exercises 1–4, use the graph at the right, which shows average weekly television viewing time for various age groups in a rural community.

Weekly TV Viewing Time 1992

1. Does the graph show that men generally watch television more than women? **no**

2. Which age group of both men and women watches the most hours of television? **55 and over**

3. Which age group of both men and women watches the fewest hours of television? **18–24**

4. ***True or false*** Viewing time for both sexes goes down steadily with increasing age. **false**

For Exercises 5–9, use the chart at the right. The road mileage between two cities can be found where the row of one city crosses the column of the other city.

	L.A.	Det.	Den.	Dal.	Cle.	Chi.	Bos.
Atlanta	2182	699	1398	795	672	674	1037
Boston	2979	695	1949	1748	628	963	
Chicago	2054	266	996	917	335		
Cleveland	529	170	1321	1159			
Dallas	1387	1143	781				
Denver	1059	1253					
Detroit	2311						

What is the mileage between each pair of cities?

5. Boston and Detroit **695**

6. L.A. and Dallas **1387**

7. Denver and Chicago **996**

8. Which two cities are farthest apart? **Boston and L.A.**

9. Which two cities are closest together? **Cleveland and Detroit**

For Exercises 10–12, use the concept map at the right.

10. What are the three large categories directly related to mathematics?

Exs. 10, 11: See below.

11. Name a concept that is related to both computers and business.

12. ***Writing*** Describe all the relationships you can that are illustrated by the concept map. **Check students' work.**

10. science, computers, and business 11. spreadsheets

Name ______________ Date ______________

Practice 2

For use with Section 1-2

1. Shape 4 / Shape 5 — **Perimeter of Shape n is $4n$.**

2. Shape 4 / Shape 5 — **Perimeter of Shape n is $3n$.**

Draw Shapes 4 and 5 in each pattern. Make a table of the perimeters of the shapes. Then write a variable expression for the perimeter of Shape n. **Ex. 1, 2. See above.**

1. Shape 1, Shape 2, Shape 3

2. Shape 1, Shape 2, Shape 3

Write a variable expression for each phrase.

3. the number of fielders x plus the number of pitchers y **$x + y$**

4. 10 times the rate r **$10r$**

5. the mass m multiplied by the velocity v **mv**

6. 0.25 times the number of quarters q **$0.25q$**

Evaluate each variable expression for $x = 3$ and $y = 15$.

7. $x + y$ **18**

8. xy **45**

9. $\frac{y}{x}$ **5**

10. $2x + y$ **21**

11. $y - x$ **12**

12. $0.5y + x$ **10.5**

13. $3y - 2x$ **39**

14. $4xy$ **180**

Write a variable expression for the perimeter of each shape.

15. **$2x + 10$**

16. **$2x + 12$**

17. **$4x + 8$**

A car can go 28 mi on one gallon of gas. Find how far the car can go on each amount of gas.

18. 5 gal **140 mi**

19. 10 gal **280 mi**

20. 50 gal **1400 mi**

21. n gal **$28n$ mi**

22. There are 1.6 km in one mile. Write a variable expression for the number of kilometers in p miles. **$1.6p$**

23. Suppose a car can go 28 mi on 1 gal of gas. How many kilometers can it go on 1 gal? **44.8 km**

24. How many kilometers can the car go on x gal? **$44.8x$ km**

Name ______________________ Date ____________

Practice 3

For use with Section 1-3

Write the product as a power. Then write how to say it.

1. $10 \cdot 10$ **10^2, ten squared**
2. $5 \cdot 5 \cdot 5$ **5^3, five cubed**
3. $2 \cdot 2 \cdot 2 \cdot 2 \cdot 2 \cdot 2$ **2^6, two to the sixth**
4. $3 \cdot 3 \cdot 3 \cdot 3 \cdot 3$ **3^5, three to the fifth**
5. $7 \cdot 7 \cdot 7 \cdot 7$ **7^4, seven to the fourth**
6. $8 \cdot 8 \cdot 8 \cdot 8 \cdot 8 \cdot 8 \cdot 8$ **8^7, eight to the seventh**
7. $n \cdot n$ **n^2, n squared**
8. $x \cdot x \cdot x \cdot x \cdot x$ **x^5, x to the fifth**
9. $y \cdot y \cdot y$ **y^3, y cubed**
10. $w \cdot w \cdot w \cdot w$ **w^4, w to the fourth**
11. $k \cdot k$ **k^2, k squared**
12. $m \cdot m \cdot m \cdot m \cdot m \cdot m$ **m^6, m to the sixth**

Write using exponents.

13. 5 to the fourth **5^4**
14. 3 squared **3^2**
15. 4 cubed **4^3**
16. the fifth power of 7 **7^5**
17. the sixth power of 2 **2^6**
18. 5 squared **5^2**
19. n to the sixth **n^6**
20. b cubed **b^3**
21. p to the seventh **p^7**
22. q squared **q^2**
23. y to the fourth **y^4**
24. the fifth power of z **z^5**

Write an expression for the area covered by each group of tiles. Evaluate each expression when $x = 3$.

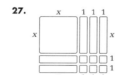

25. **$x^2 + 2x$, 15**

26. 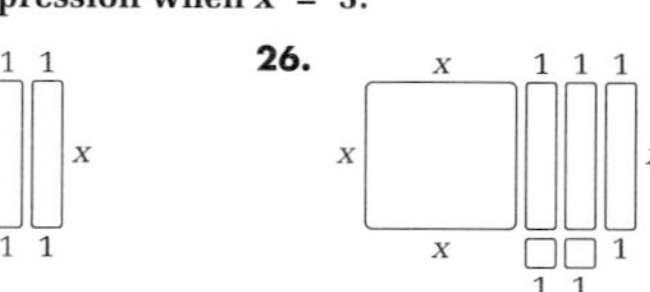

$x^2 + 3x + 2$, 20

27. **$x^2 + 5x + 6$, 30**

Write as a power of ten.

28. $10^2 \cdot 10^3$ **10^5**
29. $10^5 \cdot 10^4$ **10^9**
30. $10^8 \cdot 10$ **10^9**
31. $10^6 \cdot 10^6$ **10^{12}**
32. $10^{15} \cdot 10^{15}$ **10^{30}**
33. $10 \cdot 10^{12}$ **10^{13}**
34. $\frac{10^3}{10^2}$ **10**
35. $\frac{10^6}{10}$ **10^5**
36. $\frac{10^{13}}{10^8}$ **10^5**
37. ***Open-ended*** Write as a power of 10: $(10^3)^2$, $(10^3)^3$, and $(10^3)^4$. Make a conjecture about what power of 10 you get for $(10^a)^b$.
10^6, 10^9, 10^{12}; $(10^a)^b = 10^{ab}$

Name ______________________ Date ____________

Practice 4

For use with Section 1-4

Calculate according to the order of operations.

1. $10 \cdot 3 + 5$ **35**
2. $6 + 12 \div 3$ **10**
3. $4 \cdot 2^3$ **32**
4. $25 - 3^2 \cdot 2$ **7**
5. $4^3 \div 8 - 2$ **6**
6. $54 - 6^2 \div 3$ **42**
7. $3 \cdot 5 - 2^2$ **11**
8. $5^3 \cdot 10 \div 2$ **625**
9. $10^4 \div 5 + 15$ **2015**
10. $5 + 20 \cdot 3 - 1$ **64**
11. $5 \cdot 2^5 - 20 \div 5$ **156**
12. $108 - 12 \cdot 3^2$ **0**
13. $200 - (11 - 3)^2$ **136**
14. $200 - 11 - 3^2$ **180**
15. $200 - (11 - 3^2)$ **198**
16. $24 + 8 \div 2^3$ **25**
17. $(24 + 8) \div 2^3$ **4**
18. $24 + (8 \div 2)^3$ **88**
19. $(3 \cdot 10)^2 \div 5 - 4$ **176**
20. $3 \cdot 10^2 \div 5 - 4$ **56**
21. $3 \cdot 10^2 \div (5 - 4)$ **300**
22. $[(5 + 3)^2 \div 4]^2 - 3$ **253**
23. $27 - [6^2 \div (10 - 6)]$ **18**

For each group of tiles, (a) write a variable expression for the perimeter, (b) write a variable expression for the area, and (c) evaluate the expressions when $x = 5$.

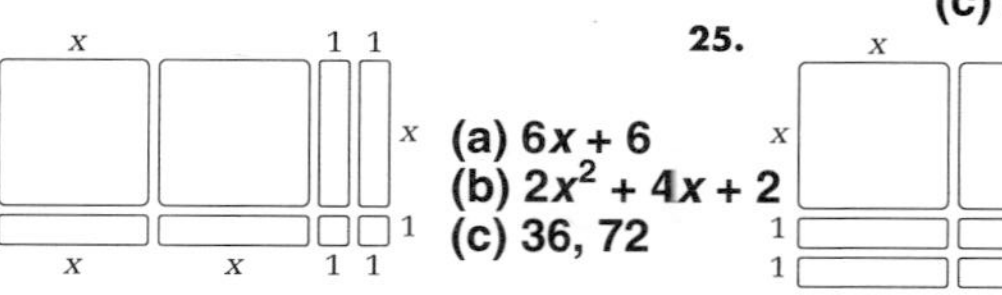

24. **(a) $6x + 6$ (b) $2x^2 + 4x + 2$ (c) 36, 72**

25. **(a) $6x + 6$ (b) $2x^2 + 5x + 2$ (c) 36, 77**

Insert parentheses to make each statement true.

26. $90 \div (5 + 4) \cdot 2 - 1 = 19$
27. $90 \div 5 + 4 \cdot (2 - 1) = 22$
28. Samia asked her friend, "What's 48 divided by 3 plus 5?" Her friend wondered whether she meant "48 divided by 3 … plus 5" or "48 divided by … 3 plus 5". Write these two interpretations as expressions and evaluate them. **$(48 \div 3) + 5 = 21$, $48 \div (3 + 5) = 6$**
29. ***Open-ended*** By inserting one pair of parentheses at different places in $100 - 3^2 + 5 \cdot 4 - 6 \div 2$, find as many different ways of evaluating the expression as you can. **Check students' work.**

Name ______________________ Date ____________

Practice 5

For use with Section 1-5

Rewrite each product as a sum or difference. Do not calculate.

1. 3(50 + 25) **3 • 50 + 3 • 25**
2. 6(200 − 30) **6 • 200 − 6 • 30**
3. 7(100 + 10) **7 • 100 + 7 • 10**
4. 5(200 − 30) **5 • 200 − 5 • 30**
5. 2(140 − 50) **2 • 140 − 2 • 50**
6. 4(500 + 15) **4 • 500 + 4 • 15**
7. 9(400 − 40) **9 • 400 − 9 • 40**
8. 8(100 + 60) **8 • 100 + 8 • 60**

Use the distributive property to find each sum or difference mentally.

9. 19 • 6 + 19 • 4 **190**
10. 22 • 13 − 22 • 3 **220**
11. 170 • 35 − 70 • 35 **3500**
12. 17 • 28 + 3 • 28 **560**
13. 45 • 21 − 45 **900**
14. 15 • 93 + 15 • 7 **1500**

Use the distributive property to rewrite each expression without parentheses.

15. $3(x + y)$ $\mathbf{3x + 3y}$
16. $5(p - 2q)$ $\mathbf{5p - 10q}$
17. $7(3a - b^2)$ $\mathbf{21a - 7b^2}$
18. $\frac{1}{2}(4w - 12)$ $\mathbf{2w - 6}$
19. $\frac{1}{7}(7u + 56v)$ $\mathbf{u + 8v}$
20. $\frac{1}{3}(24 - 15n)$ $\mathbf{8 - 5n}$

Combine like terms.

21. $5x - 2x$ $\mathbf{3x}$
22. $7a^2 - 3 + 2a^2$ $\mathbf{9a^2 - 3}$
23. $8y + 5y^3 - 3y$ $\mathbf{5y + 5y^3}$
24. $6(r + 8) - r$ $\mathbf{5r + 48}$
25. $10m + 4(3 - m)$ $\mathbf{6m + 12}$
26. $9(2j^2 - j) - 3j^2$ $\mathbf{15j^2 - 9j}$
27. $2(3x + 2y) + 10(x + 2y)$ $\mathbf{16x + 24y}$
28. $5(2a - 3) + 7(a + 6)$ $\mathbf{17a + 27}$

For Exercises 29 and 30, use the diagram.

29. The diagram contains a large rectangle and small rectangles. Write expressions for the areas of the small rectangles and for the whole figure. $\mathbf{3x, 3y, 12x + 30y}$

30. Write expressions for the length and width of the whole figure. Using these expressions, write an expression for the area of the whole figure. Is this expression equal to what you got in Exercise 29? $\mathbf{2x + 5y, 6; (2x + 5y)6;}$ **yes**

Name ______________________ Date ____________

Practice 6

For use with Section 1-6

14. Quad. $KWBP \cong$ Quad. $CMQY$
Any three: $\overline{KW} \cong \overline{CM}$, $\overline{WB} \cong \overline{MQ}$, $\overline{BP} \cong \overline{QY}$, $\overline{PK} \cong \overline{YC}$

What kind of (*slide*, *turn*, or *flip*) shows that the two shaded polygons are congruent?

1. 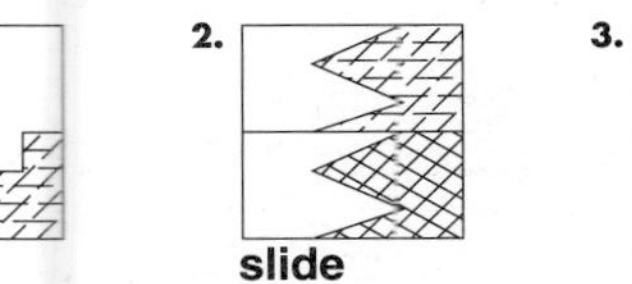 **turn**
2. 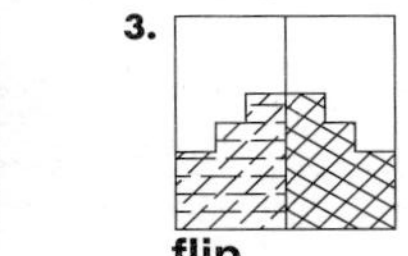 **slide**
3. 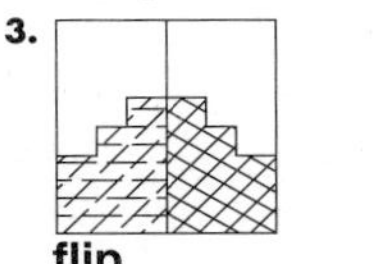 **flip**
4. 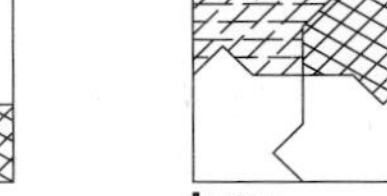 **turn**

What kind of movement (*slide*, *turn*, or *flip*) shows that the two symbols are congruent?

5. ≤ ≥ **flip**
6. N Z **turn**
7. M M **slide or flip**
8. ? ¿ **flip**
9. 9 6 **turn**
10. ó ò **flip**
11. ± ∓ **turn**
12. ” „ **slide**

For Exercises 13 and 14, name the two congruent polygons and name three pairs of congruent sides. **13. $\triangle ABE \cong \triangle BCD$ 14. See top of page.**

$\overline{AB} \cong \overline{BC}$
$\overline{BE} \cong \overline{CD}$
$\overline{AE} \cong \overline{BD}$

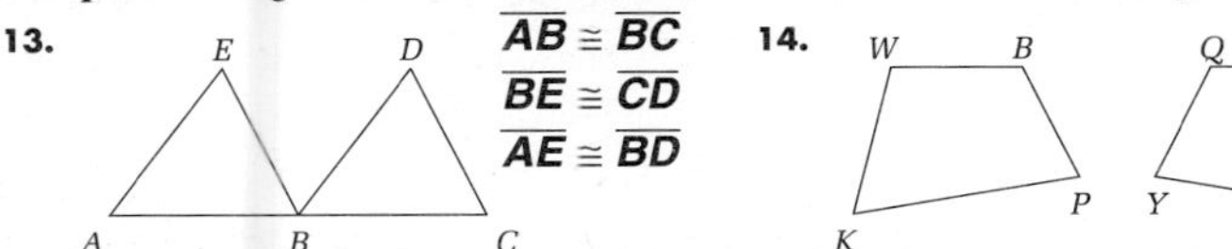

Exs. 13, 14: Students need not use bar notation for segments.

For Exercises 15–17, mark congruent lengths with tick marks and with letters, and write a variable expression for the perimeter of the polygon.

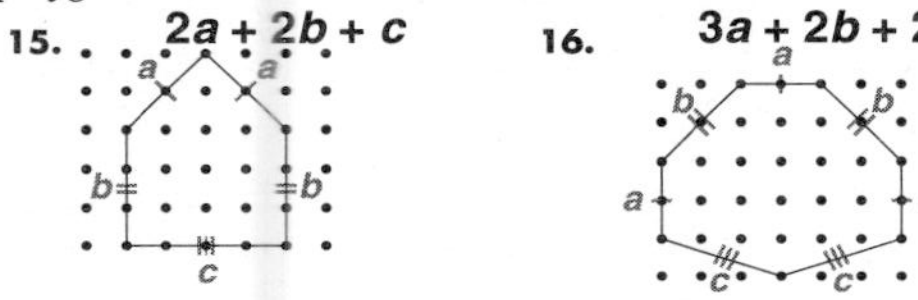

18. ***Writing*** Suppose you are shown a diagram of two congruent polygons. Explain how you would decide which vertices and which sides are corresponding. **Check students' work.**

Name ______________________ Date ____________

Practice 7

For use with Section 1-7

What name best describes each quadrilateral?

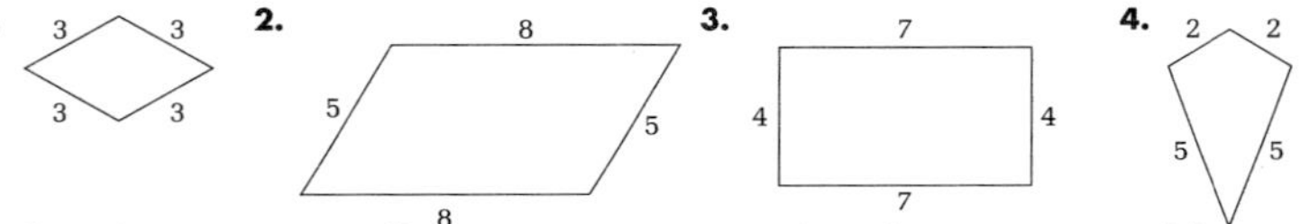

1. **rhombus** **2.** **parallelogram** **3.** **rectangle** **4.** **kite**

Copy each diagram. Draw the lines of symmetry for each polygon, or write *no symmetry*.

5. **6.** **7.**

8. **9.** no symmetry **10.**

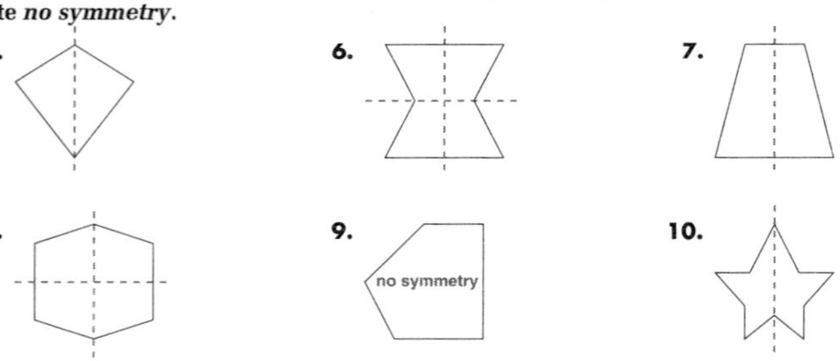

For each pair of triangles, name all the quadrilaterals from the list below that can be made by putting the triangles together, without flipping.

a. parallelogram **b.** rhombus **c.** rectangle **d.** kite

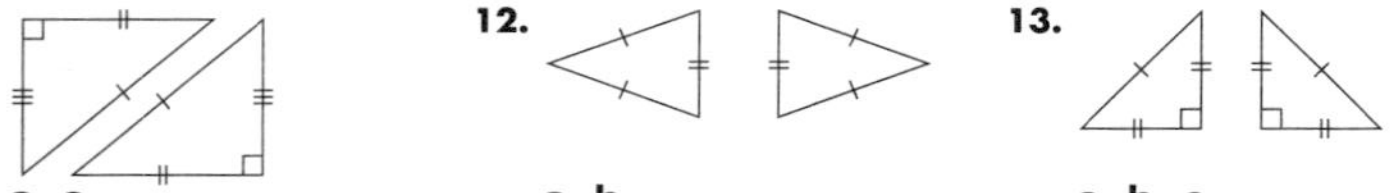

11. **a, c** **12.** **a, b** **13.** **a, b, c**

Draw a quadrilateral of each type. Draw one line that divides the quadrilateral into two congruent triangles. **Check students' work.**

14. rectangle **15.** kite **16.** parallelogram

17. ***Writing*** Suppose you have two congruent triangles cut out of paper, and suppose neither triangle contains a right angle. Can you put the two triangles together to make a rectangle? Tell how, or explain why you cannot do it. **Check students' work.**

Name ______________________ Date ____________

Practice 8

Cumulative Practice through Unit 1

Write a variable expression for each phrase.

1. Angelo's weekly earnings s divided by the number of hours h that he works each week. **$s \div h$ or $\frac{s}{h}$**

2. Miao's speed r times the numbers of hours h she drove. **rh**

Evaluate each variable expression for $x = 12$ and $y = 25$.

3. $x + 2y$ **62** **4.** $\frac{x}{y}$ **$\frac{12}{25}$** **5.** xy **300** **6.** $\frac{0.3y}{x}$ **$\frac{5}{8}$**

Write as a power of ten.

7. $10^8 \cdot 10^3$ **10^{11}** **8.** $10 \cdot 10^5$ **10^6** **9.** $\frac{10^7}{10^3}$ **10^4** **10.** $\frac{10^{20}}{10^{12}}$ **10^8**

Calculate according to the order of operations.

11. $4 + 6 \div 2 + 5$ **12** **12.** $37 - (8 + 5)$ **24** **13.** $7 \cdot 2 - 3(10 - 9)$ **11**

Combine like terms.

14. $3c + 4d - c + 2d$ **$2c + 6d$** **15.** $5x^2 + (x - 3x^2)$ **$2x^2 + x$** **16.** $8(m + n) + 2(m + 2n)$ **$10m + 12n$**

Name the congruent polygons. Then list three pairs of congruent sides. **Exs. 17, 18: Students need not use special notation for triangles and segments.**

17. **18.**

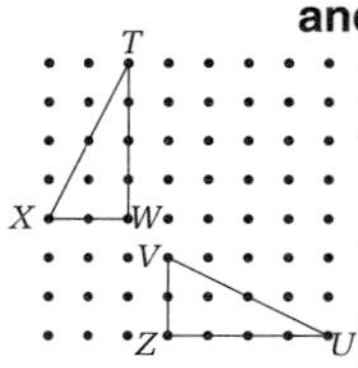

***17.* $\triangle XTW \cong \triangle VUZ$**
$\overline{XT} \cong \overline{VU}$, $\overline{TW} \cong \overline{UZ}$, $\overline{WX} \cong \overline{ZV}$

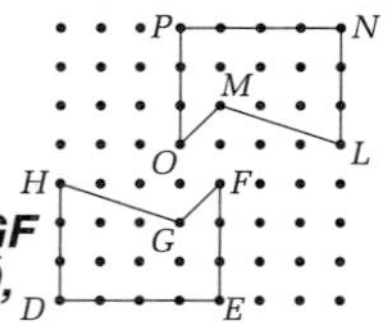

***18.* $PNLMO \cong EDHGF$**
Any three: $\overline{PN} \cong \overline{ED}$, $\overline{NL} \cong \overline{DH}$, $\overline{LM} \cong \overline{HG}$, $\overline{MO} \cong \overline{GF}$, $\overline{OP} \cong \overline{FE}$

Draw all lines of symmetry for each figure or write *no symmetry*.

19. **20.** **21.** no symmetry **22.**

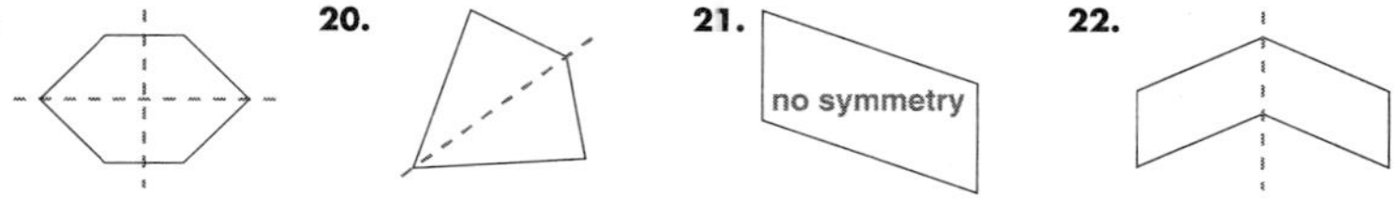

Name ______________________ Date ____________

Practice 9

For use with Section 2-1

Tell whether each number is used for *identifying*, or *ordering*, or as a *count* or a *measure*. Tell whether each number is likely to be exact or estimated.

1. The population of Austin, Texas **count, estimate**
2. The position of a song in the Top 40 **ordering, exact**
3. The distance traveled by a home-run ball **measure, estimate**
4. A score on a science true-false quiz **count, exact**
5. The land area of Earth **measure, estimate**
6. The attendance at a free outdoor concert **count, estimate**

Classify each quantity as *discrete* or *continuous*.

7. An amount of rainfall **continuous**
8. The attendance at a football game **discrete**
9. The number of stars you can see **discrete**
10. A person's weight **continuous**

Exercises 11–13 refer to the diagram at the right.

11. Without counting black squares, is the number of black squares in the tens, hundreds, or thousands? **hundreds**
12. Describe a method for estimating the number of black squares. **12. Count the squares along one row and multiply by a count or estimate of the number of rows.**
13. Use your method to estimate the number of black squares. **13. about 270 or 280 black squares**

For Exercises 14–16, refer to the following scale.

impossible 0%	unlikely 25%	possible 50%	likely 75%	certain 100%
0	0.25	0.5	0.75	1

Use a number anywhere along the scale to estimate the probability of each event.

14. One of your teachers will be absent tomorrow. **Answers may vary.**
15. It will be dark at 11:00 P.M. tomorrow night. **100%**
16. A coin that you toss will land heads up. **50%**
17. ***Writing*** Arlene wanted to estimate the number of words in the English language. She counted all the words in her pocket dictionary that started with the letter Z. Then she multiplied by 26. Was this a good plan? Explain your answer. **Check students' work.**

Name ______________________ Date ____________

Practice 10

For use with Section 2-2

Find the opposite and the absolute value of each number.

1. 5 **−5, 5**
2. $-\frac{2}{3}$ **$\frac{2}{3}, \frac{2}{3}$**
3. −4.7 **4.7, 4.7**
4. 0 **0, 0**
5. 8.4 **−8.4, 8.4**
6. $-5\frac{1}{2}$ **$5\frac{1}{2}, 5\frac{1}{2}$**

Simplify.

7. $|-3|$ **3**
8. $|4.3|$ **4.3**
9. $|-0.6|$ **0.6**
10. $|-17|$ **17**
11. −5 + 17 **12**
12. −22 + 9 **−13**
13. 15 + (−16) **−1**
14. 4 − (−1) **5**
15. −7 − 29 **−36**
16. 33 − (−33) **66**
17. 12 − 12 **0**
18. 19 + (−23) **−4**
19. −5.8 + 100 **94.2**
20. −4.2 − (−5) **−9.2**
21. −3 − (−7.8) **4.8**
22. −6.2 + 10.3 **4.1**
23. (3)(−7) **−21**
24. (−4)(−13) **52**
25. (180)(−1) **−180**
26. (−2.5)(16) **−40**

Simplify. Show every step. **For steps in calculations, check students' work.**

27. −5 + (−3)(4) − 7 **−24**
28. 15 − (−9 + 4) − 2 **18**
29. −7 − 6(5 − 17) **65**
30. 16 − 7 • 5 + 8 **−11**
31. 24 • 3 − (9)(−8) **144**
32. 5 + 0.5(−28 + 12) **−3**
33. (0.2)(50) − (5 + 19) **−14**
34. −2(4 − 7) + 15 **21**
35. (−1.5)(6) − 2(3)(−8) **39**
36. $\frac{-17 + 9}{3}$ **$-\frac{8}{3}$**
37. $\frac{5 \cdot 6}{3 - (-4)}$ **$\frac{30}{7}$**
38. $\frac{-1 + 10}{-3 - 11}$ **$-\frac{9}{14}$**

Evaluate each expression for the given values of the variable.

39. $5 - c$ when $c = -12$ **17**
40. $\frac{-p - 13}{4}$ when $p = -6$ **$-\frac{7}{4}$**
41. $x^2 - 3$ when $x = 4$ **13**
42. $-y^2 + y$ when $y = -2$ **−6**
43. $\frac{n - 8}{7}$ when $n = 1$ **−1**
44. $\frac{3 + k}{3 - k}$ when $k = 0$ **1**
45. $10 - ab$ when $a = 3$ and $b = -4$ **22**
46. $0.5xy - x^2$ when $x = 4$ and $y = 6$ **−4**
47. $\frac{c + d}{cd}$ when $c = 5$ and $d = -2$ **$-\frac{3}{10}$**
48. $\frac{5}{9}(F - 32)$ when $F = -40$ **−40**
49. "Par for the course" in golf means the number of strokes a good golfer is expected to take to go around the course. One golfer shoots 5 strokes above par and another shoots 4 strokes below par. What is the difference between their scores? **9**

Name ____________________ Date ____________

Practice 11

For use with Section 2-3

Write each number in scientific notation.

1. 567,000 **5.67×10^5**
2. 45.8 **4.58×10^1**
3. 0.0019 **1.9×10^{-3}**
4. 0.0596 **5.96×10^{-2}**
5. 7,000,000,000 **7×10^9**
6. 84 **8.4×10^1**
7. 453.5 **4.535×10^2**
8. 0.000228 **2.28×10^{-4}**
9. 7050 **7.05×10^3**
10. 0.05 **5×10^{-2}**
11. 50,600 **5.06×10^4**
12. 6,000,000 **6×10^6**

Write each number in decimal notation.

13. 3.62×10^{-3} **0.00362**
14. 5.8×10^7 **58,000,000**
15. 6.43×10^3 **6430**
16. 1.98×10^1 **19.8**
17. 3.07×10^{-2} **0.0307**
18. 9.5×10^{-6} **0.0000095**
19. 5.638×10^0 **5.638**
20. 8×10^4 **80,000**
21. 4.875×10^{-1} **0.4875**

Simplify. Write each answer in scientific notation.

22. $(1.2 \times 10^3)(3 \times 10^2)$ **3.6×10^5**
23. $(3.6 \times 10^{-4})(1.5 \times 10^{-3})$ **5.4×10^{-7}**
24. $\frac{4.5 \times 10^8}{9 \times 10^{-3}}$ **5×10^{10}**
25. $\frac{8.4 \times 10^{-6}}{7 \times 10^5}$ **1.2×10^{-11}**
26. $\frac{1.28 \times 10^7}{1.6 \times 10^6}$ **8×10^0**
27. $300(5.6 \times 10^{-4})$ **1.68×10^{-1}**
28. $0.18(3.2 \times 10^7)$ **5.76×10^6**
29. $16(1.8 \times 10^{-8})$ **2.88×10^{-7}**
30. $\frac{4.9 \times 10^6}{7}$ **7×10^5**
31. $\frac{4 \times 10^{12}}{25}$ **1.6×10^{11}**
32. $\frac{2.7 \times 10^{-3}}{5000}$ **5.4×10^{-7}**

33. Sound travels about 340 m in one second. How far would sound travel in a minute and a half? Express your answer in scientific notation. **3.06×10^4 m**

34. An India paper edition of an unabridged dictionary is 2.75 inches thick, not including the covers. There are 3210 numbered pages in the dictionary. How many sheets of India paper is this (two pages are printed on each sheet)? What is the thickness of one sheet of India paper? Express your answer in scientific notation. **1605 sheets about 1.713×10^{-3} inches**

35. During the year 1988, the average American ate an average of 31 eggs. There were about 246 million Americans at that time. How many eggs were eaten by all Americans during 1988? Express your answer in scientific notation. **about 7.626×10^9 eggs**

36. ***Writing*** Suppose you were given two numbers in scientific notation. Describe a method for deciding which one is larger. Describe a way to estimate quickly how many times larger one number is than the other. **Check students' work.**

Name ____________________ Date ____________

Practice 12

For use with Section 2-4

Estimate the length of each side of quadrilateral *ABCD* in both U.S. customary units and metric units. **Estimates may vary.**

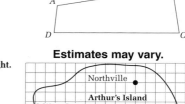

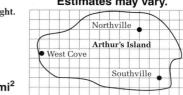

1. *AB* **2 in., 5 cm**
2. *BC* **1 in., 2 cm**
3. *CD* **2 in., 5 cm**
4. *AD* **$\frac{1}{2}$ in., 1 cm**

Estimate each distance by using the map at the right. Each grid square is 5 mi on a side. **Estimates may vary.**

5. Northville to Southville **25 mi**
6. Southville to West Cove **60 mi**
7. Northville to West Cove **50 mi**
8. Estimate the area of Arthur's Island. **2200 mi²**

In the diagram for Exercises 9–12, *P* is the midpoint of $\overline{JK}$ and *Q* is the midpoint of $\overline{KL}$.

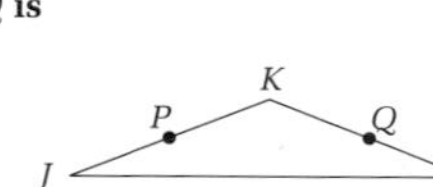

9. Suppose $JK = 18$. What is *PK*? **9**
10. Suppose $KQ = 10$. What is *KL*? **20**
11. Suppose $JK = KL$. Will *PK* equal *KQ*? **yes**
12. Suppose $JP = LQ = 12$ and $JL = 35$. Find the perimeter of triangle *JKL*. **83**
13. Draw a rectangle and draw the two diagonals of the rectangle. Call the point where the two diagonals meet *X*. Does *X* appear to be the midpoint of each diagonal? **yes**
14. The Tigers plan to have a stitched block letter "T" on their baseball uniforms, as shown at the right. What area must be covered by stitching? (You can sketch a figure like this on graph paper if you wish.) **75 cm²**
15. ***Open-ended*** On graph paper, draw several rectangles with the same perimeter. Do your rectangles all have the same area? Draw another rectangle with the same perimeter, but make the area as large as you can. How large can it be? Draw one more rectangle with the same perimeter, but make the area as small as you can. How small can it be? **Check students' work.**

Name ______________________ Date ____________

Practice 13

For use with Section 2-5

Exercises 1–5 refer to the diagram at the right.

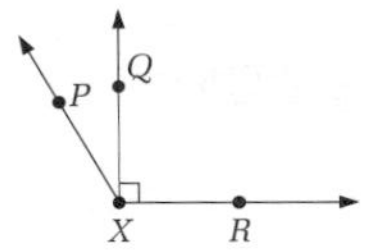

1. Name a right angle. **$\angle QXR$**

2. Name an obtuse angle. **$\angle PXR$**

3. Name an acute angle. **$\angle PXQ$**

4. Estimate the measure of $\angle PXQ$. **about 30°**

5. Suppose $\angle PXQ$ has measure 32°. Find the measure of $\angle PXR$. **122°**

In the diagram, $\angle CKD$ is a right angle, and $\overrightarrow{KE}$ bisects $\angle DKF$. Find the measure of each angle without estimating or using a protractor.

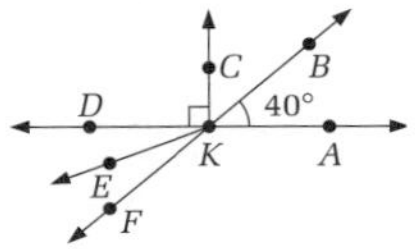

6. $\angle CKB$ **50°** **7.** $\angle FKA$ **140°** **8.** $\angle DKF$ **40°**

9. $\angle DKE$ **20°** **10.** $\angle CKF$ **130°** **11.** $\angle BKE$ **160°**

For each set of given information, find the missing angle measure.

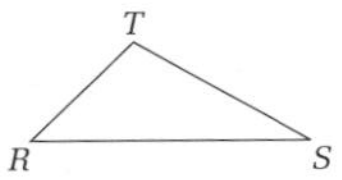

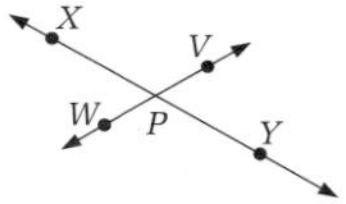

12. $\angle R = 45°$; $\angle T = 100°$; $\angle S =$ __?__ **35°**

13. $\angle S = 32°$; $\angle T = 108°$; $\angle R =$ __?__ **40°**

14. $\angle R = 56°$; $\angle S = 33°$; $\angle T =$ __?__ **91°**

15. $\angle XPW = 75°$; $\angle WPY =$ __?__ **105°**

16. $\angle XPV = 115°$; $\angle XPW =$ __?__ **65°**

17. $\angle WPY = 125°$; $\angle VPX =$ __?__ **125°**

21. Possible answer: The shortest side is opposite the angle with the smallest measure, and the longest side is opposite the angle with the greatest measure.

The circle graph at the right shows the distribution of household electricity use in the United States in 1987.

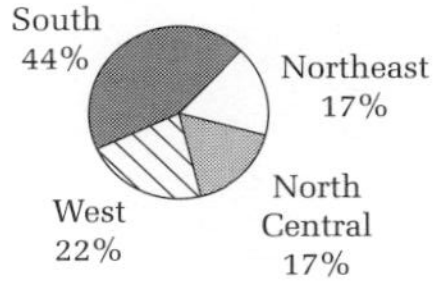

18. Which region is shown by an obtuse angle? **South**

19. Which regions have central angles of equal measure?

20. Which region's angle is closest to a right angle? **West**

21. *Open-ended* Draw a scalene triangle or cut one out of paper. Measure the three sides and list the measures in a column from largest to smallest. Do the same for the three angles. What do you notice about the side-angle pairs that are in the same slot in each list? Try the same procedure for several more triangles. Make a conjecture. **See above.**

19. Northeast and North Central

Name ______________________ Date ____________

Practice 14

For use with Section 2-6

Simplify.

1. $(3x)(3x)$ $\mathbf{9x^2}$ **2.** $(5a)(6b)$ $\mathbf{30ab}$ **3.** $(-2p)(7q)$ $\mathbf{-14pq}$

4. $5(3n^2)$ $\mathbf{15n^2}$ **5.** $(2r)(2r)(2r)$ $\mathbf{8r^3}$ **6.** $(-4t)(6t)(-2t)$ $\mathbf{48t^3}$

7. $7x + 2x$ $\mathbf{9x}$ **8.** $9y - 6y$ $\mathbf{3y}$ **9.** $-8z^2 + 3z^2$ $\mathbf{-5z^2}$

10. $3n - 5n^2 + 8n$ $\mathbf{11n - 5n^2}$ **11.** $-2k^2 + k - k^2 + 5k$ $\mathbf{-3k^2 + 6k}$

12. $x^3 - 4x^2 - 3x^3 + 7x + 4x^2$ $\mathbf{-2x^3 + 7x}$ **13.** $2y^2 - 3y + 4y - y^2 + 10$ $\mathbf{y^2 + y + 10}$

Write and simplify an expression for (a) the perimeter and (b) the area of a rectangle with the given dimensions.

14. $3n, 5n$ $\mathbf{16n, 15n^2}$ **15.** $7v, 4$ $\mathbf{14v + 8, 28v}$

16. $6t^2, 3t$ $\mathbf{12t^2 + 6t, 18t^3}$ **17.** $6y, 4y + 5$ $\mathbf{20y + 10, 24y^2 + 30y}$

Write and simplify an expression for the volume of a box with the given dimensions.

18. $3c, c, 2c$ $\mathbf{6c^3}$ **19.** $5, w, 3w$ $\mathbf{15w^2}$

20. $4, a, a^2$ $\mathbf{4a^3}$ **21.** $d, 2d, 3d + 1$ $\mathbf{6d^3 + 2d^2}$

Write and simplify an expression for the sum of the angles in each figure.

22. 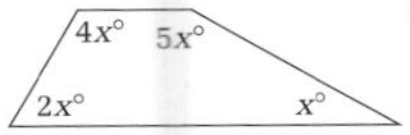

12x°

23. 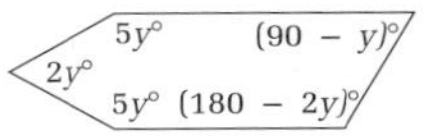

(9y + 270)°

24. Packing boxes are made with dimensions $6x$ in., $8x$ in., and x in., for various values of x. Write and simplify an expression for the volume of a box, and find the volume of boxes in which $x = 2$, $x = 3$, and $x = 5$. $\mathbf{48x^3}$**; 384 in.³, 1296 in.³, 6000 in.³**

The box at the right is to be made from six rectangles, two of each of the rectangles shown.

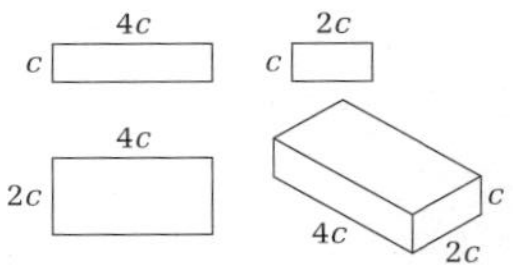

25. Write and simplify an expression for the total area of the outside of the box. $\mathbf{28c^2}$

26. Write and simplify an expression for the volume of the box. $\mathbf{8c^3}$

Name ______________________ Date ____________

Practice 15

For use with Section 2-7

Solve each equation.

1. $a + 25 = 13$ **−12**
2. $b + 12 = -8$ **−20**
3. $r - 15 = -2$ **13**
4. $7 + d = 22$ **15**
5. $-3 + q = 5$ **8**
6. $u + 17 = 17$ **0**
7. $5j = 60$ **12**
8. $7p = 63$ **9**
9. $10y = 180$ **18**
10. $2n - 5 = 17$ **11**
11. $9 + 2m = 35$ **13**
12. $3x - 7 = 41$ **16**
13. $6 = 4k - 30$ **9**
14. $y + y - 9 = 55$ **32**
15. $c + 10 + c = 18$ **4**
16. $8 + 7w = 29$ **3**
17. $3b - b + 5 = 7$ **1**
18. $8t - 19 + t = 35$ **6**

Write and solve an equation to find each unknown angle measure in each figure. (*Note:* The sum of the measures of the angles of a quadrilateral is 360°.)

19. **71°**

22. **84°**

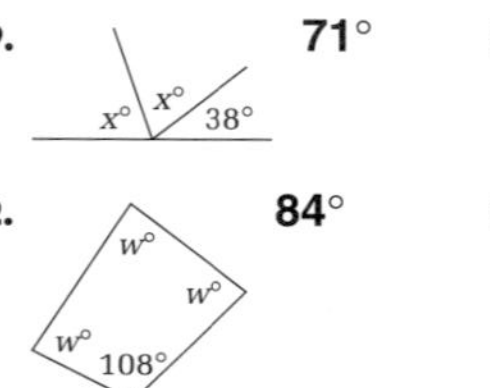

20. **47°**

23. **105°**

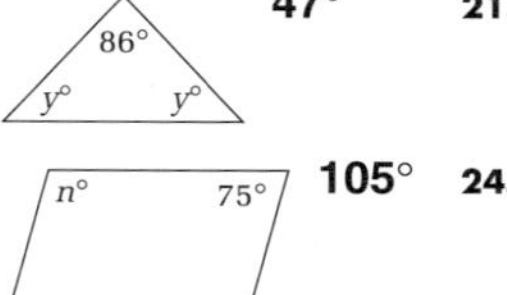

21. **80°**

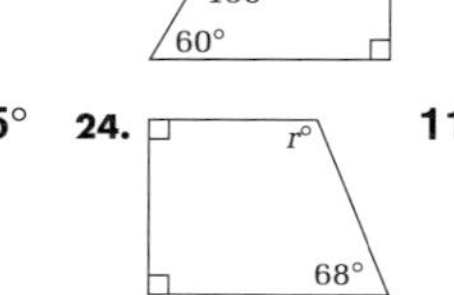

24. **112°**

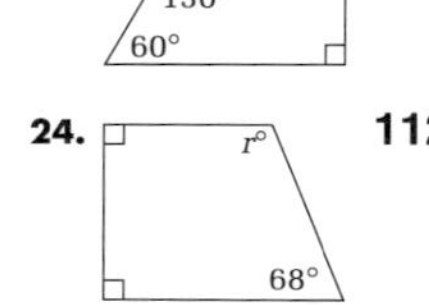

25. The perimeter of a trapezoid is 25 cm. Three sides of the trapezoid have length x cm. The fourth side has length 7 cm. Write and solve an equation to find the value of x. **6**
26. Two sides of a kite are each 34 in. long. Each of the other two sides has length y in. Suppose the perimeter of the kite is 104 in. Write and solve an equation to find y. **18**

Yi-Qian jogs around her block to keep in shape. Her block is a rectangle. She has found that one side of the rectangle is twice as long as the other. Suppose x stands for the length of the shorter side of the rectangle.

27. Write an expression for the length of the longer side, using x. **2x**
28. Suppose the perimeter of the rectangle is 1440 ft. Write an equation to find x, and solve the equation. **240 ft**

Name ______________________ Date ____________

Practice 16

For use with Section 2-8

Solve.

1. $4a + 3a = -35$ **−5**
2. $2n - 17 = 15$ **16**
3. $-5c + 39 = -6$ **9**
4. $\frac{d}{2} + 6 = 8$ **4**
5. $5 + 3x = -19$ **−8**
6. $\frac{y}{4} + 7 = 9$ **8**
7. $\frac{k}{3} - 5 = 4$ **27**
8. $-2n + 17 = -5$ **11**
9. $3a - 7a = 52$ **−13**
10. $5p - 63 = 12$ **15**
11. $6q + 13 = -20$ **$-\frac{11}{2}$**
12. $-9 = \frac{m}{6} + 2$ **−66**
13. $1.2w - 5 = 10$ **12.5**
14. $5.5v - 3.3v = 7.7$ **$\frac{7}{2}$**
15. $8 - \frac{x}{4} = 2.5$ **22**
16. $3.2z + 4 = -0.8$ **−1.5**
17. $-3.6t + 7.6 = 0.4$ **2**
18. $0.06x - 5 = 16$ **350**
19. $5.3y + 6.5y = 53.1$ **4.5**
20. $\frac{m}{2} - 3.4 = -6.5$ **−6.2**
21. $-\frac{k}{5} + 0.8 = 1.2$ **−2**
22. $\frac{x}{1.5} - \frac{x}{3} = 7$ **21**
23. $5.2b + 15 = 8.5$ **−1.25**
24. $12a - 51 = -53$ **$-\frac{1}{6}$**
25. $-6.4k + 3.5 = -7.7$ **1.75**
26. $\frac{c}{1.2} - 6.5 = 7$ **16.2**
27. $8 - \frac{m}{4.5} = 2.6$ **24.3**
28. Felipe bought two compact discs. He gave the cashier at the store \$30 and got \$2.10 change. One disc cost \$11.95. How much did the other disc cost? Let c = the cost of the other disc. **\$15.95**
29. Mike Wei's construction company has a project that Mike figures will take his workers 182 hours to complete. His workers work 7 hours a day. How many working days will it take to complete the project? Let k = the number of working days to complete the project. **26**
30. Sumi bought the same number of bran muffins and bagels at the bakery. Bran muffins cost \$.35 each, and bagels cost \$.45 each. Sumi spent \$5.60 altogether. How many of each item did she buy? Let n = the number of muffins or the number of bagels she bought. **7**
31. Anna Gallagher and two friends want to rent an apartment. The three of them will split the rent evenly. Anna figures that food will cost her \$225 each month, and she can afford to spend a total of \$400 on food and her share of the rent. What should be the rent on an apartment in order for it to fit Anna's budget? Let r = the rent on the apartment. **\$525**

Name ______________________ Date ____________

Practice 17

For use with Section 2-9

25. between 2 and 3; 2.47
26. between 3 and 4; 3.27
27. between 1 and 2; 1.71
28. between 10 and 11; 10.06

Find the square roots of each number.

1. 49 **7, –7**
2. $\frac{1}{64}$ **$\frac{1}{8}$, $-\frac{1}{8}$**
3. 1.69 **1.3, –1.3**
4. $\frac{4}{81}$ **$\frac{2}{9}$, $-\frac{2}{9}$**
5. 0.0036 **0.06, –0.06**
6. 2500 **50, –50**
7. 0.0121 **0.11, –0.11**
8. 90,000 **300, –300**

Find the cube root of each number.

9. 27 **3**
10. $\frac{1}{1000}$ **$\frac{1}{10}$**
11. $\frac{8}{125}$ **$\frac{2}{5}$**
12. 0.008 **0.2**
13. 0.027 **0.3**
14. 64,000 **40**
15. 0.125 **0.5**
16. 0.216 **0.6**

Tell whether each number is rational or irrational.

17. 23.6 **rational**
18. $\frac{3}{7}$ **rational**
19. $\sqrt{10}$ **irrational**
20. $1.6\overline{3}$ **rational**

Estimate each square root within a range of two integers. Then use a calculator to find each square root to the nearest hundredth.

21. $\sqrt{30}$ **between 5 and 6; 5.48**
22. $\sqrt{12}$ **between 3 and 4; 3.46**
23. $\sqrt{106}$ **between 10 and 11; 10.30**
24. $\sqrt{0.5}$ **between 0 and 1; 0.71**

Estimate each cube root within a range of two integers. Then use a calculator to find each cube root. **Exs. 25–28: See top of page.**

25. $\sqrt[3]{15}$
26. $\sqrt[3]{35}$
27. $\sqrt[3]{5}$
28. $\sqrt[3]{1020}$

29. The current I (in amps) drawn by an appliance is given by the formula $I = \sqrt{\frac{P}{R}}$, where P is the power rating of the appliance (in watts) and R is its resistance (in ohms). What current is drawn by a 1500-watt toaster-oven with a resistance of 9.6 ohms? **12.5 amps**

30. The approximate time T (in seconds) for a pendulum L meters long to make a full swing is given by the formula $T = 6.3\sqrt{\frac{L}{10}}$.
How many seconds will it take a pendulum 2 meters long to make a full swing? **about 2.82 s**

31. ***Open-ended*** Convert several fractions to decimals on your calculator. First try fractions with small denominators, like 3, 7, 9, and 11. Then try fractions with larger denominators. Are all the numbers that you are using rational? Can you always tell from the calculator's display that the decimals are repeating? Explain. **Check students' work.**

Name ______________________ Date ____________

Practice 18

Cumulative Practice through Unit 2

Some Mayan numerals and their modern equivalents are shown below.

•• 2   8   10   16

Tell what number each Mayan symbol represents.

1. • • • **3**
2. **6**
3. **14**
4. **20**

Write as a power of 10.

5. 10 • 10 • 10 • 10 • 10 **10^5**
6. $10^5 \cdot 10^3$ **10^8**
7. $10 \cdot 10^8$ **10^9**
8. $10^5 \cdot 10^2 \cdot 10^3$ **10^{10}**
9. $\frac{10^7}{10}$ **10^6**
10. $\frac{10^{15}}{10^3}$ **10^{12}**

Simplify.

11. –5 – 31 **–36**
12. 17 – (–12) **29**
13. –26 ÷ 2 **–13**
14. (–4)(–18) **72**
15. (–29 + 8) ÷ 3 **–7**
16. 5 + (–3)(6) – 4 **–17**
17. 15 – 2(–8 + 14) ÷ 3 **11**

Write and solve an equation to find each unknown angle measure.

18. (45°, 105°, $x°$) **$x° = 30°$**
19. (32°, $x°$) **$x° = 58°$**
20. (77°, $x°$) **$x° = 103°$**

21. The edges of a rectangular box have lengths k cm, $3k$ cm, and $5k$ cm. Write and simplify an expression for the volume of the box. **$k(3k)(5k) = 15k^3\ cm^3$**

22. A triangle has sides of length x^2 in., $2x^2$ in., and $5x$ in. Write and simplify an expression for the perimeter of the triangle. **$x^2 + 2x^2 + 5x = 3x^2 + 5x$ in.**

23. Gregory Chan bought 10 ft of copper tubing and fittings to upgrade his hot-water system. The fittings cost \$5.25, and the total for the fittings and tubing came to \$12.75. What was the cost per foot of the copper tubing? **\$0.75 per foot**

24. Felipe Peña brought 3 water bottles, all filled to the same level, on a day hike. During the hike, he drank 35 oz of water. At the end of the day, he had 16 oz of water left. At the start of the day, how many ounces of water were there in each water bottle? **17 oz**

Name ______________________ Date ____________

Practice 19

For use with Section 3-1

Federal Aid to Education (in billions of dollars)

	1984	1988	1990	1992
Elem. & Sec.	4.3	5.7	7.2	8.8
Handicapped	2.4	3.1	3.5	5.3
Voc. & Adult	1.0	1.0	1.1	1.9
College Aid	7.5	8.8	11.1	15.3

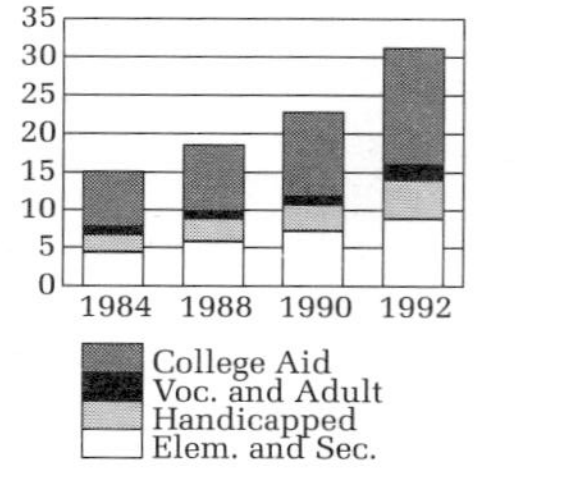

For Exercises 1–7 use the matrix and the stacked bar graph. The graph was drawn using the data in the matrix.

How much in rederal aid was spent in each category?

1. Elementary and wecondary aid in 1988 **$5.7 billion**

2. Aid for handicapped in 1992 **$5.3 billion**

3. Aid for vocational and adult education in 1984 **$1.0 billion**

4. Aid for college education in 1990 **$11.1 billion**

Tell what each number represents.

5. The second number in the fourth row **College Aid in 1988**

6. Which category of federal aid grew the least (in dollars) between 1984 and 1992? **Voc. & Adult**

7. Which category grew the fastest (in dollars)? **College**

For Exercises 8–12 use the matrix and graph on population of U.S. cities.

Population of U.S. cities (in millions)

	1900	1950	1970	1990
New York	3.4	7.6	7.9	7.3
L. A.	0.1	2.0	2.8	3.5
Chicago	1.7	3.6	3.4	2.8
Houston	0.04	0.6	1.2	1.6

8. Which two cities lost population between 1970 and 1990? **New York and Chicago**

9. Did the same two cities lose population between 1950 and 1970? **New York, no Chicago, yes**

10. Which city gained most in population between 1950 and 1990? **L.A.**

11. What was the ranking of the cities from largest to smallest population in 1970? **New York, Chicago, L.A., Houston**

12. Which two cities traded rankings between 1970 and 1990? **L.A. and Chicago**

Name ______________________ Date ____________

Practice 20

For use with Section 3-2

For Exercises 1–4, use the table of National League home run leaders.

National League Home Run Leaders (1985–1992)

Year	Leader	HRs
1985	Dale Murphy	37
1986	Mike Schmidt	37
1987	Andre Dawson	49
1988	Darryl Strawberry	39
1989	Kevin Mitchell	47
1990	Ryne Sandberg	40
1991	Howard Johnson	38
1992	Fred McGriff	35

1. Find the mean, the median, and the mode(s) of the home run data. **40.25, 38.5, 37**

2. Which of the three numbers that you found in Exercise 1 gives the least accurate indication of the typical number of home runs hit by a home run leader? **mean**

3. Are there any outliers in the data? **no**

4. What is the range of the data? **14**

For each set of data, find the mean, the median, and the mode(s).

5. Judges' scores for one contestant at a diving competition: 7.8, 5.6, 8.3, 6.4, 8.3, 7.5, 7.8, 7.8, 3.2, 8.5, 8.3 **7.2, 7.8, 7.8 and 8.3**

6. Number of cars washed each day of a school event to raise money for a local charity: 35, 44, 31, 56, 53, 45, 60, 62, 56, 41, 56 **49, 53, 56**

7. Price of a pound of spaghetti at different supermarkets: $.89, $.79, $1.19, $.79, $.59, $.99, $.79, $.89, $.69, $.69 **$.83, $.79, $.79**

8. Attendance at school basketball games: 135, 230, 150, 185, 165, 110, 173, 224, 272 **186, 173, 165**

9. Normal precipitation for each month in Tampa, Florida (in inches): 2.2, 3.0, 3.5, 1.8, 3.4, 5.3, 7.4, 7.6, 6.2, 2.3, 1.9, 2.1 **3.9, 3.2, no mode**

Ho Chan's scores on math tests so far this term are 86, 88, 68, 93, 84, 90, and 86.

10. What is the mean of her scores? **85**

11. Name an outlier among the scores. **68**

12. Suppose there is one more test in math this term. What will Ho Chan's score on this test have to be in order for her to end up with a mean score of 86? **93**

13. ***Writing*** In a conversation with his math teacher, Mark argued that his score of 52 on one test was an outlier among the data and should not be counted in his average. Do you agree with his argument? How might his teacher counter this reasoning? **Check students' work.**

Name ______________________ Date ____________

Practice 21

For use with Section 3-3

Write an inequality that fits each graph.

1. (number line: −4, −2, 0, 2, 4) $x \geq 1$
2. (number line: −20, −10, 0, 10, 20) $x < 15$
3. (number line: −4, −2, 0, 2, 4) $-3 < x \leq 2$
4. (number line: −200, −100, 0, 100, 200) $-150 \leq x < 150$

Graph each inequality on a number line.

5. $x \leq 5$ (5)
6. $x \geq -2$ (−2)
7. $x \geq 3$ (3)
8. $-4 \leq x \leq 3$ (−4, 0, 3)
9. $0 < x \leq 6$ (0, 2, 6)
10. $-5 < x < -1$ (−5, 0, −1)
11. $x > 2.5$ (0, 2)
12. $\frac{1}{3} \leq x < 1\frac{2}{3}$ (0, 1)
13. $-\frac{1}{2} < x \leq 3\frac{1}{2}$ (0, 2)

Write an inequality to describe the shortest interval of the number line than contains all the numbers in each group.

14. 5, −7, 3, −1, 8, 6, 2 $-7 \leq x \leq 8$
15. 0, −1, 3, −9, −2, −4, −8 $-9 \leq x \leq 3$
16. −1, −0.5, −1.6, −0.2, −1.2, 0 $-1.6 \leq x \leq 0$
17. $\frac{1}{2}, -\frac{1}{3}, -\frac{1}{6}, \frac{1}{4}, -\frac{3}{4}, \frac{1}{5}$ $-\frac{3}{4} \leq x \leq \frac{1}{2}$

Write an inequality to describe each statement.

18. All temperatures in the universe are above "absolute zero," which is −273°C. $x > -273$
19. In a school zone, cars can go no more than 20 mi/h. $0 \leq x \leq 20$
20. Any year beginning with "19", such as 1956, is in the twentieth century. $1900 \leq x \leq 1999$
21. The smallest distance between Earth and Mars is 35 million miles, and the greatest distance between the two planets is 248 million miles. $35{,}000{,}000 \leq x \leq 248{,}000{,}000$
22. Altitudes in the Death Valley area range from 282 ft below sea level to about 11,000 ft above sea level. $-282 \leq x \leq 11{,}000$
23. Water can be in a liquid form between 32°F and 212°F. $32 < x < 212$
24. Natural land formations on Earth vary from 29,028 ft above sea level (Mt. Everest) to 36,198 ft below sea level (the Mariana Trench in the Pacific Ocean). $-36{,}198 \leq x \leq 29{,}028$

Name ______________________ Date ____________

Practice 22

For use with Section 3-4

15.

Stem	Leaves
0	7
1	8
2	0 2 5 7 9 9
3	0 0 0 2 2 3 3 3 4 6 7 8 8 9
4	0 0 0 0 4
5	0 2 3 4
6	1

For Exercises 1–9, use the histogram at the right, showing the results of an experiment to find out the heights of specimens of a kind of tree after 3 years.

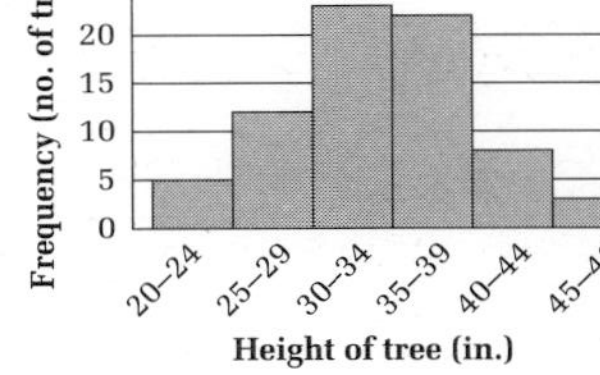

How many trees were in each interval?

1. 20–24 in. **5**
2. 25–29 in. **12**
3. 30–34 in. **23**
4. 35–39 in. **22**
5. 40–44 in. **8**
6. 45–49 in. **3**
7. What was the total number of trees in the experiment? **73**
8. What interval contains the greatest number of trees? **30–34**
9. What interval contains the smallest number of trees? **45–49**

For Exercises 10–15, use the table below, listing the number of stories in buildings in Philadelphia, PA that are over 340 ft tall.

Number of Stories in Philadelphia Buildings							
30	29	34	30	61	52	54	53
30	33	32	44	50	40	40	7
29	37	20	33	40	40	38	39
27	33	22	18	36	38	32	25

10. Make a frequency table for the data. **Check students' work.**
11. Draw a histogram for the data. **Check students' work.**
12. What interval in your histogram has the tallest bar? **12. If intervals of 0–9, 10–19, etc. are used, the tallest bar is for 30–39.**
13. What numbers would you use for the stems of a stem-and-leaf plot? **0, 1, 2, 3, 4, 5, 6**
14. List all the leaves for the stem 2. **0, 2, 5, 7, 9, 9**
15. Make a stem-and-leaf plot of the data in the table. **See top of page.**
16. ***Open-ended*** Ask as many students in your school as you can how many hours they spend watching television in a typical week. Organize the data into intervals. Plot the data in a histogram. Think of other surveys you might make of numbers that each student might report. Construct a histogram or a stem-and-leaf plot of your data. **Check students' work.**

Name ______________ Date ______________

Practice 23

For use with Section 3-5

Exercises 1–7 refer to the box-and-whisker plot below.

Brite-Glo Paint Employee Commuting Times (minutes)

0 5 10 15 20 25 30 35 40 45 50 55 60

Morning Commute

Evening Commute

1. What were the median morning commuting time and the median evening commuting time? **35 min, 40 min**

2. What were the upper and lower extremes of the morning times? **50 min, 10 min**

3. What were the upper and lower extremes of the evening times? **60 min, 10 min**

4. About what percent of the morning commuting times fell between 25 and 40 minutes? **50%**

5. What percent of the evening commuting times fell between 40 and 50 minutes? **25%**

6. What percent of the evening commuting times fell above the median morning commuting time? **75%**

7. What percent of the morning commuting times fell below the lower quartile of the evening commuting times? **50%**

Henry Suarez grows two kinds of tomatoes, Great Northern and Red Giant. The tables at the right show the number of tomatoes produced by each of his plants.

8. Find the extremes, the upper and lower quartiles, and the median of the Great Northern data. **6 and 32, 14 and 24, 19**

9. Construct a box-and-whisker plot for the Great Northern data. **Check students' work.**

10. Find the extremes, the upper and lower quartiles, and the median of the Red Giant data. **12 and 28, 16 and 24, 20**

11. Copy the box-and-whisker plot you made for Exercise 9. Add to the copy a box-and-whisker plot for the Red Giant data. **Check students' work.**

Great Northern			
6	20	22	24
28	12	20	18
26	28	20	30
15	15	8	24
27	26	16	18
32	18	11	16
21	10	12	13
8	22	23	17

Red Giant			
15	18	16	22
19	21	22	16
17	21	12	23
28	25	16	26
22	14	19	15
18	25	26	25

Name ______________ Date ______________

Practice 24

For use with Section 3-6

For each kind of graph, tell whether or not each statement describes the given kind of graph.

Histogram:

1. Displays each item of data **no**

2. Is good for data organized in intervals **yes**

3. Shows relationship of parts to whole **no**

4. Displays frequencies **yes**

Circle graph:

5. Shows division of a whole into parts **yes**

6. Shows trends in the data **no**

7. Angle of each "slice" indicates percent **yes**

8. Displays outliers clearly **no**

Stem-and-leaf plot:

9. Shows trends in the data **no**

10. Shows individual items of data **yes**

11. Shows the quartiles of the data **no**

12. Shows the median of the data **no**

Tell which type of graph best suits each situation.

13. A company's finance officer wants to show how the company spends its money and what percent is used for each purpose. **circle graph**

14. An agricultural researcher wants to compare the weights of feed consumed by six different kinds of farm animals in a month. **bar graph**

15. A bird-watching club wants to show the bird counts that its individual members achieved on a hike. **stem-and-leaf plot**

16. A city historian wants to display the changes in the population of two neighboring towns between 1900 and 1990. The graph should show upward and downward trends of the two populations clearly. **line graph**

17. A statistician in a high school testing service wants to display the distribution of scores on a test, the median of the scores, and the interval that contained the middle half of the scores. **box-and-whisker plot**

18. ***Writing*** Name two types of graph that you might use to display the data in the table at the right, and explain the advantages and disadvantages of each type. **Check students' work.**

Household Average Daily Electricity Usage (kWh)			
7.5	8.2	13.4	10.6
12.0	10.1	9.3	8.5
9.6	9.4	11.8	12.2
10.5	10.2	9.7	9.8

Name ______________________ Date ____________

Practice 25

For use with Section 3-7

The graph at the right compares the fuel economy of vehicles made by Consolidated Motors Company (CMC) with vehicles made by National Motors (NM). Use the graph for Exercises 1–8.

Fuel Economy of Vehicles

Miles per Gallon (mi/gal): 25, 26, 27

pick-up, van, car, wagon

NM, CMC

1. About how many times longer is the bar for the CMC pickup than the bar for the NM pickup? **3 times**
2. What is the actual ratio of the CMC pickup's fuel economy to the NM pickup's fuel economy? **See above.**

   2. $\frac{27}{25}$ **or 1.08**
3. Does the graph give an accurate picture of the relationship between these two fuel economies? **no**
4. How much greater is the fuel economy of CMC's car than the fuel economy of NM's car? Choose the correct letter. **b**

   a. 1.5 mi/gal **b.** 2.5 mi/gal **c.** 25 mi/gal **d.** 27.5 mi/gal
5. What percent of the fuel economy of NM's car does the answer to Exercise 4 represent? **about 10%**
6. Does the graph give an accurate picture of the true relationship between the fuel economies of the two cars? **no**
7. Do the other vehicle categories show accurately the relationship between corresponding fuel economies? **no**
8. Suppose one of the two companies, NM or CMC, used this graph in a magazine ad. Which one do you think it was? **CMC**

In Exercises 9–13, use the graph at the right, showing sales of computer disks in one area of the country.

Computer Disk Sales (millions of dollars)

$16.7 — 1988; $31.5 — 1990

9. About how many times greater were the 1990 sales of disks than the 1988 sales? **2 times**
10. Suppose the shapes are approximately square and that the width of the square for 1988 sales is *x*. Write an expression for the width of the square for 1990 sales, using *x*. **2x**
11. Using *x*, write expressions for the areas of the squares that represent 1988 sales and 1990 sales. x^2, $4x^2$
12. How many times greater is the area of the larger square? **4 times**
13. Does the graph give an accurate picture of the relationship between the two sales figures? **no**

Name ______________________ Date ____________

Practice 26

Cumulative Practice through Unit 3

For Exercises 1–4, use a number anywhere along the scale below to estimate the probability of each event.

impossible 0%	unlikely 25%	possible 50%	likely 75%	certain 100%
0	0.25	0.5	0.75	1

1. A human being will walk on Mars within ten years. **Answers may vary.**
2. Thanksgiving will fall on a Thursday this year. **100%**
3. You will have no homework in math for the rest of this year. **0%**
4. You will see a cat on the way home from school today. **Answers may vary.**

For Exercises 5–9, use rectangle *ABCD* at the right. *M* is the midpoint of $\overline{AB}$ and *N* is the midpoint of $\overline{BC}$. Find each measure.

D, C, N, 10, A, M, 8, B

5. *AB* **16**
6. *BC* **10**
7. *CN* **5**
8. the perimeter of *ABCD* **52 units**
9. the area of *ABCD* **160 square units**

Rewrite the numbers in order from least to greatest.

10. $\sqrt{10}$, 5, $\sqrt{22}$, $\sqrt{5}$, 4, 3, $\sqrt{15.1}$, $\sqrt{6}$ **$\sqrt{5}$, $\sqrt{6}$, 3, $\sqrt{10}$, $\sqrt{15.1}$, 4, $\sqrt{22}$, 5**
11. 6, $\sqrt[3]{29}$, 4, $\sqrt[3]{1001}$, $\sqrt{65}$, $\sqrt[3]{65}$, $\sqrt{75}$ **$\sqrt[3]{29}$, 4, $\sqrt[3]{65}$, 6, $\sqrt{65}$, $\sqrt[3]{75}$, $\sqrt[3]{1001}$**

Find the mean, the median, and the mode(s) of each set of data.

12. Sizes of men's shoes sold on a particular day at Walker's Shoe Store: 8, 7, 9.5, 10.5, 9.5, 6, 7.5, 7, 7, 8, 9.5 **8.1, 8, 7**
13. Points scored by a high school football team in each game: 9, 28, 20, 10, 16, 9, 17, 21, 20, 35 **18.5, 18.5, 9 and 20**

Graph each inequality on a number line.

14. $x > 5$
15. $x \leq 2$
16. $-1 < x \leq 3$

Write an inequality to describe each situation.

17. At sea level, water boils at or above 100°C. $x \geq 100$
18. A middleweight boxer must weight 160 lb or less. $0 < x \leq 160$
19. Bus passengers over 12 and under 65 years of age pay full fare. $12 < x < 65$

Name ______________________ Date ______________

Practice 27

For use with Section 4-1

For Exercises 1–9, use the map below.

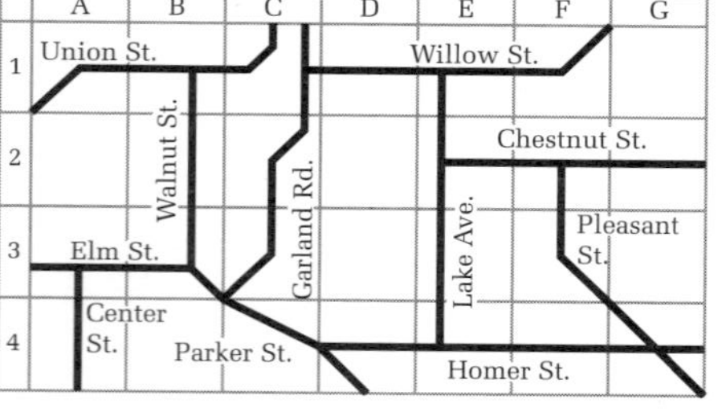

Name the street that goes through each group of squares.

1. C1, C2, C3 **Garland Rd.** **2.** F2, F3, G4 **Pleasant St.** **3.** B1, B2, B3 **Walnut St.**

Name all the squares that each street runs through.

4. Elm St. **A3, B3**
5. Homer St. **D4, E4, F4, G4**
6. Union St. **A1, B1, C1**
7. Willow St. **C1, D1, E1, F1**
8. Parker St. **B3, C4, D4**
9. Center St. **A3, A4**

For Exercises 10–29, use the diagram at the right. Name the quadrant each point is in.

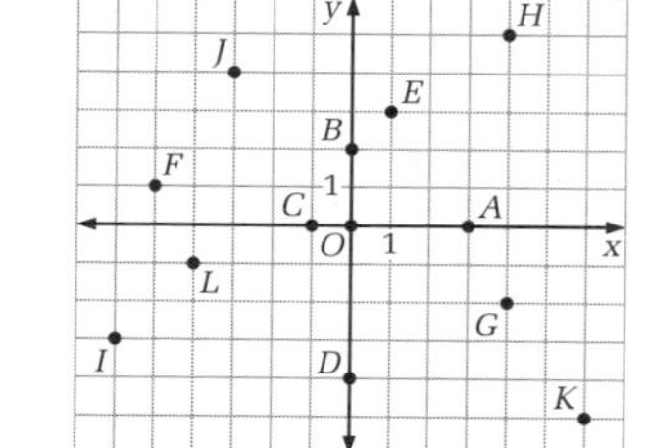

10. E **I** **11.** F **II** **12.** G **IV** **13.** H **I**
14. I **III** **15.** J **II** **16.** K **IV** **17.** L **III**

Name the coordinates of each point.

18. A **(3, 0)** **19.** B **(0, 2)** **20.** C **(–1, 0)** **21.** D **(0, –4)**
22. E **(1, 3)** **23.** F **(–5, 1)** **24.** G **(4, –2)** **25.** I **(–6, –3)**
26. J **(–3, 4)** **27.** K **(6, –5)** **28.** L **(–4, –1)** **29.** O **(0, 0)**

30. ***Open-ended*** Draw a map of some of the streets near your home or school. Draw a grid and label your grid with letters across the top and numbers down the left side. Make up a street index, telling the labels of the squares through which each street runs. **Check students' work.**

Name ______________________ Date ______________

Practice 28

For use with Section 4-2

Find the area of each polygon.

1.

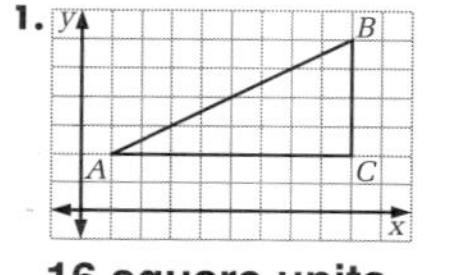

16 square units

2. **21 square units**

3. **16 square units**

4.

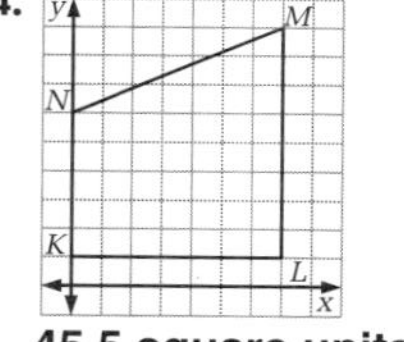

45.5 square units

5. **30 square units**

6. **31 square units**

Follow these steps for Exercises 7–12. **For drawings, check students' work.**

a. **Plot the points on a coordinate plane. Connect the points in order and connect the last point to the first.**

b. **Write the specific name of the polygon you formed.**

c. **List all pairs of congruent sides.**

7. $A(1, -1)$, $B(7, -1)$, $C(4, 4)$ **isosceles triangle**

8. $U(-3, 4)$, $V(1, 1)$, $W(5, 4)$ **isosceles triangle**

9. $D(-1, 2)$, $E(3, 2)$, $F(3, 5)$, $G(-1, 5)$ **rectangle**

10. $S(-3, 1)$, $T(5, 1)$, $U(3, 5)$, $V(-1, 5)$ **trapezoid**

11. $W(1, 0)$, $X(5, 2)$, $Y(4, 5)$, $Z(0, 3)$ **parallelogram**

12. $L(-1, 1)$, $M(2, -2)$, $N(5, -2)$, $O(-1, 4)$ **trapezoid**

7. $\overline{AC} \cong \overline{BC}$ **8.** $\overline{UV} \cong \overline{WV}$ **9.** $\overline{GD} \cong \overline{FE}$, $\overline{DE} \cong \overline{GF}$ **10.** $\overline{VS} \cong \overline{UT}$ **11.** $\overline{ZW} \cong \overline{YX}$, $\overline{ZY} \cong \overline{WX}$ **12.** $\overline{LO} \cong \overline{MN}$

13. Find the areas of the regions labeled I, II, III, and IV in the diagram at the right. Use these areas to find the area of quadrilateral $ABCD$. **See top of page.**

13. Sum of areas = 12 + 14 + 12 + 7.5 = 45.5 square units

14. ***Open-ended*** On a coordinate plane, graph three points that are the vertices of a triangle. Can you locate a fourth point in such a way that the four points are the vertices of a parallelogram? Is there more than one way to locate such a fourth point? How many such fourth points are there? Try the same experiment with a different set of three points. Write your results. **For drawings, check students' work. For each triangle, there are three possibilities for the fourth point.**

Name ____________________ Date ____________________

Practice 29

For use with Section 4-3

2. A′(–3, –1), B′(3, –5), C′(2, 2)

4. A′(–8, 1), B′(– 2, –3), C′(–3, 4)

Find the coordinates of each vertex of $\triangle ABC$ after each translation.

1. 1 unit right **A′(–2, 1), B′(4, –3), C′(3, 4)**
2. 2 units down **See above.**
3. 3 units up **A′(–3, 4), B′(3, 0), C′(2,7)**
4. 5 units left **See above.**
5. 2 units right and 3 units down **A′(–1, –2), B′(5,–6), C′(4, 1)**
6. 3 units left and 4 units up **A′(–6, 5), B′(0,1), C′(–1, 8)**
7. 5 units right and 2 units up **A′(2, 3), B′(8,–1), C′(7, 6)**

A(–3, 1) C(2, 4) B(3, –3)

Write the coordinates of P' after each translation of the given point P.

8. $P(4, 1)$; $(x, y) \to (x - 1, y)$ **P′(3, 1)**
9. $P(3, 5)$; $(x, y) \to (x, y + 2)$ **P′(3, 7)**
10. $P(2, 3)$; $(x, y) \to (x + 3, y - 5)$ **P′(5, –2)**
11. $P(1, 4)$; $(x, y) \to (x - 2, y + 4)$ **P′(–1, 8)**
12. $P(-1, 5)$; $(x, y) \to (x + 2, y - 3)$ **P′(1, 2)**
13. $P(0, -2)$; $(x, y) \to (x, y + 6)$ **P′(0, 4)**
14. $P(-3, 0)$; $(x, y) \to (x - 7, y - 2)$ **P′(–10, –2)**
15. $P(1, 6)$; $(x + 4, y - 3)$ **P′(5, 3)**
16. $P(-2, -4)$; $(x, y) \to (x + 5, y - 4)$ **P′(3, –8)**
17. $P(-5, 1)$; $(x + 4, y - 1)$ **P′(–1, 0)**

Describe each translation by showing the change in the coordinates (x, y) of any point.

18. 2 units right **$(x, y) \to (x + 2, y)$**
19. 3 units down **$(x, y) \to (x, y - 3)$**
20. 5 units up **$(x, y) \to (x, y + 5)$**
21. 1 unit left and 4 units up **$(x, y) \to (x - 1, y + 4)$**
22. 2 units right and 6 units up **$(x, y) \to (x + 2, y + 6)$**
23. 3 units right and 2 units down **$(x, y) \to (x + 3, y - 2)$**
24. 7 units left and 8 units down **$(x, y) \to (x - 7, y - 8)$**
25. $(3, 7) \to (4, 5)$ **$(x, y) \to (x + 1, y - 2)$**
26. $(2, -9) \to (5, -7)$ **$(x, y) \to (x + 3, y + 2)$**

Tell whether the pattern you find in each of the following has translational symmetry.

27. The rings of an archery target **no**
28. The checkered flag at a car race **yes**
29. A straight brick wall **yes**
30. A basketball court **no**
31. A maple leaf **no**
32. A bicycle wheel **no**
33. The lines on a page of ruled notebook paper **yes**
34. The wire fencing of a baseball backstop **yes**

Name ____________________ Date ____________________

Practice 30

For use with Section 4-4

14. yes; 45°, 90°, 135°, 180°, 225°, 270°, and 315°

15. yes; 60°, 120°, 180°, 240°, and 300°

The graphs show rotations around the origin. Describe the direction and amount of rotation of each graph.

1. 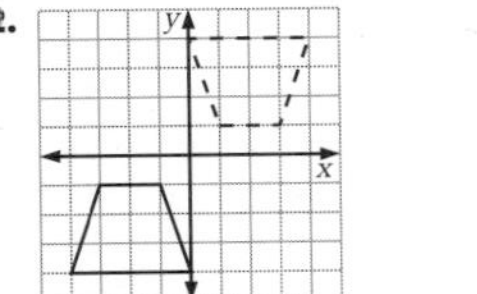
90° counterclockwise

2. 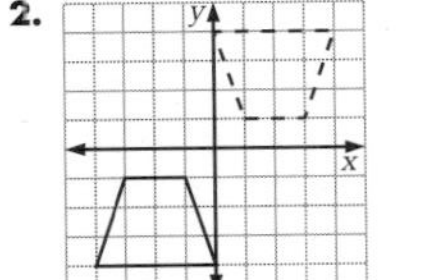
180°

3. 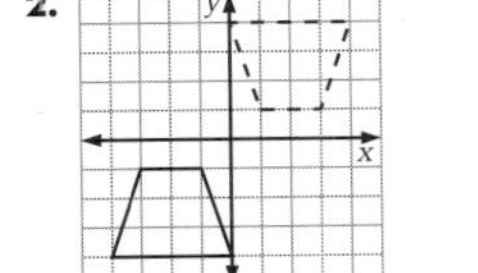
90° clockwise

Copy the figure on polar graph paper. Draw each indicated rotation of the figure around the origin.

4. 30° counterclockwise
5. 90° clockwise
6. 180°
7. 90° counterclockwise
8. 120° clockwise
9. 60° clockwise

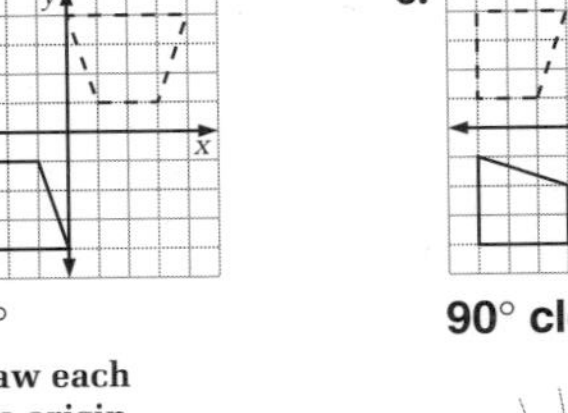
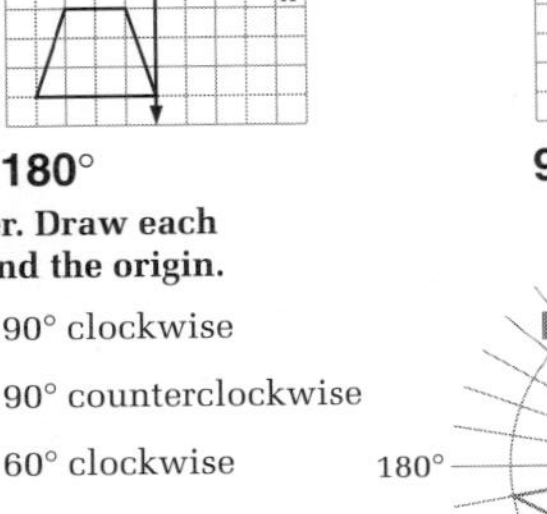
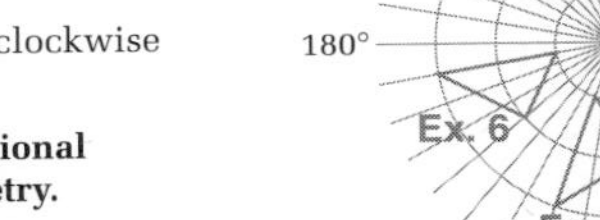

Tell whether or not each object has rotational symmetry. If it does, describe the symmetry.

10. The pattern of 5 dots on a die **yes; 90°, 180°, and 270°**
11. The capital letter "N" **yes; 180°**
12. A window fan with three blades **yes; 120° and 240°**
13. The heads side of a penny **no**
14. The outline of a stop sign
15. The head of a bolt with 6 sides

14, 15. See top of page.

Tell whether or not each figure has rotational symmetry. If it does, describe the symmetry.

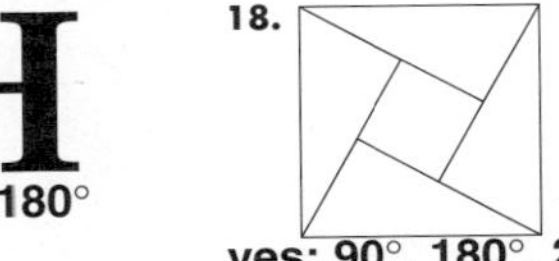

16. **yes; 120°, 240°**
17. **yes; 180°**
18. **yes; 90°, 180°, 270°**
19. **no**

20. ***Open-ended*** Make up a table listing vehicles you see every day together with a description of the symmetry of their wheels. You can find the symmetry by counting the identical "pie slices" in the wheel and dividing 360° by this number. **Check students' work.**

Name ______________________ Date ____________

Practice 31

For use with Section 4-5

State whether each scatter plot shows a positive correlation, a negative correlation, or no correlation.

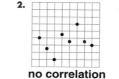

1. 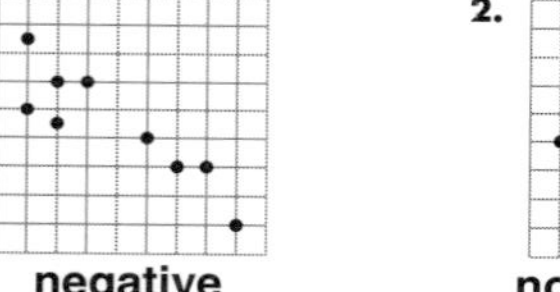
negative

2. **no correlation**

3. **positive**

For Exercises 4 and 5, use the table at the right to make each scatter plot.

Date	Av. Temp. (°F)	Air Cond. Sales	Sweater Sales
March 10	35	3	45
March 20	40	1	42
April 1	52	5	35
April 12	63	10	21
April 30	55	16	12
May 5	76	22	5
May 15	72	26	8
May 25	85	35	2

4. Air conditioner sales versus average temperature **Check students' work.**
5. Sweater sales versus average temperature **Check students' work.**
6. State whether each of the scatter plots you made for Exercises 4 and 5 shows a positive correlation, a negative correlation, or no correlation. **positive, negative**

Exs. 7–9: For scatter plots, check students' work.

For Exercises 7–11, use the table at the right, which lists data on laptop computers produced by various companies.

For Exercises 7–9, make a scatter plot of each relationship. State whether each scatter plot shows a positive correlation, a negative correlation, or no correlation.

Manufacturer	Price ($)	Weight (lb)	Ad Costs (mil. $)	Sales (units)
Leapfrog	1600	9.3	25	32,000
EZ Compr	2400	5.4	37	45,000
Link Inc.	1750	10.2	32	30,000
Future Pro	2900	6.0	50	47,000
Tec Trek	1300	11.5	20	18,000
Key Byte	2300	8.6	42	38,000
Disk Corp.	3000	5.2	24	19,000
Micro Power	2500	7.5	12	15,000
Star	2800	6.2	35	29,000
Laserkiss	1900	9.2	30	26,000

7. Price versus weight **negative correlation**
8. Ad costs versus sales **positive correlation**
9. Weight versus sales **no correlation**
10. For each of the scatter plots you drew in Exercises 7–9 that shows a positive or a negative correlation, draw a fitted line. **Check students' work.**
11. Based on your scatter plot for Exercise 7, predict the weight of a laptop computer that costs $2600. **about 7.0 lb**
12. *Writing* What conclusion can you draw from the scatter plot you drew in Exercise 9? **Check students' work.**

Name ______________________ Date ____________

Practice 32

For use with Section 4-6

Tell whether each graph represents a function.

1. **no**
2. **yes**
3. **yes**
4. **no**
5. **yes**
6. **yes**

Graph each function. **For graphs, check students' work.**

7. Average Height (Girls)

Age	Height (in.)
1	29
2	33
3	36
4	39
5	41
6	44
7	47
8	50
9	52
10	54

8. Wind Chill (Temp. 35°F)

Wind Speed (mi/h)	Wind Chill Factor (°F)
5	33
10	22
15	16
20	12
25	8
30	6
35	4
40	3
45	2

9. Distance of Free Fall

Time (s)	Dist. (m)
0	0
1	4.9
2	19.6
3	44.1
4	78.4
5	122.6
6	176.5
7	240.2

10. Use the graph you drew in Exercise 7 to estimate the average height of a girl at $6\frac{1}{2}$ years of age. **about 45 in.**
11. Use the graph you drew in Exercise 9 to estimate the time required for a free-falling object to fall 120 m. **about 5 s**
12. Use the graph you drew in Exercise 8 to estimate the windchill factor for a temperature of 35°F and a 50 mi/h wind. **about 1°F**
13. *Writing* Some graphs of functions consist of dots. Others are lines or curves. How do you know whether or not to connect the dots when graphing a real-life function? **Check students' work.**

Name ____________________ Date ____________

Practice 33

For use with Section 4-7

5–19b. The shapes for the graphs are described briefly. Two checkpoints are also given below. **5–7. Line 8–10. Line 11–13. U-shape 14–16. V-shape 17–19. Two "facing" branches**

Write an equation to represent each function.

1.

x	y
−3	3
−2	2
−1	1
0	0
1	−1
2	−2
3	−3

$y = -x$

2.

x	y
−3	0
−2	1
−1	2
0	3
1	4
2	5
3	6

$y = x + 3$

3.

x	y
−3	−9
−2	−6
−1	−3
0	0
1	3
2	6
3	9

$y = 3x$

4.

x	y
−3	−8
−2	−7
−1	−6
0	−5
1	−4
2	−3
3	−2

$y = x - 5$

In Exercises 5–19, (a) make up a table of values, using values from −3 to 3 for the control variable (use 0.5 and −0.5 instead of 0 in Exercises 17–19), and (b) graph each function. **Exs. 5–19a: Two checkpoints are given below. Exs. 5–19b: See top of page.**

5. $y = x + 1$ **(0, 1), (3, 4)**

6. $y = x - 2$ **(0, −2), (3, 1)**

7. $y = -x + 3$ **(0, 3), (3, 0)**

8. $y = 2x$ **(0, 0), (3, 6)**

9. $y = \frac{1}{2}x$ **(0, 0), (2, 1)**

10. $y = -3x$ **(0, 0), (3, −9)**

11. $y = -x^2$ **(0, 0), (−3, −9)**

12. $y = \frac{1}{4}x^2$ **(0, 0), (2, 1)**

13. $y = 2x^2$ **(0, 0), (−2, 8)**

14. $y = -|x|$ **(−3, −3), (3, −3)**

15. $y = |x| + 1$ **(−2, 3), (3, 4)**

16. $y = \frac{1}{2}|x|$ **(0, 0), (−2, 1)**

17. $y = -\frac{1}{x}$ **(0.5, −2), (−0.5, 2)**

18. $y = \frac{6}{x}$ **(0.5, 12), (2, 3)**

19. $y = -\frac{4}{x}$ **(−0.5, 8), (2, −2)**

Write each function as an equation. Then graph the function. **Exs. 20–23: For graphs, check students' work.**

20. Suppose you drive a car at a steady speed of 50 mi/h. The distance (in miles) that you cover depends on the driving time (in hours). **$y = 50x$**

21. The fare on city buses is being raised by $.25. The new fare depends on the old fare. **$y = x + 0.25$**

22. In Springfield, 40% of the money collected in taxes goes to support education. The money used for education depends on the money collected in taxes. **$y = 0.4x$**

23. An amusement park has an admission charge of $2.00, and each ticket for a ride costs $.50. The total amount that a person spends at the amusement park depends on the number of tickets bought. **$y = 2 + 0.5x$**

Name ____________________ Date ____________

Practice 34

Cumulative Practice through Unit 4

Simplify. Write each answer in scientific notation.

1. $3.2(4.5 \times 10^5)$ **1.44×10^6**

2. $(9.25 \times 10^3)(6.4 \times 10^4)$ **5.92×10^8**

3. $\frac{1.8 \times 10^{-3}}{3000}$ **6×10^{-7}**

In Exercises 4–7, use the graph at the right, which shows the prices turkey farmers received for their turkeys at 10-year intervals from 1930 to 1990.

Average Turkey Price per Pound (received by farmers)

4. In which year did farmers receive the highest price per pound for their turkeys? **1980**

5. In which year did farmers receive the lowest price per pound for their turkeys? **1940**

6. In which two 10-year spans did the prices increase most rapidly? **1940–1950 and 1970–1980**

7. Does the graph show a steady increase in the prices turkey farmers received, a steady decrease in these prices, or neither? **neither**

The table at the right lists counts of a certain kind of bird at a wildlife preserve on successive days. Use the table for Exercises 8–10.

Bird Counts			
12	24	40	35
21	33	27	42
25	32	11	14
20	16	30	34
27	32	35	24

8. Make a stem-and-leaf plot using the data. **Check students' work.**

9. Find the median of the data. **27**

10. Make a histogram from the data using the intervals 10–19, 20–29, 30–39, and 40–49. **Check students' work.**

The circle graph at the right compares audience share for four radio stations during a one-hour time period. Use this graph in Exercises 11–14.

11. From the wedges in the graph, does it appear from the graph that WTOP has half of the audience during the time period? **yes**

12. Is it really true that WTOP has more than half of the audience? **no**

13. Does WPDQ have one-fourth of the audience? Does this appear to be true from the graph? Why is this so? **yes; no; The circle is seen at an angle.**

14. Suppose one of the four radio stations made this graph to show prospective advertisers? Which station do you think it was? **WTOP**

Name ______________________ Date ______________

Practice 35

For use with Section 5-1

For spreadsheets or tables, check students' work.

Model each situation using a spreadsheet or table and then solve.

1. Your summer job pays $4.50 per hour. How many hours of work will it take to earn a total of $35 for a pair of concert tickets? **8 hours**

2. An earthmoving company must move 80 tons of dirt from a construction site. Each of the company's trucks carries 14 tons. How many loads would one driver have to carry to do the job alone? **6 loads**

3. A lumber mill has 15 ft of a certain custom molding on hand. The mill can produce 18 ft of the molding per hour. How many hours will it take to fill an order for 175 ft? **9 hours**

4. David Jackson's job pays him $20,000 this year. Suppose that in every future year he works, his salary is 1.1 times what it was the year before. After how many years will his salary be over $32,000? **5 years**

Model each situation using a graph and then solve.

5. A jetliner has completed 225 miles of a 3000-mile flight. At an airspeed of 475 mi/h, how long will it take the jetliner to reach its destination? **about 6 hours**

6. A package of tomato plant seeds states that about 85% of the seeds can be expected to sprout. Jo Stillwater wants to have 80 tomato plants. How many seeds should she plant? **95 seeds**

Model each situation using an equation and then solve.

7. Emily Niquette pays a monthly charge of $3.40 for electricity and in addition there is a $.07 charge for each kilowatt-hour she uses. One month her bill was $12.50. How many kilowatt-hours did she use? **$3.4 + 0.07x = 12.5$; 130 kilowatt-hours**

8. On May 5, there are 14 h 4 min of daylight in Denver, Colorado. The amount of daylight goes up by about 2 min each day. On what day in May should there be 14 h 36 min of daylight in Denver? **$4 + 2x = 36$; May 21**

9. Goncalves Textiles pays an employee when the employee uses his or her own car for business. Each employee is entitled to $12.50 plus $1.80 for every mile driven. One employee is paid $228.50 for a business trip. How many miles did the employee drive? **$12.5 + 1.8x = 228.5$; 120 miles**

10. ***Writing*** Describe as many situations as you can that could be modeled by the equation $7.5 = 1.5 + 0.25x$. **Check students' work.**

Name ______________________ Date ______________

Practice 36

For use with Section 5-2

Simplify.

1. $-(-4r)$ **$4r$**
2. $-(5 - y)$ **$-5 + y$**
3. $-(10 - 2z)$ **$-10 + 2z$**
4. $6 - (-3p + 1)$ **$5 + 3p$**
5. $x - (0.4 + 0.7x)$ **$0.3x - 0.4$**
6. $12 - (-m - 8)$ **$m + 20$**
7. $a^2 - (5 - 9a^2)$ **$10a^2 - 5$**
8. $3 + c - (4 + c)$ **-1**
9. $3 - b - (b - 3)$ **$6 - 2b$**
10. $n - 2(-n + 4)$ **$3n - 8$**
11. $6t - t^2 - 5(t - t^2)$ **$t + 4t^2$**
12. $10v - v(6 - 4v)$ **$4v + 4v^2$**

Solve.

13. $9 - x = 16$ **-7**
14. $-32 - n = -7$ **-25**
15. $2z - 5 + z = 43$ **16**
16. $y + 17 - 4y = -4$ **7**
17. $-2d + 6 - 5d = 62$ **-8**
18. $-(4 - t) = 15$ **19**
19. $-(7 + 6w) = -19$ **2**
20. $-(5 - 2g) = -11$ **-3**
21. $4(8 - m) = 56$ **-6**
22. $-7(5 - y) = 49$ **12**
23. $6 - (3 + 2n) = 25$ **-11**
24. $5 - 2(a + 7) = 32$ **-20.5**
25. $8 + 3(5 - b) = -10$ **11**
26. $k - 3(6 - k) = -14$ **1**
27. $6(3 - z) - 5z = -4$ **2**
28. $(5 + r) - (6 - r) = 13$ **7**
29. $-2(u - 5) - (u + 1) = -18$ **9**

Find the measure of each angle.

30. $2x°$, $3(x - 5)°$ — **78°**, **102°**

31. $11x°$, $6(x - 4)°$ — **132°**, **48°**

32. $2x°$, $110°$, $5(x - 7)°$ — **30°**, **40°**

33. The sum of the measures of the angles of a convex polygon is 1980°. How many sides does the polygon have? **13 sides**

Lin Hsia plans to invest $1400 in two stocks: Consolidated Industries (CI) and Amalgamated Manufacturing (AM).

34. Let x = the amount she invests in CI. Write an expression for the amount Lin has left to invest in AM. **$1400 - x$**

35. Suppose that after 5 years Lin's CI stock does not change in value, but her AM stock triples, making her stocks worth $3300. Write an equation that expresses this fact. **$x + 3(1400 - x) = 3300$**

36. Find out how much she invested in each company by solving the equation you wrote in Exercise 35. **$450 in CI, $950 in AM**

Name ______________________ Date ______________

Practice 37

For use with Section 5-3

Solve.

1. $3x = 4x - 5$ **5**
2. $-5t = t + 12$ **−2**
3. $2w + 70 = -3w$ **−14**
4. $4y + 33 = 15y$ **3**
5. $26 - 4a = 9a$ **2**
6. $-3n + 28 = -7n$ **−7**
7. $2(b - 21) = -5b$ **6**
8. $-3(8 - c) = 7c$ **−6**
9. $7(m - 56) = -m$ **49**
10. $-6(m + 5) = 9m$ **−2**
11. $8x = -11(6 - x)$ **22**
12. $z = 5(12 + z)$ **−15**
13. $0.5(102 - p) = 2.5p$ **17**
14. $0.3t = 0.8(t - 5)$ **8**
15. $5k = -2(21 + k)$ **−6**
16. $-5 - d = 3(7 - d)$ **13**
17. $29 + q = -2(q - 13)$ **−1**
18. $-2r - 3 = 7(11 - r)$ **16**
19. $4(n - 3) - 18 = -n$ **6**
20. $-6(8 - b) - 20 = 5b$ **68**
21. $-2(c + 7) - 30 = 9c$ **−4**

Find x in each diagram.

22. $(x + 10)°$, $4(x - 26)°$ **x = 38**

23. $3(x - 5)$ cm, $(37 - x)$ cm **x = 13**

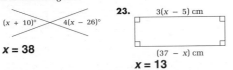

24. x cm, $(4x - 51)$ cm **x = 17**

Marissa left her apartment at 7:00 A.M. riding her bike at 12 mi/h. At 7:30 A.M. Marissa's roommate Kim realized that Marissa had forgotten her lunch and set off after her, by the same route, riding her moped at 18 mi/h.

25. Let t = Marissa's travel time. Write an expression for Kim's travel time, using t. Write expressions for Marissa's distance and for Kim's distance, using t. **$t - 0.5$; $12t$ and $18(t - 0.5)$**

26. Write and solve an equation to find the time it took Kim to catch up to Marissa. **$12t = 18(t - 0.5)$; $t = 1.5$; 1.5 hours**

Chesterton's population is 37,500 and is growing by 650 each year. Melville has a population of 36,300 and is growing by 800 each year.

27. Write expressions for the populations after x years. **$37{,}500 + 650x$ and $36{,}300 + 800x$**

28. Write and solve an equation to determine how many years it will take before the two towns have the same population. **$37{,}500 + 650x = 36{,}300 + 800x$; $x = 8$; 8 years**

29. ***Writing*** Tell whether you think the expressions you wrote for Exercise 27 would be useful in predicting the populations of the towns a hundred years from now. Explain your thinking. **Check students' work.**

Name ______________________ Date ______________

Practice 38

For use with Section 5-4

Solve and graph each inequality. **For graphs, check students' work.**

1. $p + 3 < 5$ **$p < 2$**
2. $c - 4 \ge 2$ **$c \ge 6$**
3. $x - 1 > -6$ **$x > -5$**
4. $7 - y \le 2$ **$y \ge 5$**
5. $-9 - q \ge -5$ **$q \le -4$**
6. $2 - v > -3$ **$v < 5$**
7. $5w \ge -35$ **$w \ge -7$**
8. $-3n > 9$ **$n < -3$**
9. $-4k \le 24$ **$k \ge -6$**
10. $-12b < 0$ **$b > 0$**
11. $0.27 < -0.06h$ **$h < -4.5$**
12. $10d \le -35$ **$d \le -3.5$**
13. $2u - 5 < 7$ **$u < 6$**
14. $8 - 2r \ge 10$ **$r \le -1$**
15. $6t + 5 > -7$ **$t > -2$**
16. $-3m + 22 > 4$ **$m < 6$**
17. $9 \le 24 - 5z$ **$z \le 3$**
18. $18 \le -8 - 13a$ **$a \le -2$**
19. $2(x - 5) \le -12$ **$x \le -1$**
20. $-4(7 - t) > -28$ **$t > 0$**
21. $3 > -3(y + 7)$ **$y > -8$**
22. $-15 \le -3(8 + v)$ **$v \le -3$**
23. $6(w - 9) < -21$ **$w < 5.5$**
24. $-10(5 - c) \le 25$ **$c \le 7.5$**

25. Fashion Statement, Inc. makes men's shirts for department stores. A store needs at least 525 shirts. The company has 84 shirts in its stock. Write and solve an inequality to find the number of shirts the company will have to make to fill the store's order. **$x + 84 \ge 525$; $x \ge 441$; at least 441 shirts**

26. An elevator has an inspection certificate stating that the maximum weight the elevator can carry is 2100 lb. Suppose each person who takes the elevator weighs 140 lb. Write and solve an inequality for the number of persons the elevator can carry. **$140n \le 2100$; $n \le 15$; at most 15 people**

27. Miguel Santos saves $65 a week out of his salary toward a vacation trip. Suppose the trip will cost at least $1430. Write and solve an inequality to find the number of weeks it will take him to pay for his vacation trip. **$65w \ge 1430$; $w \ge 22$; at least 22 weeks**

28. Dugungi's hardware store has 17 pitchforks in its inventory. The store manager estimates that the store will need over 65 pitchforks for the coming growing season. Pitchforks are packed 4 to a box. Write and solve an inequality to find the number of boxes of pitchforks Dugungi's should order. **$17 + 4b > 65$; $b > 12$; more than 12 boxes**

29. Mei Ling Won wants to keep her local telephone bill under $20. The phone company charges a base rate of $5.60 each month and $.24 for each message unit used. Write and solve an inequality to find how many message units she can use. **$5.6 + 0.24m < 20$; $m < 60$; fewer than 60 message units**

30. A supermarket manager wants to price a box of cereal. During a sale in which each box is marked $1.50 off, the manager wants 5 boxes to sell for less than 3 boxes did before the sale. Write and solve an inequality to find the price the supermarket should charge for a box of cereal. **$5(p - 1.5) < 3p$; $p < 3.75$; less than $3.75**

Name ____________________ Date ____________

Practice 39

For use with Section 5-5

Solve each equation for the variable indicated.

1. $C = 2\pi r$ for r $\quad r = \frac{C}{2\pi}$
2. $V = \pi r^2 h$ for h $\quad h = \frac{V}{\pi r^2}$
3. $T = kPV$ for P $\quad P = \frac{T}{kV}$
4. $E = k + p$ for p $\quad p = E - k$
5. $y = mx + b$ for b $\quad b = y - mx$
6. $E = I^2R$ for R $\quad R = \frac{E}{I^2}$
7. $ax + by = c$ for x $\quad x = \frac{c - by}{a}$
8. $v = s + at$ for t $\quad t = \frac{v - s}{a}$
9. $w = 3m - 4k$ for k $\quad k = \frac{3m - w}{4}$
10. $s = \frac{a}{1 - r}$ for r $\quad r = \frac{s - a}{s}$
11. $I = p(1 + r)$ for r $\quad r = \frac{I}{p} - 1$
12. $m = \frac{360}{n}$ for n $\quad n = \frac{360}{m}$

For Exercises 13 and 14, suppose there is an 8% sales tax on all items purchased at a craft supplies store.

13. Write a formula to show the total amount T, including tax, that you would pay for items at the store that cost c dollars altogether. $T = 1.08c$
14. Brian Chung wants to spend $81, including tax, for a gift certificate. What amount will the gift certificate show? **$75**

For Exercises 15–17, suppose Felicia has saved $140 and plans to save an additional $15 each week out of the salary she makes at her part-time job.

15. Write a formula to show the total amount d that she has saved after w weeks. $d = 140 + 15w$
16. Rewrite the formula you found in Exercise 15 to show the number of weeks w it will take Felicia to save d dollars. $w = \frac{d - 140}{15}$
17. Use the formula you found in Exercise 16 to calculate how many weeks it will take Felicia to save $410 to buy a guitar. **18 weeks**

For Exercises 18 and 19, suppose Takeisha has made 34 free throws so far this season in basketball. She has made 75% of her free-throw shots.

18. Suppose she continues to hit 75% of her free-throw shots. Write a formula to show the total number of free throws f that Takeisha can expect to have made after her next s shots. $f = 34 + 0.75s$
19. Use the formula you found in Exercise 18 to find how many more shots Takeisha needs to take if she wants to equal the league record of 55. **28 shots**

Name ____________________ Date ____________

Practice 40

For use with Section 5-6

Solve.

1. $-6x = 15$ $\quad -2.5$
2. $\frac{3}{4}w = -24$ $\quad -32$
3. $-\frac{2}{3}k = -18$ $\quad 27$
4. $14 = \frac{3}{5}y - 1$ $\quad 25$
5. $-\frac{5}{6}p + 2 = -23$ $\quad 30$
6. $8 = -\frac{3}{7}c - \frac{1}{7}$ $\quad -19$

Solve each equation for the indicated variable.

7. $A = \frac{1}{2}bh$ for b $\quad b = \frac{2A}{h}$
8. $V = \frac{1}{3}b^2h$ for h $\quad h = \frac{3V}{b^2}$
9. $p = \frac{1}{2}mv^2$ for m $\quad m = \frac{2p}{v^2}$
10. $V = \frac{1}{6}lwh$ for w $\quad w = \frac{6V}{lh}$
11. $A = \frac{2}{5}k$ for k $\quad k = \frac{5}{2}A$
12. $m = -\frac{3}{4}v$ for v $\quad v = -\frac{4}{3}m$
13. $y = -\frac{2}{3}x + b$ for x $\quad x = -\frac{3}{2}(y - b)$
14. $A = \frac{1}{2}(a + b)h$ for a $\quad a = \frac{2A}{h} - b$
15. $g = \frac{v^2}{2h}$ for h $\quad h = \frac{v^2}{2g}$

Roberto and two roommates ordered take-out shrimp, and the three agreed to split the cost (c) equally. Let s = Roberto's share of the cost.

16. Write an equation that describes this situation. $s = \frac{c}{3}$
17. Rewrite the formula to solve for c. $c = 3s$
18. Suppose Roberto's share was $2.63. Find the total cost of the shrimp. **$7.89**

Carlotta Mendez overhauled her tractor and mowed two of her five equal-sized fields. Overhauling the tractor took her 1.5 h. Let t = the time it takes her to mow all five fields, and let s = the time for the work she has already done.

19. Write an equation that describes this situation. $s = 1.5 + \frac{2}{5}t$
20. Rewrite the equation to solve for t. $t = \frac{5}{2}(s - 1.5)$
21. Suppose the work she has already done took Carlotta 6.5 h. How long does it take her to mow all five fields? **12.5 h**
22. *Open-ended* On a calculator, enter any number other than 0 or 1. Press the reciprocal key. Press the reciprocal key again. What do you notice? Try this with other numbers. What can you say in general about pressing the reciprocal key twice? Try starting with the number $\frac{\sqrt{5} + 1}{2}$. What is unusual about the reciprocal of this number and the number itself?

22. If you enter a nonzero number and then press the reciprocal key twice, you return to the original number. $\frac{\sqrt{5}+1}{2}$ and its reciprocal differ by exactly 1.

Practice Bank, INTEGRATED MATHEMATICS 1
Copyright © by Houghton Mifflin Company. All rights reserved.

Name ______________________ Date ____________

Practice 41

For use with Section 5-7

Find the area of each figure.

1. 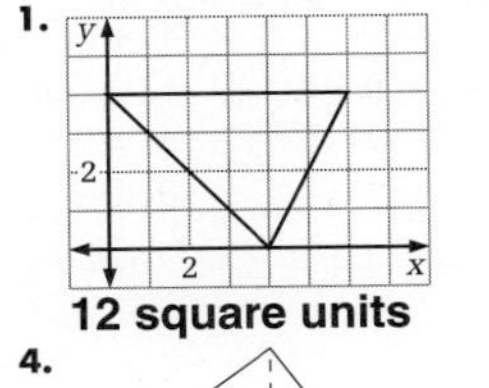

12 square units

2. 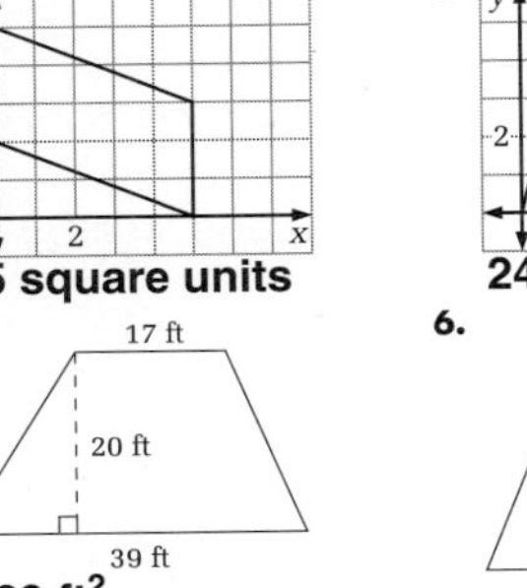

15 square units

3. 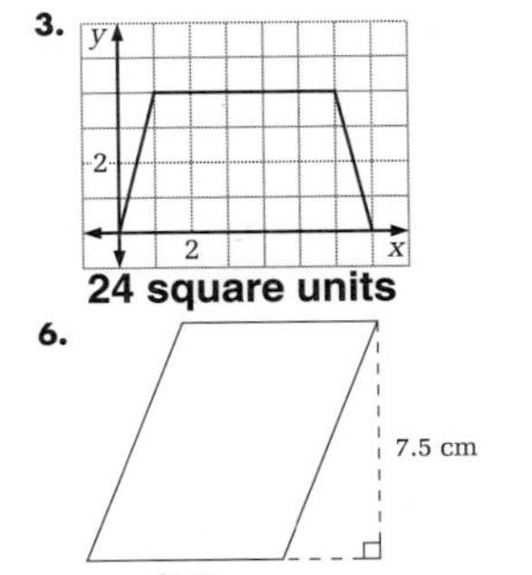

24 square units

4. 8 in.; 17 in.
68 in.^{2}

5. 17 ft; 20 ft; 39 ft
560 ft^2

6. 7.5 cm; 6 cm
45 cm^2

Find the area of a parallelogram having the given dimensions.

7. Base 15.8 cm; height 6.5 cm **102.7 cm^2**

8. Base 3.5 in.; height 6.8 in. **23.8 in.^{2}**

9. Find the base of a parallelogram having area 25.6 cm^2 and height 8 cm. **3.2 cm**

Each entry in the following tables gives information about a different trapezoid. Find x for each trapezoid.

	Base 1	Base 2	Height	Area
10.	14	18	x **5**	80
12.	17	x **25**	8	168

	Base 1	Base 2	Height	Area
11.	27	35	x **8**	248
13.	x **19**	15	6	102

14. One side of a parallelogram has length 10 in. With this side as base, the height of the parallelogram is 9 in. Another side of the parallelogram has length 15 in. What is the height of the parallelogram using this other side as the base? **6 in.**

15. A parallelogram has a base of $3(n - 4)$ in. The height of the parallelogram is 5 in. and its area is $7n$ in.^{2}. Find n. **7.5**

16. A trapezoid has bases of length $(3x - 2)$ cm and $(4x + 1)$ cm. The height of the trapezoid is 5 cm, and its area is 120 cm^2. Find x. **7**

Name ______________________ Date ____________

Practice 42

For use with Section 5-8

Solve each system of equations.

1. $y = 3x$
$2x + y = 5$ **(1, 3)**

2. $7a - b = 32$
$b = 3a$ **(8, 24)**

3. $m = -5n$
$m + 2n = 18$ **(30, −6)**

4. $p = 2q + 1$
$3p - q = -12$ **(−5, −3)**

5. $v = 4u - 3$
$u - v = 27$ **(−8, −35)**

6. $3d - 5e = 30$
$d = 2e + 7$ **(25, 9)**

7. $w = 5 - 3z$
$-4w + 2z = 50$ **(−10, 5)**

8. $8x - 3y = 49$
$y = 2x - 5$ **(17, 29)**

9. $10c - 7d = -9$
$d = 3c + 6$ **(−3, −3)**

Rewrite one of the equations in each system to get one of the variables alone on one side of the equation. Then solve the system of equations.

10. $2x + y = 12$
$3x - 4y = 7$ **(5, 2)**

11. $5c - 2d = -11$
$2c + d = 1$ **(−1, 3)**

12. $-3j + k = -7$
$2j - 3k = 7$ **(2, −1)**

Find x and y in each diagram, using a system of equations.

13. 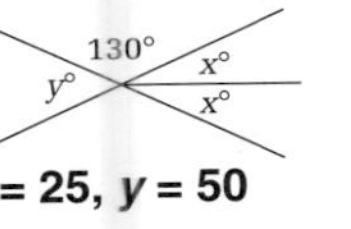

x = 25, y = 50

14. 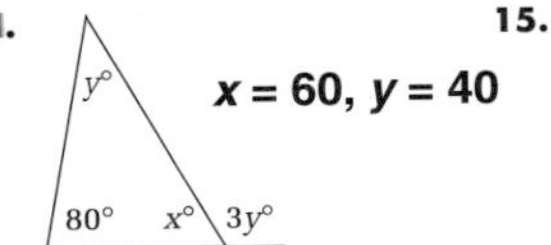

x = 60, y = 40

15. 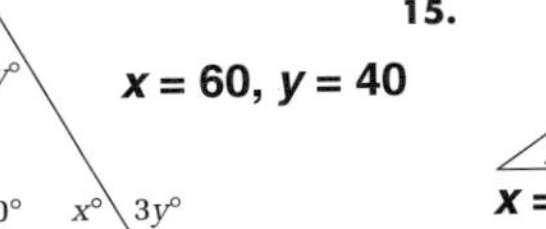

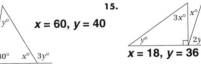

x = 18, y = 36

16. One angle of a triangle is 4 times as large as another angle of the same triangle. The third angle of the triangle has measure 60°. What are the measures of the other two angles of the triangle? **24° and 96°**

17. One acute angle of a right triangle is 5 times as large as the other. What are the measures of the two acute angles of the triangle? **15° and 75°**

18. The width of a rectangle is 3 in. less than its length. The perimeter is 24 in. Find the length and width of the rectangle. **7.5 in. and 4.5 in.**

19. In isosceles triangle *ABC*, each of the base angles is twice as large as the third angle. What are the measures of the three angles of the triangle? **72°, 72°, and 36°**

20. ***Open-ended*** What happens when you try to solve the system

$$y = 3x$$
$$6x - 2y = 5 \quad ?$$

Suppose the number 5 in the second equation is changed to 0. What happens when you try to solve the new system? Make up some other systems like these two. **Check students' work.**

Name ______________________ Date ____________

Practice 43

Cumulative Practice through Unit 5

Make a box-and-whisker plot of the set of data.

1. Passengers entering a public transit system station per hour (weekday): 50, 165, 272, 441, 324, 266, 295, 195, 180, 220, 233, 310, 470, 368, 310, 275, 163, 152, 85, 70 **Check students' work.**

Find the area of each polygon.

2. 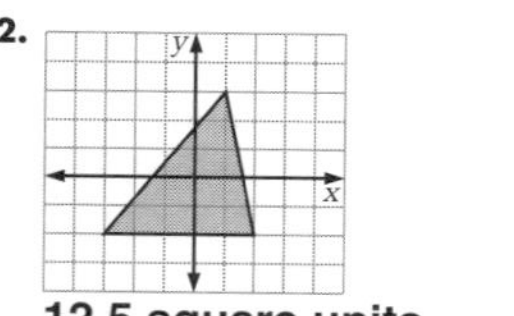

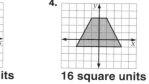

12.5 square units

3. 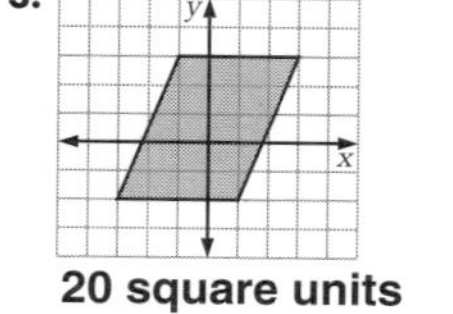

20 square units

4. 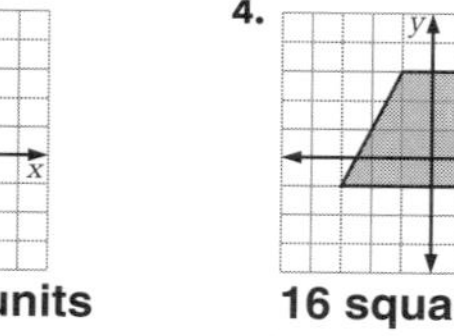

16 square units

In a laboratory experiment, plants were given a certain number of hours of light per day, and their heights were measured.

Hours of light (h)	1	2	2	4	4	6	6	8	8	10
Height of plant (cm)	10	22	16	24	30	28	35	44	32	36

5. Make a scatter plot for the data in the table. Tell whether there is a positive correlation, a negative correlation, or no correlation.
For scatter plots, check students' work.; positive correlation

Solve.

6. $15 - 2c = -7$ **11** 7. $-5 + 0.5b = 12$ **34** 8. $-4(2 - x) = 28$ **9**

Solve and graph each inequality. **For graphs, check students' work.**

9. $5x + 3 < -2$ **$x < -1$** 10. $24 \geq -3(x + 2)$ **$x \geq -10$** 11. $5x \leq 7x - 8$ **$x \geq 4$**

12. x = no. of guests, y = no. of cookies left, $y = 48 - 3x$

Write an equation to represent each function. Explain your variables.

12. Kameisha made 48 oatmeal cookies for a party. She estimates that each guest will eat 3 cookies. The number of cookies left after the party depends on the number of guests. **See above.**

13. An empty elevator cab weighs 500 lb. Suppose each person in the cab weighs 160 lb. The total weight of the elevator cab depends on the number of people in the cab.
x = no. of riders, y = total weight; $y = 500 + 160x$

Name ______________________ Date ____________

Practice 44

For use with Section 6-1

Express each ratio as a fraction in simplest form.

1. 11 : 55 **$\frac{1}{5}$** 2. 175 : 50 **$\frac{7}{2}$** 3. 12 to 18 **$\frac{2}{3}$** 4. 14 to 35 **$\frac{2}{5}$**

5. 3 min : 2 h **$\frac{1}{40}$** 6. 9 in. : 2 ft **$\frac{3}{8}$** 7. 63¢ : $9 **$\frac{7}{100}$** 8. 40 s : 2 min **$\frac{1}{3}$**

Give the unit price of each item.

9. 8 pears cost $1.20 **$.15 per pear**
10. 3 rolls of paper towels cost $1.29 **$.43 per roll**
11. 4 tires cost $236 **$59 per tire**
12. 12 ball-point pens cost $2.76 **$.23 per pen**

13. On a certain day of stock market trading, losing stocks outnumbered gaining stocks by a ratio of 7 to 3. What percent of all stocks gained in price on that day? **30%**

14. The number of miles a car can go on one gallon of fuel (mpg) is called its fuel economy. What is the fuel economy of a car that goes 224 miles on 8 gallons of fuel? **28 mpg**

15. A photographic enlargement made from a negative measuring 24 mm by 36 mm is to have the same width to length ratio as the negative. Which of these sizes are possible for the enlargement? (There may be more than one.) **c and d**

a. 8 in. by 10 in. b. 16 in. by 20 in. c. 6 in. by 9 in. d. 10 in. by 15 in.

16. A television news program contains 18 minutes of news and 12 minutes of commercials. What percent of program time is devoted to news? **60%**

The ratio of the volume inside one of a car's cylinders when the piston is down to the volume inside the cylinder when the piston is up is called the *compression ratio* of the engine. Find each compression ratio.

17. Down: 56 cm^3 Up: 7 cm^3 **8 : 1** 18. Down: 63 cm^3 Up: 9 cm^3 **7 : 1**

19. A salad dressing company found that the ratio of buyers who preferred its onion flavor to buyers who preferred its salsa flavor was 7 : 5. The company plans to produce 1,800,000 bottles of salad dressing next year. How many should be onion flavor? **1,050,000 bottles**

20. ***Writing*** Starting with the third number, each number in the sequence 1, 1, 2, 3, 5, 8, 13, 21, 34, 55, ... is the sum of the two numbers just before it. (So the number after 55 will be 89.) Use a calculator to investigate the ratios of two numbers next to each other, such as 2 : 3, 8 : 13, and so on. What do you notice about the ratios? **Check students' work.**

Name ____________________ Date ____________

Practice 45

For use with Section 6-2

A spinner with the numbers 1 through 12 is spun. Find each probability.

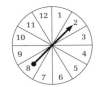

1. $P(7)$ $\frac{1}{12}$ **2.** $P(5 \text{ or } 6)$ $\frac{1}{6}$ **3.** $P(\text{odd number})$ $\frac{1}{2}$

4. $P(\text{multiple of three})$ $\frac{1}{3}$ **5.** $P(\text{even number})$ $\frac{1}{2}$ **6.** $P(13)$ **0**

A compact disc player randomly chooses a track to play out of the 18 tracks on a disc. Find the probability that the chosen track is of each kind.

7. track 6 $\frac{1}{18}$ **8.** before track 5 $\frac{2}{9}$ **9.** after track 9 $\frac{1}{2}$

Tags containing the 9 letters of the word ACOUSTICS are placed in a hat and a tag is selected at random. Find each probability.

10. $P(C)$ $\frac{2}{9}$ **11.** $P(A \text{ or } S)$ $\frac{1}{3}$ **12.** $P(\text{vowel})$ $\frac{4}{9}$

13. $P(\text{consonant})$ $\frac{5}{9}$ **14.** $P(\text{letter after W})$ **0** **15.** $P(\text{letter before V})$ **1**

Exercises 16–18 use the table at the right, which shows the number of vehicles passing a certain intersection in an hour. Find the probability that a vehicle passing the intersection is of each type.

	Cars	Trucks	Vans
Pre-1988	28	14	4
Post-1988	49	7	10

16. a truck $\frac{3}{16}$ **17.** a pre-1988 vehicle $\frac{23}{56}$ **18.** a post-1988 car $\frac{7}{16}$

Use the following information for Exercises 19–21. Fred bought 5 tickets out of 100 sold on the first day of a charity raffle.

19. What was the probability of his winning the prize at that point? $\frac{1}{20}$

20. Another 140 tickets were sold on the second and final day of the raffle. Suppose Fred did not buy any more tickets. What was the probability of his winning? $\frac{1}{48}$

21. How many of the 140 tickets sold on the second day would Fred have had to buy in order to keep the probability of his winning the same as it was after the first day? **7 tickets**

22. At Emma's school, the probability of having a locker on the 3rd-floor is $\frac{1}{3}$ and of having one on the 2nd-floor is $\frac{1}{2}$. All 1740 lockers are on the first three floors of the building. How many lockers are on the 1st floor? **290 lockers**

Name ____________________ Date ____________

Practice 46

For use with Section 6-3

Solve each proportion.

1. $\frac{5}{4} = \frac{t}{36}$ **45** **2.** $\frac{w}{45} = \frac{4}{9}$ **20** **3.** $\frac{15}{32} = \frac{x}{96}$ **45** **4.** $\frac{12}{0.12} = \frac{u}{27}$ **2700**

5. $\frac{75}{z} = \frac{57}{19}$ **25** **6.** $\frac{1.25}{y} = \frac{3.6}{144}$ **50** **7.** $\frac{28}{48} = \frac{35}{n}$ **60** **8.** $\frac{84}{q} = \frac{6}{5}$ **70**

9. $\frac{6}{1.5} = \frac{18}{z}$ **4.5** **10.** $\frac{1000}{19} = \frac{j}{1.9}$ **100** **11.** $\frac{125}{s} = \frac{25}{16}$ **80** **12.** $\frac{280}{56} = \frac{h}{15}$ **75**

13. $\frac{a}{0.56} = \frac{48}{0.128}$ **210** **14.** $\frac{12}{26} = \frac{18}{k}$ **39** **15.** $\frac{15}{2000} = \frac{m}{3200}$ **24** **16.** $\frac{7.5}{r} = \frac{13}{78}$ **45**

17. Using the numbers x, 8, 12, 15, write four proportions that each have the solution $x = 10$.
any four: $\frac{x}{15} = \frac{8}{12}, \frac{15}{x} = \frac{12}{8}, \frac{x}{8} = \frac{15}{12}, \frac{8}{x} = \frac{12}{15}, \frac{8}{12} = \frac{x}{15}, \frac{12}{8} = \frac{15}{x}, \frac{15}{12} = \frac{x}{8}, \frac{12}{15} = \frac{8}{x}$

In Exercises 18–21, solve the proportion

$$\frac{x}{12} = \frac{p}{60},$$

using each of the given values for p.

18. $p = 5$ **1** **19.** $p = 35$ **7** **20.** $p = 65$ **13** **21.** $p = 170$ **34**

22. In one month Margarethe earned \$540 at her part-time job, and \$81 was withheld for federal income tax. Suppose she earns \$620 next month. How much will be withheld for federal income tax? **\$93**

23. A television rating service found that out of a sample of 100 households, 35 were watching Town Talk during its time slot. Suppose there are 210,000 households in a marketing region. How many of them would you expect to be watching Town Talk? **73,500 households**

24. José Balboa left his office at 12 00 noon, and by 3:00 P.M. he had driven 126 of the 189 miles between his office and the office of a client. If he continues driving at the same speed, at what time could he expect to arrive at the client's office? **4:30 P.M.**

25. A 3 lb bag of lawn seed covers 5000 ft². Lawn seed comes in 6 lb bags costing \$7.50 and 3 lb bags costing \$4.50. What is the smallest amount it would cost to cover a 24,000 ft² area with lawn seed? **\$19.50**

26. ***Writing*** The speed of a computer's processor is measured in millions of cycles (operations) per second, or *megaherz*. If you were using a computer with a 4.77 megaherz processor for your work and you switched to one with a 25 megaherz processor, how would it affect the time it took you to do your job? Explain. **Check students' work.**

Name ______________________ Date __________

Practice 47

For use with Section 6-4

1. In a capture-recapture study, a biologist tagged and released 300 deer. A month later she captured 50 deer, 12 of which had tags. About how many deer were in the population? **about 1250**

2. Suppose the margin for error in Exercise 1 was ±2%. Give an interval for the population. **$1225 \le d \le 1275$**

3. In a semiconductor company's quality control test, a machine found that 12 out of a sample of 300 computer chips were defective. How many of the 4200 such chips that the company makes each month would you expect to be defective? **168 chips**

4. If the margin for error in Exercise 3 was ±1%, give an interval for the number of defective chips produced each month. **$166 \le c \le 170$**

For Exercises 5–9, use the graph at the right, showing the weekly mileages of bicycle riders. The graph is based on a sample of 200 responses to a helmet maker's registration questionnaire. Suppose the helmet maker sells 48,000 helmets each year. How many are sold to riders who ride each weekly mileage?

Weekly Mileages

No. of Riders: 0, 20, 40, 60, 80, 100, 120

Distance (mi): Under 10, 10–19, 20–49, 50 & over

5. Less than 10 miles **4800 riders**

6. 10 to 19 miles **7200 riders**

7. 20 to 49 miles **28,800 riders**

8. 50 or more miles **7200 riders**

9. How many of the helmets sold each year go to riders who ride less than 20 mi per week? **12,000 helmets**

For Exercises 10–13, use the table showing voter preference of a sample of the voting-age population in a district. The voting-age population is 65,000.

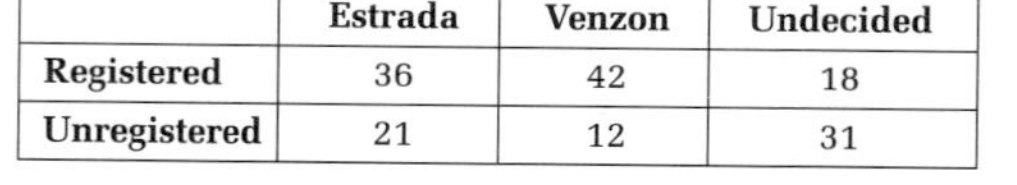

	Estrada	Venzon	Undecided
Registered	36	42	18
Unregistered	21	12	31

10. About how many people have not yet registered? **26,000**

11. About how many registered voters intend to vote for Estrada? How many of the registered voters intend to vote for Venzon? **14,625; 17,063**

12. Of all the voters in the population, how many intend to vote for Estrada? How many intend to vote for Venzon? Would a registration drive be a good idea for Estrada supporters? **23,156; 21,938; yes**

13. ***Writing*** Discuss ways the undecided vote may affect the election. **Check students' work.**

Name ______________________ Date __________

Practice 48

For use with Section 6-5

5. yes; They each have a right angle and they share ∠*F*.

In the diagram, *ABCD* ~ *PQRS*. Find each measure.

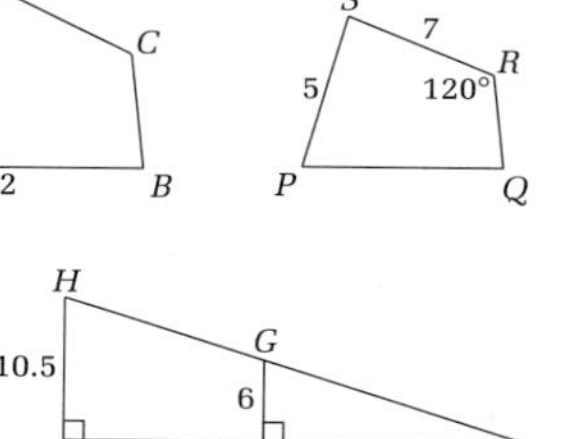

1. $\angle P$ **75°**

2. $\angle C$ **120°**

3. PQ **7.5**

4. CD **11.2**

For Exercises 5–8, refer to the diagram at the right.

5. In the diagram, is triangle FDH similar to triangle FEG? Explain your answer. **See above.**

6. If $EF = 8$, find DF. **14**

7. If $FH = 21$, find FG. **12**

8. If $DF = 17.5$, find EF. **10**

A scale drawing of a proposed recreation center has a scale of 1 in. : 20 ft. Find the actual measurement corresponding to each measurement in the drawing.

9. the length of a basketball court: 4.5 in. **90 ft**

10. the length of a wrestling room: 2.6 in. **52 ft**

11. the width of a hockey rink: 4.25 in. **85 ft**

12. the height of a ceiling: 1.4 in. **28 ft**

On a map with a scale of $\frac{1}{2}$ in. : 10 mi, find the length on the map corresponding to each actual length.

13. 60 mi **3 in.**

14. 150 mi **7.5 in.**

15. 85 mi **4.25 in.**

16. 64 mi **3.2 in.**

17. An illustration of a microorganism in a biology book has a scale of 200 : 1. That is, each measurement in the illustration is 200 times as large as the actual measurement. What is the width of the actual microorganism if the width of the illustration is 8 cm? **0.04 cm**

18. At 3:00 P.M. the shadow of a 4 ft pole is 7 ft long. At the same time the shadow of a tree is 56 ft long. How tall is the tree? **32 ft**

19. Northport and Southport are 120 mi apart. If you want to draw a map on which the two cities are 8 in. apart, what should the scale of the map be? **1 in. : 15 mi**

20. ***Open-ended*** Suppose you wanted to build a scale model of your school building. Find out the actual height, length, and width of the building, and propose a scale that will allow the model to fit on the top of a table. Calculate the length, width, and height of your model. Construct the model out of cardboard or construction paper, if you can. **Check students' work.**

Name ______________________ Date ______________

Practice 49

For use with Section 6-6

Tell whether each diagram shows a dilation, a rotation or a translation.

1. **rotation**

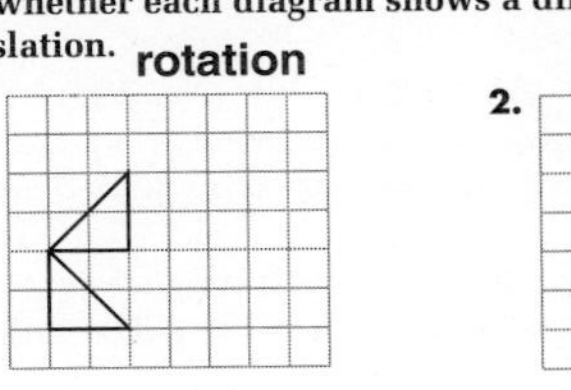

2. **dilation**

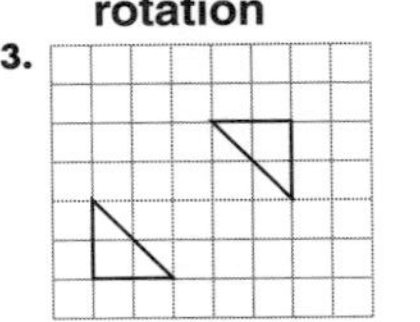

3. **rotation**

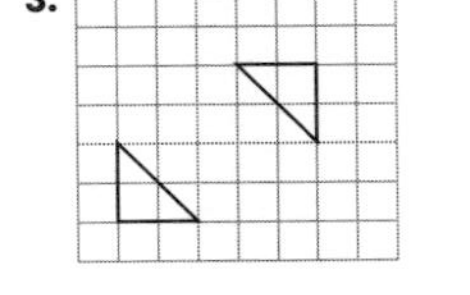

In each dilation, the smaller figure is the original figure. For each, find

a. the center of the dilation

b. the scale factor

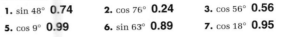

4. **center (0, 0), scale factor 2**

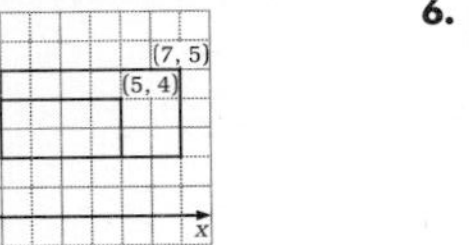

5. **center (1, 2), scale factor $\frac{3}{2}$**

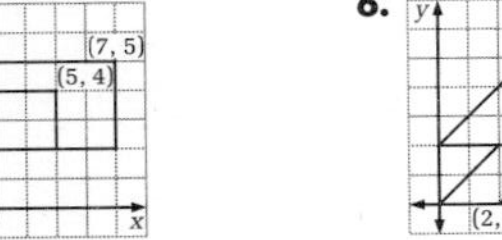

6. **center (0, –2), scale factor 2**

Draw a dilation of the polygon with the given vertices, using the given center of dilation and the given scale factor. **Ex. 7–10. See bottom of page.**

7. $A(0, 0)$, $B(1, 2)$, $C(-1, 2)$; center $A(0, 0)$; scale factor 3 **$A'(0, 0)$, $B'(3, 6)$, $C'(-3, 6)$**

8. $A(2, 1)$, $B(3, 3)$, $C(1, 4)$; center $P(-1, 2)$; scale factor 2 **$A'(5, 0)$, $B'(7, 4)$, $C'(3, 6)$**

9. $A(4, 0)$, $B(8, 0)$, $C(9, 4)$, $D(1, 4)$ center $P(-1, 0)$; scale factor $\frac{1}{2}$ **$A'(1.5, 0)$, $B'(3.5, 0)$, $C'(4, 2)$, $D'(0, 2)$**

10. $A(3, 0)$, $B(0, 3)$, $C(-3, 0)$, $D(0, -3)$; center $P(9, 6)$; scale factor $\frac{2}{3}$ **$A'(5, 2)$, $B'(3, 4)$, $C'(1, 2)$, $D'(3, 0)$**

11. ***Writing*** Suppose $\triangle KLM$ is a dilation of $\triangle ABC$ with center P and scale factor 5. Suppose also that $\triangle XYZ$ is a dilation of $\triangle ABC$ with center P and scale factor 3. Is it possible that $\triangle KLM$ is a dilation of $\triangle XYZ$? Explain your thinking. **Check students' work.**

Ex. 7–10: Coordinates of the new vertices are given.

Name ______________________ Date ______________

Practice 50

For use with Section 6-7

Use a calculator to find each value as a decimal rounded to hundredths.

1. sin 48° **0.74**
2. cos 76° **0.24**
3. cos 56° **0.56**
4. sin 21° **0.36**
5. cos 9° **0.99**
6. sin 63° **0.89**
7. cos 18° **0.95**
8. sin 67° **0.92**

Express each ratio as a decimal rounded to hundredths.

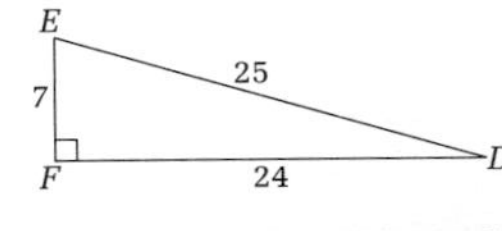

9. sin E **0.96**
10. cos E **0.28**
11. sin D **0.28**
12. cos D **0.96**

For each set of data about right triangle ABC, **For equations, check students' work.**

a. **Write an equation, involving sine or cosine, that you would use to find the value of x, using the given measures.**

b. **Use your equation to find the value of x to the nearest tenth.**

13. $\angle A = 38°$; $AB = 2.6$; $BC = x$ **1.6**
14. $\angle B = 63°$; $AB = 5.5$; $BC = x$ **2.5**
15. $\angle B = 72°$; $BC = 4.2$; $AB = x$ **13.6**
16. $\angle A = 14°$; $BC = 2.3$; $AB = x$ **9.5**
17. $\angle B = 54°$; $AC = 5.5$; $AB = x$ **6.8**
18. $\angle A = 25°$; $AB = 8.3$; $BC = x$ **3.5**

19. A support wire for a telephone pole must make an angle of 78° with the level ground and reach to a point on the pole 27 ft above the ground. How long should the wire be, to the nearest tenth of a foot? **26.4 ft**

20. The diagonal of a rectangular computer chip is 54.0 mm and makes an angle of 23° with one edge of the chip. Find the length and width of the chip, to the nearest 0.1 mm. **49.7 mm and 21.1 mm**

21. Refer to the diagram below. At high tide, a 40-ft gangplank makes an angle of 77° with the pier. At low tide this angle is 65°. To the nearest tenth of a foot, how far does the water fall between high and low tides? **7.9 ft**

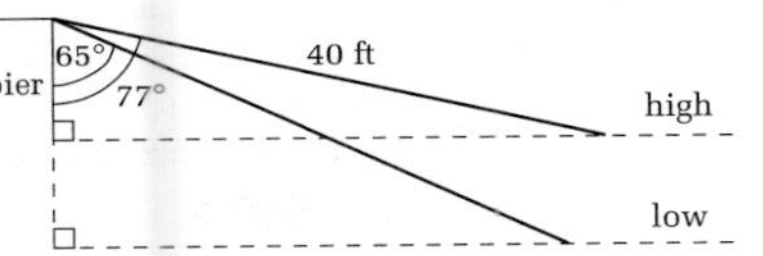

Name ________________ Date ________

Practice 51

Cumulative Practice through Unit 6

What type of graph is a good choice for displaying each data set: a *bar graph*, a *histogram*, a *circle graph*, a *line graph*, a *stem-and-leaf plot*, or a *box-and-whisker plot*?

1. The changes in the consumer price index between 1970 and 1990. **line graph**

2. The percents of the different gases that make up our atmosphere. **circle graph**

3. The average number of movies attended per person per month by age group (under 20, 20–29, 30–39, and so on), from among a sample of 1000 persons. **histogram**

4. The distribution of the ages of major-league baseball players, showing the median age and the range within which the middle 50% of all ages falls. **box-and-whisker plot**

5. The numbers of students in your class choosing each of the colors red, orange, yellow, green, blue, or violet as their favorite color. **bar graph**

Solve.

6. $\frac{n}{3} - 5 = 8$ **39** **7.** $9 - 3.2y = -55$ **20** **8.** $41 = 13 - 2.5x - 4.5x$ **−4**

Solve each equation for the indicated variable.

9. $3x - 6y = 15$ for y $\mathbf{y = 0.5x - 2.5}$ **10.** $y = -\frac{1}{4}x + 8$ for x $\mathbf{x = -4y + 32}$ **11.** $x - \frac{3}{5}y = \frac{1}{5}$ for y $\mathbf{y = \frac{5}{3}x - \frac{1}{3}}$

12. The measures of two angles of a triangle are equal. The third angle of the triangle has measure 34°. What is the measure of the two angles of equal measure? **73°**

13. Two angles are supplementary. One angle is 5 times as large as the other. Find the measures of the two angles. **30° and 150°**

Use the part of a spreadsheet at the right for Exercises 14–19. Name the contents of each cell.

	A	B	C	D
1	1985	$25	$80	31.25%
2	1987	$32	$86	37.21%
3	1989	$50	$125	40%
4	1991	$62	$220	28.18%

14. B4 **$62** **15.** D2 **37.21%** **16.** A3 **1989**

Tell which cell contains each item.

17. $125 **C3** **18.** 31.25% **D1** **19.** 1991 **A4**

Find the coordinates of the point (−1, 3) after each translation.

20. 4 units to the left and 6 units up **(−5, 9)** **21.** 5 units to the right and 4 units down **(4, −1)**

Name ________________ Date ________

Practice 52

For use with Section 7-1

For each direct variation equation:
a. Rewrite the equation so that it does not have a fraction in it.
b. Find the value of a when $b = 5$.
c. Find the value of b when $a = 24$.

1. $\frac{a}{b} = 36$ $\mathbf{a = 36b;\ 180;\ \frac{2}{3}}$ **2.** $\frac{a}{b} = 1.6$ $\mathbf{a = 1.6b;\ 8;\ 15}$ **3.** $\frac{a}{b} = 4.8$ $\mathbf{a = 4.8b;\ 24;\ 5}$ **4.** $\frac{a}{b} = 720$ $\mathbf{a = 720b;\ 3600;\ \frac{1}{30}}$

For Exercises 5–7, find each tangent ratio.

5. tan ∠A **0.4** **6.** tan ∠R **1.6** **7.** tan ∠H **1.25**

A, B, C, 5 cm, 2 cm; P, Q, R, 4 cm, 2.5 cm; H, J, K, 32 cm, 40 cm

Find each value to the nearest hundredth, using a calculator.

8. tan 38° **0.78** **9.** tan 54° **1.38** **10.** tan 15° **0.27** **11.** tan 87° **19.08**

For Exercises 12–17, use the diagram at the right. For each set of data, express the tangent of the given angle as a ratio of the lengths of two sides of triangle ABC. Find the length of the missing side to the nearest 0.1 cm.

A, B, C

12. ∠A = 34°; AC = 8 cm; BC = _?_ **5.4 cm**

13. ∠A = 22°; AC = 75 cm; BC = _?_ **30.3 cm**

14. ∠A = 18°; BC = 9 cm; AC = _?_ **27.7 cm**

15. ∠B = 57°; BC = 50 cm; AC = _?_ **77.0 cm**

16. ∠B = 73°; BC = 62 cm; AC = _?_ **202.8 cm**

17. ∠B = 61°; AC = 3.6 cm; BC = _?_ **2.0 cm**

For Exercises 18 and 19, use the diagram at the right. A lamppost $\overline{EC}$ casts a shadow $\overline{AC}$. A 30-cm ruler $\overline{DB}$ has been moved from A so that its shadow falls just within the shadow of the lamppost.

E, D, A, B, C

18. Suppose the length of the ruler's shadow is 42 cm. What is the slope of the imaginary line $\overline{AE}$? $\mathbf{\frac{5}{7}}$ **or about 0.71**

19. Suppose the lamppost's shadow is 15 m long. How tall is the lamppost? **about 10.7 m**

Name ______________________ Date ______________

Practice 53

For use with Section 7-2

11. yes; Equations may vary. Possible answer: $y = 0.85x$, where x = number of seeds planted, y = number of plants produced
13. Answers may vary. Possible answer: slope is about 0.85.
14. Answers may vary. Possible answer: about 162 seeds

For Exercises 1–6, decide whether direct variation is a good model for the data in each table. If it is, write an equation that includes the variation constant.

1. **$y = 1.5x$**

x	y
3	4.5
4	6
5	7.5
10	15

2. **$y = 0.4x$**

x	y
15	6
20	8
28	11.2
36	14.4

3. **no**

x	y
1	3
2	6
4	18
8	66

4. **$y = \frac{7}{3}x$**

x	y
4.5	10.5
15	35
21	49
102	238

5. **no**

x	y
7	17.5
20	30.5
15.5	26
19.5	30

6. **$y = 3.6x$**

x	y
5	18
15	54
17.5	63
21.5	77.4

For each direct variation relationship, find the missing value.

7. $\frac{a}{b} = 2.4$; $b = 35$; $a = \underline{?}$ **84**

8. $\frac{p}{q} = 0.6$; $p = 33$; $q = \underline{?}$ **55**

9. $\frac{c}{d} = 2.2$; $c = 18.7$; $d = \underline{?}$ **8.5**

10. $\frac{v}{w} = 16.8$; $w = 3.5$; $v = \underline{?}$ **58.8**

For Exercises 11–14, use the table at the right, which shows the results of an experiment in re-introducing a certain type of plant into a region.

Seeds Planted	Plants Produced
50	41
75	63
100	88
125	100
150	127
175	149

11. Do these data seem to show direct variation? If so, write an equation to model the situation. **See top of page.**

12. Plot these data on a graph and draw a fitted line. **Check students' work.**

13. Find the slope of the line you have drawn. **See top of page.**

14. About how many seeds would have to be planted to produce 136 plants? **See top of page.**

Exs. 15, 16: Answers may vary.

For Exercises 15 and 16, use the graph at the right.

Weight of Panes of Glass

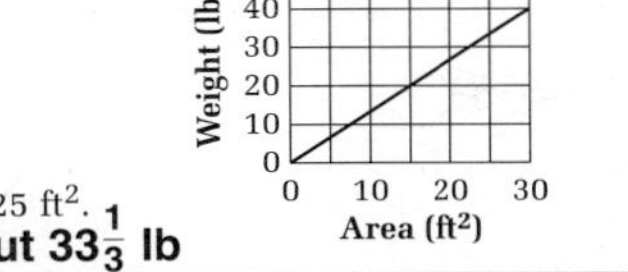

15. Estimate the variation constant. **about $\frac{4}{3}$**

16. Estimate the weight of a pane of glass whose area is 25 ft². **about $33\frac{1}{3}$ lb**

Name ______________________ Date ______________

Practice 54

For use with Section 7-3

Find the circumference of each circle.

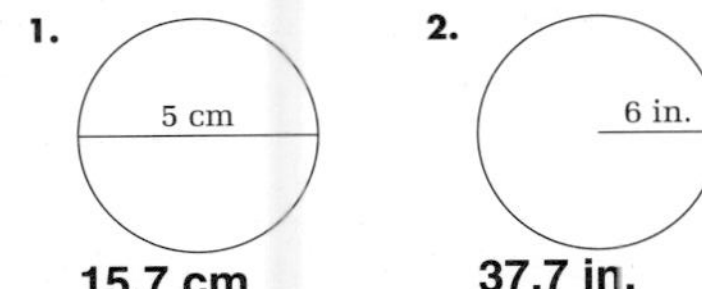
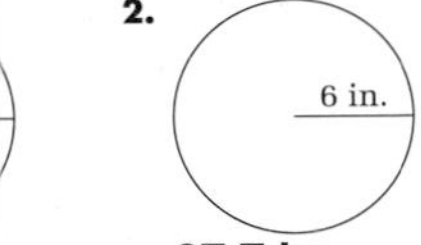
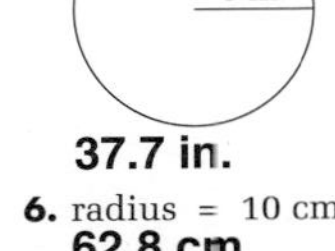

1. 5 cm **15.7 cm**

2. 6 in. **37.7 in.**

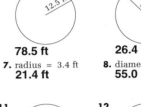

3. 12.5 ft **78.5 ft**

4. 8.4 m **26.4 m**

5. diameter = 14 m **44.0 m**

6. radius = 10 cm **62.8 cm**

7. radius = 3.4 ft **21.4 ft**

8. diameter = 17.5 m **55.0 m**

Find each arc length.

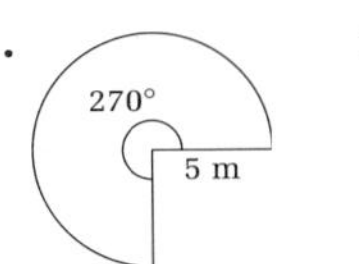

9. 8 cm **12.6 cm**

10. 2 ft **3.1 ft**

11. 270°, 5 m **23.6 m**

12. 135°, 10 in. **23.6 in.**

Find the length of the arc with each central angle and each radius.

13. central angle = 40°; radius = 12 cm **8.4 cm**

14. central angle = 36°; radius = 15 in. **9.4 in.**

15. central angle = 210°; radius = 30 ft **110.0 ft**

16. central angle = 315°; radius = 24 cm **131.9 cm**

A regular octagon is drawn inside a circle of radius 14 cm. Its vertices are on the circle.

17. Suppose a radius is drawn to each vertex of the octagon. What is the smallest central angle between two radii? **45°**

18. Find the length of the arc connecting two consecutive vertices. **11.0 cm**

A bicycle wheel has a radius of 35 cm. Each time the wheel makes one complete turn, the bicycle goes a distance equal to the circumference of the wheel.

19. What distance does the wheel go in one turn? **219.9 cm**

20. What distance does the wheel go in kilometers in 2000 turns? **4.4**

21. How many times does the wheel turn in a trip of 15 km? **about 6821 times**

Name ______________________ Date ____________

Practice 55

For use with Section 7-4

Write an equation of the form $y = kx$ to describe each line.

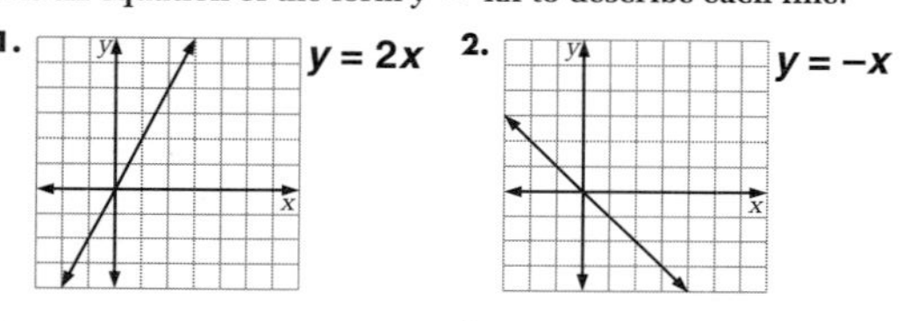

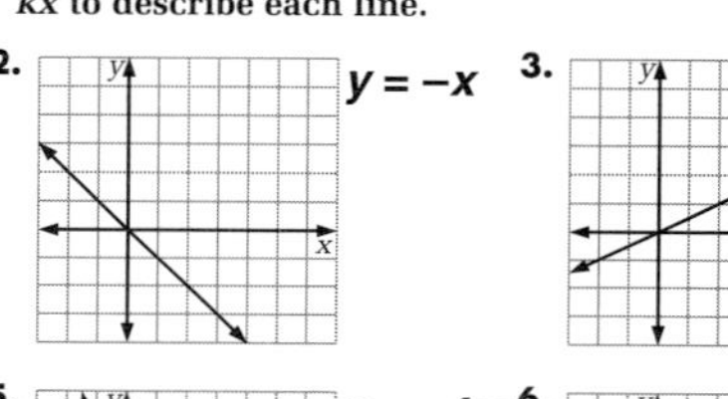

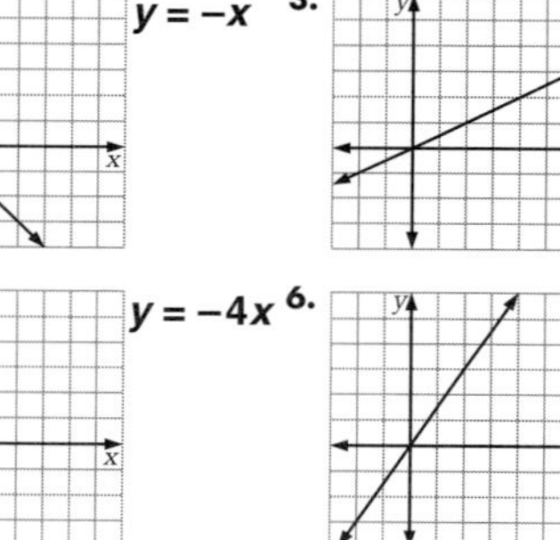

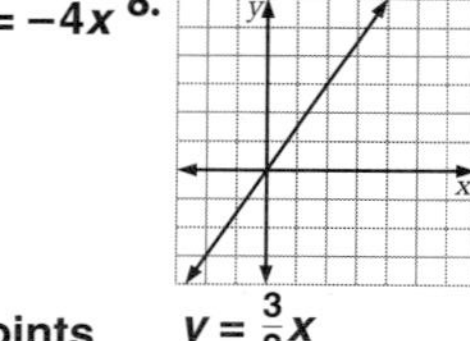

1. $y = 2x$
2. $y = -x$
3. $y = \frac{1}{2}x$
4. $y = -\frac{2}{3}x$
5. $y = -4x$
6. $y = \frac{3}{2}x$

Graph each equation. **Exs. 7–14: All graphs are lines. Two checkpoints are given for each graph.**

7. $y = -2x$ **(0, 0), (2, –4)**
8. $y = \frac{2}{3}x$ **(0, 0), (3, 2)**
9. $y = -1.5x$ **(0, 0), (2, –3)**
10. $y = 4x$ **(0, 0), (1, 4)**
11. $y = 3x$ **(0, 0), (1, 3)**
12. $y = -\frac{4}{3}x$ **(0, 0), (3, –4)**
13. $y = -0.25x$ **(0, 0), (4, –1)**
14. $y = \frac{1}{5}x$ **(0, 0), (5, 1)**

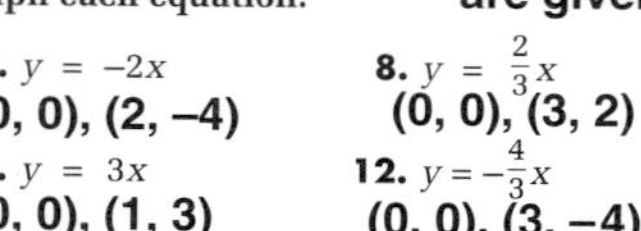

The rise and run from (0, 0) to another point are given. Plot the other point using the directions below. Then draw the line, and find its slope. **For graphs, check students' work.**

15. rise = 4, run = 5 **(5, 4), slope = $\frac{4}{5}$**
16. rise = –4, run = 6 **(6, –4), slope = $-\frac{2}{3}$**
17. rise = 3, run = –2 **(–2, 3), slope = $-\frac{3}{2}$**
18. The wavelength of a clarinet note varies directly with the length of the air column that produces the note. A note with a wavelength of 7.5 ft is produced by an air column 22.5 in. long. How long an air column is needed to produce a wavelength of 4.75 ft? What wavelength is produced by an air column 9.5 in. long? **14.25 in.; about 3.17 ft**
19. *Open-ended* Suppose the number of students in your school started to increase. Give some examples of quantities that might vary directly with the number of students. Estimate the variation constant for each quantity, and write an equation of each variation. **Check students' work.**

Name ______________________ Date ____________

Practice 56

For use with Section 7-5

For Exercises 1–6, each expression shows the units of a conversion problem. Use dimensional analysis to find the unit(s) of the answer.

1. $\frac{\text{mi}}{\text{h}} \times \text{h} = \underline{?}$ **mi**
2. $\frac{\text{mi}}{\text{min}} \times \frac{\text{min}}{\text{h}} = \underline{?}$ $\mathbf{\frac{mi}{h}}$
3. $\frac{\text{ft}}{\text{s}} \times \frac{\text{s}}{\text{min}} = \underline{?}$ $\mathbf{\frac{ft}{min}}$
4. $\frac{\text{in.}^2}{\text{ft}^2} \times \frac{\text{ft}^2}{\text{yd}^2} = \underline{?}$ $\mathbf{\frac{in.^2}{yd^2}}$
5. $\frac{\text{mm}}{\text{in.}} \times \frac{\text{in.}}{\text{ft}} \times \frac{\text{ft}}{\text{yd}} = \underline{?}$ $\mathbf{\frac{mm}{yd}}$
6. $\frac{\text{cm}^3}{\text{L}} \times \frac{\text{L}}{\text{qt}} \times \frac{\text{qt}}{\text{gal}} = \underline{?}$ $\mathbf{\frac{cm^3}{gal}}$

For Exercises 7–10, identify the control variable and the dependent variable. Express the variation constant as a rate.

7. The weight of a quantity of water varies directly with its volume. 2 ft^3 of water weighs 125 lb. **control: volume, dependent: weight; 62.5 lb/ft³**
8. The price of an amount of sliced turkey at the delicatessen varies directly with its weight. 1.5 lb of sliced turkey costs $7.47. **control: weight, dependent: price; $4.98/lb**
9. The diameter of a tree trunk varies directly with the age of the tree. A 45-year-old tree has a trunk diameter of 18 in. **control: age, dependent: diameter; 0.4 in./yr**
10. The number of words Julio can type on his word processor varies directly with time. In 17.5 min he typed 250 words. **control: time, dependent: number of words; about 14.3 words/min**
11. How many cubic centimeters are there in 25 $in.^3$? ($1\ in.^3 = 16.4\ cm^3$) **410**
12. Earth travels at 66,636 mi/h in its orbit. How many feet per second is this? (1 mile = 5280 ft) **97,732.8**

Sonya bought 8.5 gal of gasoline for $11.38. She then drove her car 161 mi and used 7 gal of gasoline.

13. What was the cost of a gallon of gasoline? How much would 11 gal cost? **$1.34; $14.74**
14. How many gallons would it take to go 120 mi? **about 5.2**
15. How much does it cost Sonya, in gasoline alone, to drive one mile? **about $0.06**
16. *Open-ended* Invent your own unit of length and a conversion factor to a standard unit of length. Then make up a table listing the conversion factors from your unit into other standard units of length, both metric and U.S. customary units. List as many as you can. **Check students' work.**

Name ______________________ Date ______________

Practice 57

For use with Section 7-6

For Exercises 1–6, find the unknown measurement for each circle.

1. radius = 12 in.
area = __?__ **452.4 in.^{2}**

2. radius = 28 m
area = __?__ **2461.8 m^2**

3. diameter = 13.9 mm
area = __?__ **151.7 mm^2**

4. area = 43 cm^2
radius = __?__ **3.7 cm**

5. area = 89 in.^{2}
radius = __?__ **5.3 in.**

6. area = 53 ft^2
diameter = __?__ **8.2 ft**

Find the area of each circle in a coordinate plane.

7. With center at (3, 4) and passing through the point (3, –2) **113.0 square units**

8. With the points (–1, 5) and (6, 5) at opposite ends of a diameter
38.5 square units

Find the area of each sector.

9. 5 ft **19.6 ft^2**

10. 130°, 7.4 yd **62.1 yd^2**

11. 110°, 14 m **119.7 m^2**

12. 8.2 m **35.2 m^2**

Find the area of each circle.

13. Perimeter of square = 144 ft
1017.4 ft^2

14. 8 cm, 18 cm
Area of trapezoid = 156 cm^2
113.0 cm^2

15. 20 in.
Area of rectangle = 268 in.^{2}
141.0 in.^{2}

For Exercises 16 and 17, use the circle graph at the right, which shows a manufacturer's costs.

16. The *Salaries* sector is 42% of the whole circle. What is the central angle of this sector? **151.2°**

17. Suppose the radius of the graph is 3 cm. What is the area of the salaries sector? **11.9 cm^2**

Costs
Energy 12%
Other 6%
Raw Materials 22%
Employee Benefits 18%
Salaries 42%

Name ______________________ Date ______________

Practice 58

Cumulative Practice through Unit 7

Tell whether each figure has rotational symmetry. If it does, describe the symmetry.

1. **180°**

2. **120°, 240°**

3. **72°, 144°, 216°, 288°**

4. **no rotational symmetry**

Model each situation using an equation and then solve.

5. Consuela would like to score the same number of points in her next 5 basketball games. So far she has scored 46 points. How many points must she score in each game in order to tie the league record of 101 points? **46 + 5*x* = 101; 11 points**

6. In a heat-loss survey of Victor Tan's house, the area of one wall was listed as 400 ft^2. There are 4 identical windows in the wall, and the siding area (not including the windows) was listed as 340 ft^2. What is the area of each window? **340 + 4*x* = 400; 15 ft^2**

Solve each equation for the variable indicated.

7. $ax - by = c$ for b $\quad$ $b = \frac{ax - c}{y}$

8. $A = \frac{1}{3}\pi r^2 h$ for h $\quad$ $h = \frac{3A}{\pi r^2}$

9. $2l + 2w = p$ for w $\quad$ $w = \frac{p - 2l}{2}$

For Exercises 10–15, players may spin the wheel only once. Find the theoretical probability of each outcome.

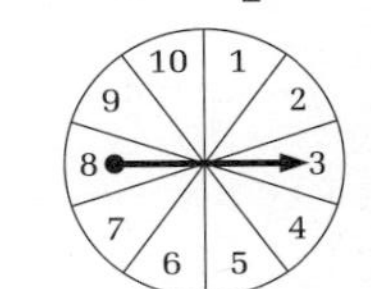

10. 7 $\frac{1}{10}$

11. an even number $\frac{1}{2}$

12. 2, 3, or 9 $\frac{3}{10}$

13. 9 or 10 $\frac{1}{5}$

14. 3, 4, 5, or 6 $\frac{2}{5}$

15. 13 **0**

For Exercises 16–18, the smaller figure is the original figure. State the coordinates of the center of dilation and find the scale factor.

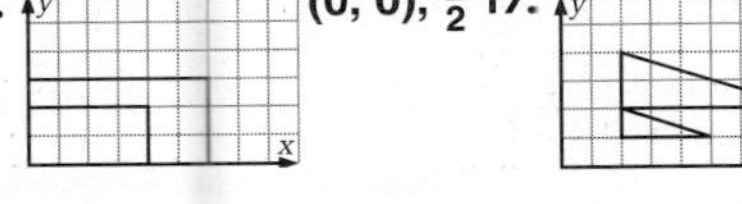

16. (0, 0), $\frac{3}{2}$

17. (2, 0), 2

18. (7, 6), 3

19. A map has a scale of 0.5 in. : 40 mi. Eastville and Westville are connected by a straight road and are 100 mi apart. How far apart are they on the map? **1.25 in.**

Name ______________________ Date __________

Practice 59

For use with Section 8-1

Without graphing, find the slope and the vertical intercept of the line modeled by each equation.

1. $y = 9x + 5$ **9, 5**
2. $y = -8x + 7$ **–8, 7**
3. $y = 11 - 4.6x$ **–4.6, 11**
4. $y = x + 15$ **1, 15**
5. $y = -2 + 12x$ **12, –2**
6. $y = -17x$ **–17, 0**

Exs. 7–12: All graphs are lines. Two checkpoints are given for each graph.

Graph each equation.

7. $y = x - 1$ **(0, –1), (1, 0)**
8. $y = -x + 3$ **(0, 3), (3, 0)**
9. $y = 0.5x - 3$ **(0, –3), (2, –2)**
10. $y = -3x + 2$ **(0, 2), (2, –4)**
11. $y = -0.2x + 4$ **(0, 4), (5, 3)**
12. $y = 4 - \frac{1}{2}x$ **(0, 4), (4, 2)**

For Exercises 13–15, find the slope and vertical intercept of each line. Write an equation of each line.

13.

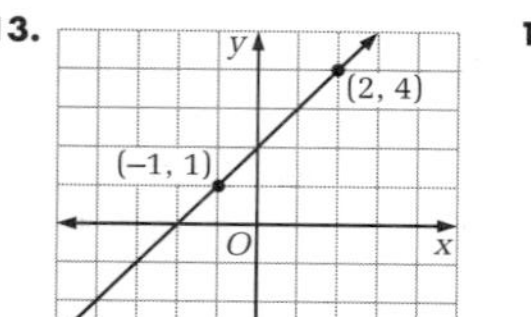

1, 2; $y = x + 2$

14.

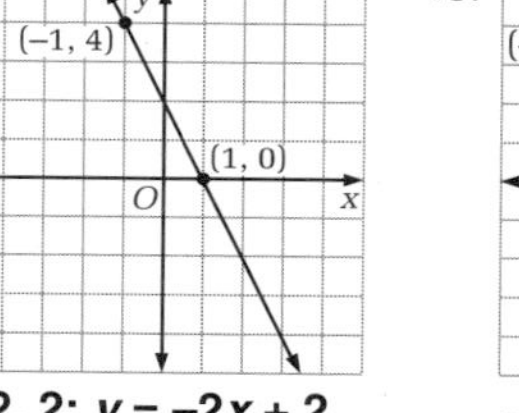

–2, 2; $y = -2x + 2$

15.

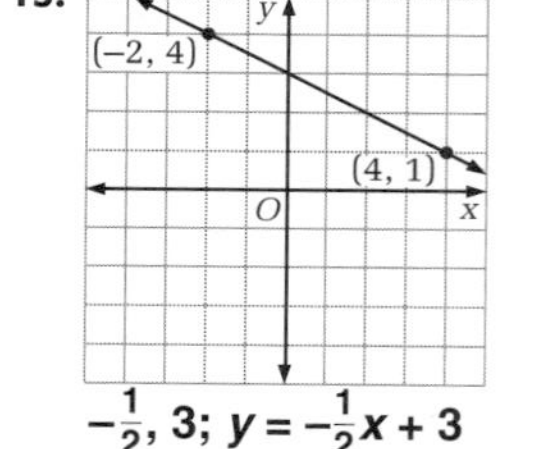
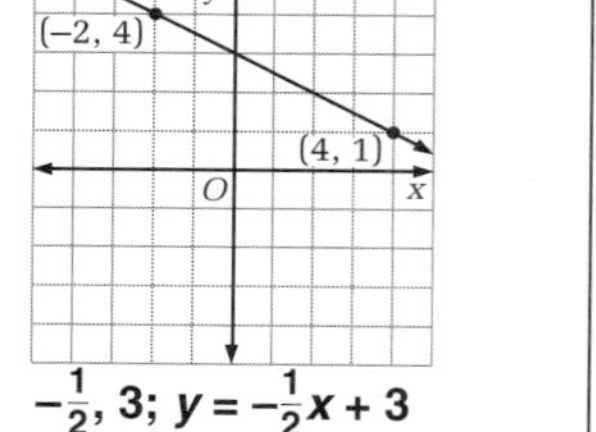

$-\frac{1}{2}$, 3; $y = -\frac{1}{2}x + 3$

Model each situation with an equation.

16. Jing walked toward his apartment at 3 mi/h from a point 5 mi from the apartment. (control variable: time; dependent variable: Jing's distance from home) **$y = 5 - 3x$**

17. A garage charges $14 for an oil change plus $1.50 for each quart of new oil. (control variable: amount of new oil; dependent variable: cost of oil change) **$y = 14 + 1.5x$**

18. The temperature of a laboratory sample of liquid oxygen is at –210°C, and it is rising at 7°C each minute. (control variable: time; dependent variable: temperature) **$y = -210 + 7x$**

19. ***Writing*** How are linear functions and direct variations related? Explain how the graphs of the two types of functions are alike and how they are different. **Check students' work.**

Name ______________________ Date __________

Practice 60

For use with Section 8-2

Find three solutions of each equation. Answers may vary.

1. $2x + y = 7$
2. $x - y = 1$
3. $3x - 2y = 6$
4. $-5x - y = 10$
5. $\frac{1}{2}x + 3y = 9$
6. $\frac{1}{3}x - 3y = 15$

Rewrite each equation in slope-intercept form.

7. $4x + y = 13$ **$y = -4x + 13$**
8. $\frac{1}{2}x + y = 25$ **$y = -\frac{1}{2}x + 25$**
9. $5x - y = -9$ **$y = 5x + 9$**
10. $3x + \frac{1}{3}y = 5$ **$y = -9x + 15$**
11. $-9x - 4y = 7$ **$y = -\frac{9}{4}x - \frac{7}{4}$**
12. $\frac{1}{2}x - 3y = 12$ **$y = \frac{1}{6}x - 4$**

Exs. 13–18: The horizontal intercept is listed first.

Find the intercepts of the graph of each equation.

13. $x + 3y = -3$ **–3, –1**
14. $4x - 3y = 18$ **$\frac{9}{2}$, –6**
15. $-2x + 7y = -28$ **14, –4**
16. $-\frac{1}{2}x - 2y = 5$ **–10, –2.5**
17. $\frac{1}{3}x + \frac{1}{2}y = 6$ **18, 12**
18. $0.6x + 1.5y = 9$ **15, 6**

Exs. 19, 20: Two checkpoints are given for each line graph.

Graph each group of equations on one set of axes.

19. $x + 3y = -3$; **(0, –1), (–3, 0)** $x + 3y = 0$; **(0, 0), (3, –1)** $x + 3y = 3$ **(3, 0), (0, 1)**

20. $3x - 2y = 6$; **(2, 0), (0, –3)** $-3x + 2y = 4$; **$\left(-\frac{4}{3}, 0\right)$, (0, 2)** $6x - 4y = 4$ **$\left(\frac{2}{3}, 0\right)$, (0, –1)**

For Exercises 21–23, write an equation relating each group of variables.

21. An isosceles triangle has a perimeter of 25 cm. Relate the length x of the two congruent sides and the length of the third side y. **$2x + y = 25$**

22. In basketball, a field goal counts 2 points, a long field goal counts 3 points, and a free throw counts 1 point. In one game, Indrani scored 14 points. Relate the number of field goals g, the number of long field goals l, and the number of free throws t she made. **$2g + 3l + t = 14$**

23. At the Smart Shop, a shirt sells for $28 and each shirt costs the store $16 at wholesale. In one month, the store made a net profit of $236 just on the new shirts it ordered that month. Relate the number of shirts s that the store sold and the number of shirts b that it bought wholesale that month. **$28s - 16b = 236$**

Name ____________ Date ____________

Practice 61

For use with Section 8-3

Find the slope of each line and write an equation for each line.

1.

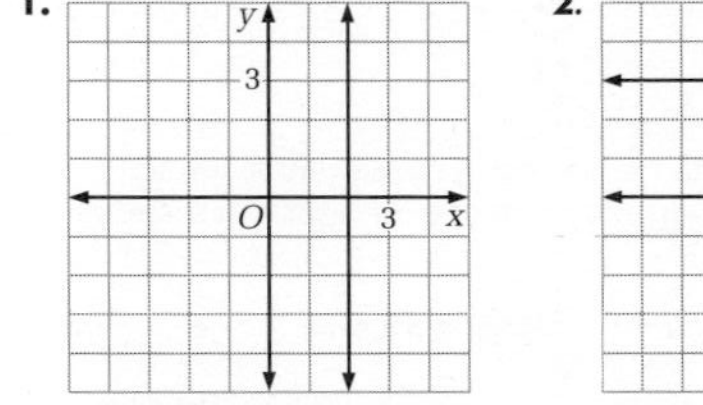

undefined, $x = 2$

2.

0, $y = 3$

3.

0, $y = -1$

Graph each equation and find the slope of each line.

4. $y = -2$ **horiz., (0, –2)**
5. $x = 3$ **vertical, (3, 0)**
6. $y = 4$ **horiz., (0, 4)**
7. $x = -1$ **vertical, (–1, 0)**
8. $x = -4$ **vertical, (–4, 0)**
9. $y = -3$ **horiz., (0, –3)**
10. $x = 1.5$ **vertical, (1.5, 0)**
11. $y = 2.5$ **horiz., (0, 2.5)**

Exs. 4–11: For graphs, check students' work. Answers tell whether line is horiz. or vertical. One checkpoint is given.

For Exercises 12–16, write an equation for each line.

12. the line through the points (6, –3) and (6, 5) **$x = 6$**
13. the line with slope 0 through the point (–2, 7) **$y = 7$**
14. the line with undefined slope through the point (8, –6) **$x = 8$**
15. the horizontal line through the point (1, 9) **$y = 9$**
16. the vertical line through the point (–5, –3) **$x = -5$**
17. What is an equation of the x-axis? What is its slope? **Possible equation: $y = 0$; 0**
18. What is an equation of the y-axis? What is its slope? **Possible equation: $x = 0$; undefined**

Tell whether a good model for each situation would be a line with 0 slope, a line with undefined slope, or neither.

19. The distance (y) of a parked car from its destination after a length of time (x). **0 slope**
20. The points (x, y) on a flagpole, where y is the height of the point above the ground and x is its distance from the side of a certain building nearby. **undefined slope**
21. The distance (y) of a jogger from her starting point after running for a length of time (x) at a constant speed. **neither**

Name ____________ Date ____________

Practice 62

For use with Section 8-4

Write an equation for the line that has each slope and each vertical intercept.

1. slope = 5; intercept = –1 **$y = 5x - 1$**
2. slope = –2; intercept = 1 **$y = -2x + 1$**
3. slope = 0.5; intercept = 3 **$y = 0.5x + 3$**
4. slope = $\frac{2}{3}$; intercept = –4 **$y = \frac{2}{3}x - 4$**
5. slope = –6; intercept = 0 **$y = -6x$**
6. slope = $-\frac{1}{3}$; intercept = $\frac{4}{3}$ **$y = -\frac{1}{3}x + \frac{4}{3}$**

Write an equation for the line that has each slope and has each point on it.

7. slope = 2; (–1, 5) on line **$y = 2x + 7$**
8. slope = –3; (2, –1) on line **$y = -3x + 5$**
9. slope = –4; (–3, 9) on line **$y = -4x - 3$**
10. slope = $\frac{1}{2}$; (2, –7) on line **$y = \frac{1}{2}x - 8$**
11. slope = $-\frac{3}{4}$; (–6, 2) on line **$y = -\frac{3}{4}x - \frac{5}{2}$**
12. slope = $-\frac{3}{2}$; (5, –4) on line **$y = -\frac{3}{2}x + \frac{7}{2}$**

Write an equation for the line that has each pair of points on it.

13. (2, 5), (6, 13) **$y = 2x + 1$**
14. (–1, 4), (1, 10) **$y = 3x + 7$**
15. (3, 6), (–5, –2) **$y = x + 3$**
16. (–1, 3), (5, 0) **$y = -\frac{1}{2}x + \frac{5}{2}$**
17. (–7, –2), (5, –6) **$y = -\frac{1}{3}x - \frac{13}{3}$**
18. (1, 0.8), (5, –4) **$y = -1.2x + 2$**

Find an equation of the line with each pair of intercepts.

19. vertical: 3; horizontal: 2 **$y = -\frac{3}{2}x + 3$**
20. vertical: –5; horizontal: 10 **$y = \frac{1}{2}x - 5$**

21. A long-distance phone call costs $1.60 for the first minute and a fixed charge for each minute after that. A 7-minute call costs $2.92. Write an equation for the cost of a call as a function of time after the first minute. **$y = 1.6 + 0.22x$**
22. A computer repair shop charges $25 to test an out-of-order computer plus an hourly charge for actual repairs. The shop charged a customer $92.50 for a job that took 1.5 h. Write an equation for the cost of a repair as a function of time. **$y = 25 + 45x$**
23. ***Open-ended*** Estimate how far your school building is from your home. Then time your trip home. Assume that you travel at a constant speed, and write an equation for your distance from home as a function of time during your trip. **Check students' work.**

Name ______________________ Date ____________

Practice 63

For use with Section 8-5

For Exercises 1–3, estimate the solution of each system of equations from the graph. Then use substitution to find the exact solution.

1.

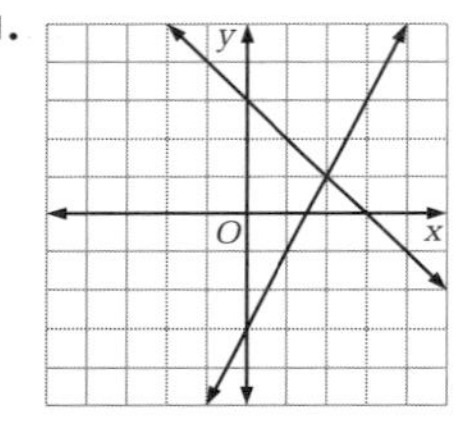

$y = -x + 3$

$y = 2x - 3$ **(2, 1)**

2.

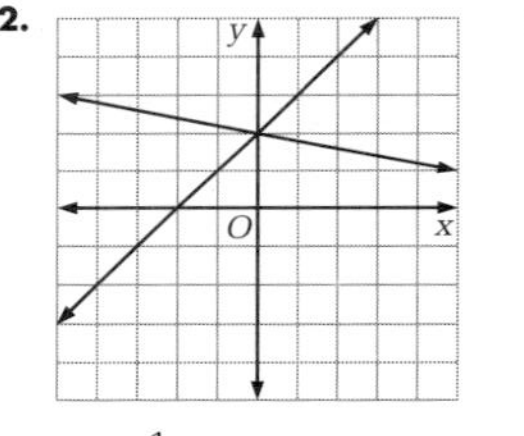
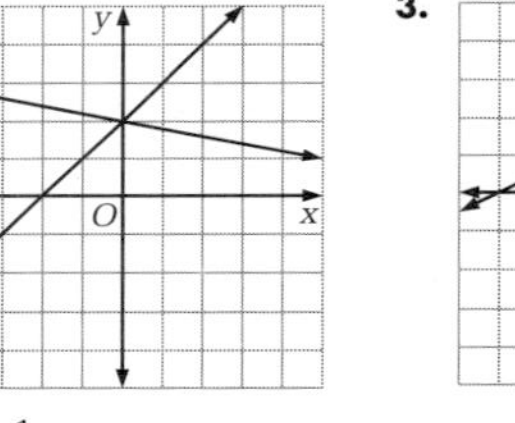

$y = -\frac{1}{5}x + 2$

$y = x + 2$ **(0, 2)**

3.

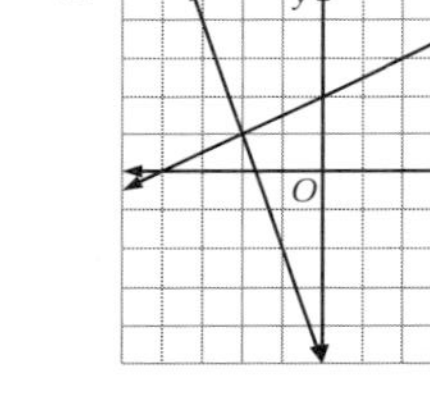
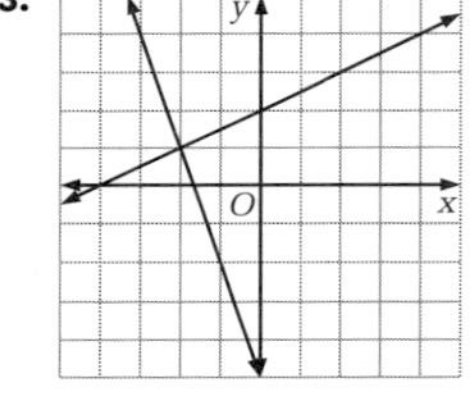
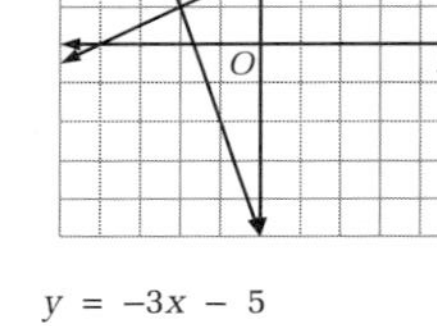

$y = -3x - 5$

$y = \frac{1}{2}x + 2$ **(−2, 1)**

Graph each system of equations. Estimate the solution of the system or write no solution. **For graphs, check students' work.**

4. $y = 2x + 1$
$y = 2x - 1$ **no solution**

5. $y = -x + 3$
$y = 3x - 1$ **(1, 2)**

6. $y = -2x + 4$
$y = \frac{1}{3}x - 3$ **(3, −2)**

Without graphing, tell whether each system of equations has a solution or no solution.

7. $y = -6x + 2$
$y = -6x - 1$ **no solution**

8. $y = -2x + 5$
$y = -x + 5$ **solution**

9. $y = 7x - 2$
$y = -7x + 2$ **solution**

For Exercises 10–12, rewrite each equation in slope-intercept form. Then tell whether each system of equations has a solution or no solution. **For equations, check students' work.**

10. $3x - y = 2$
$6x - 2y = 2$ **no solution**

11. $6x + 2y = 1$
$9x - 3y = 2$ **solution**

12. $4x - 10y = 5$ **no**
$-2x + 5y = 5$ **solution**

13. Carlos was climbing a mountain that Vijay was descending when they met. Carlos had left at 8 A.M. from an altitude of 3350 ft and gained 100 ft/h. Vijay had left at 8 A.M. from an altitude of 4850 ft and had lost 150 ft/h. What time did Carlos and Vijay meet? At what altitude? **They met at 2 P.M., at an altitude of 3950 ft.**

Name ______________________ Date ____________

Practice 64

For use with Section 8-6

Fill in the blank with one of the signs: >, <, ≥, or ≤.

1.

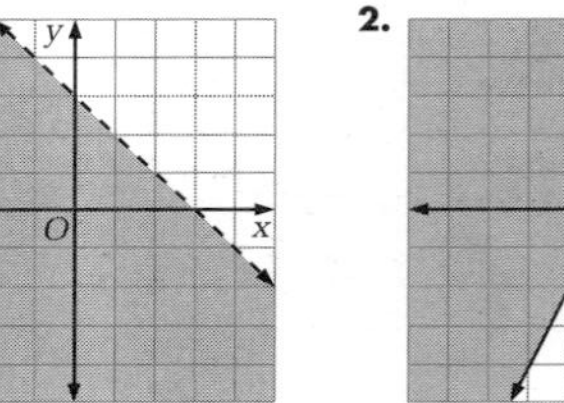

$y \underline{\ ?\ } -x + 3$ **<**

2.

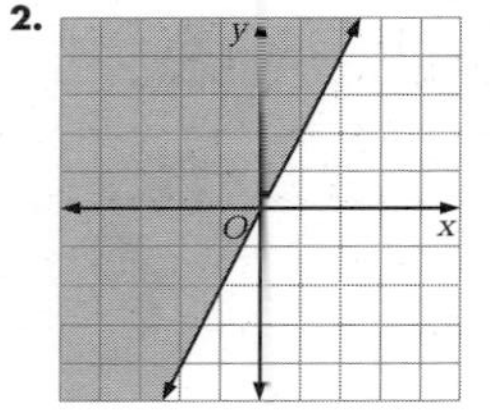

$y \underline{\ ?\ } 2x$ **≥**

3.

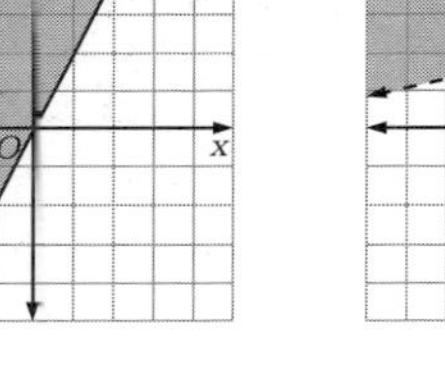

$y \underline{\ ?\ } \frac{1}{4}x + 2$ **>**

Tell whether each point is a solution of each inequality.

4. $(3, -1); y > x - 2$ **no**

5. $(1, 0); y \le 5x - 3$ **yes**

6. $(2, -3); y < -2x + 4$ **yes**

7. $(5, -3); y \ge -2x + 8$ **no**

8. $(-4, -5); y > 2x + 1$ **yes**

9. $(-1, 6); y \le -5x + 1$ **yes**

Graph each inequality. **Exs. 10–18: Answers show two checkpoints on the boundary line of the graph and tell where solution points lie relative to the boundary.**

10. $y > 4x$
(0, 0), (1, 4), above

11. $y \le x + 1$
(−1, 0), (2, 3), below, on

12. $y > -x - 4$
(0, −4), (−4, 0), above

13. $y < -\frac{1}{2}x + 3$
(−2, 4), (2, 2), below

14. $y \ge 2x + 2$
(−2, −2), (2, 6), above, on

15. $y \le -3x + 1$
(0, 1), (2, −5), below, on

16. $x - 3y < 6$
(6, 0), (0, −2), below

17. $2x + 0.5y \ge 1$
(0, 2), (−1, 6), above, on

18. $3x - 2y > 4$
(0, −2), (4, 4), below

The ticket machine for the rapid transit train gives change if you put in too much money. Juan's trip costs $1.25, and he has only dimes and quarters.

19. Suppose Juan puts x dimes and y quarters into the machine. Write a linear combination that expresses the value of the money he puts in. $\mathbf{0.1x + 0.25y}$

20. Write an inequality that relates the number of dimes and the number of quarters he must put into the machine in order to buy the ticket he wants. Graph the inequality.
$\mathbf{0.1x + 0.25y \ge 1.25}$**; For graph, check students' work.**

21. Dynell plans to go at least 6 miles in a charity walkathon, walking part of the way and jogging the rest. She walks at 3 mi/h and jogs at 9 mi/h. Write an inequality that models the situation. Graph the inequality. $\mathbf{3x + 9y \ge 6}$**; For graph, check students' work.**

Name ______________________ Date ____________

Practice 65

For use with Section 8-7

For Exercises 1–6, tell whether each ordered pair is a solution of each system. Write yes or no.

1. (1, 2); $y \geq 1$, $x < 5$ **yes**
2. (−3, 2); $y > x + 1$, $y \leq -x - 1$ **yes**
3. (5, −2); $y \geq 2x - 9$, $y < x - 5$ **no**
4. (−1, −4); $x + 2y < -5$, $x - y \geq 4$ **no**
5. (0, 5); $5x + 2y > 7$, $-3x - y < -5$ **no**
6. (−1, 6); $5x + 2y \geq 1$, $-7x - y < 2$ **yes**

Fill in each blank with one of the signs: >, <, ≥, or ≤.

7. 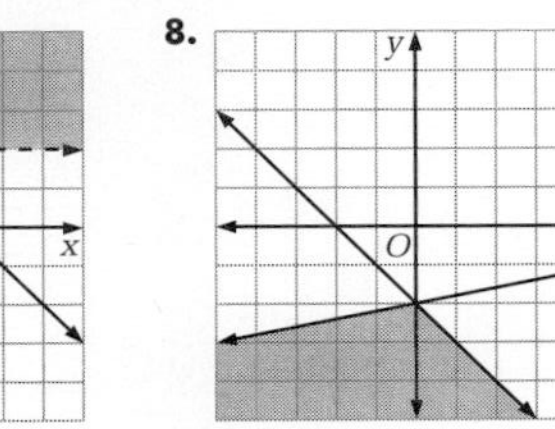

$y \ \underline{?}\ -x + 2$ **≥**

$y \ \underline{?}\ 2$ **>**

8. 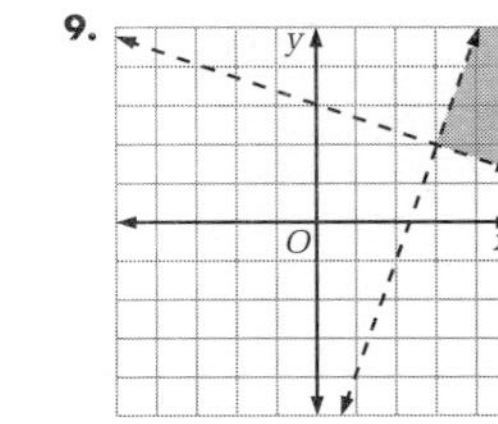

$y \ \underline{?}\ \frac{1}{5}x - 2$ **≤**

$y \ \underline{?}\ -x - 2$ **≤**

9. 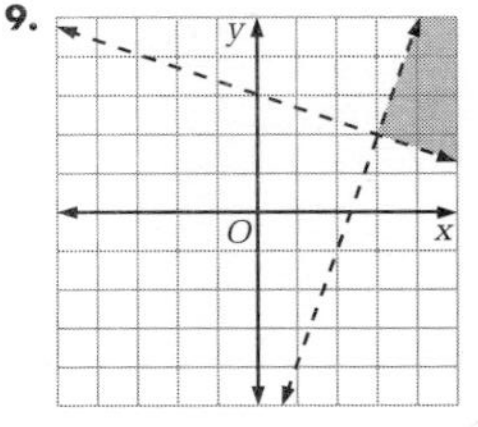
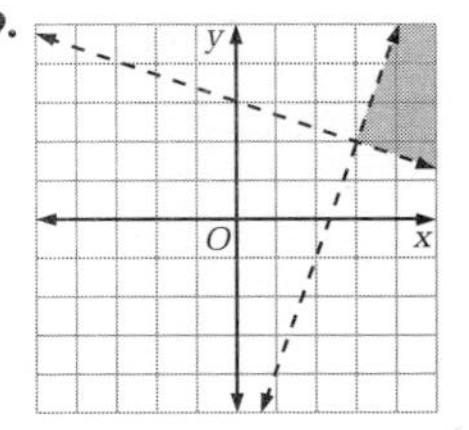

$y \ \underline{?}\ -\frac{1}{3}x - 3$ **>**

$y \ \underline{?}\ 3x - 7$ **>**

Exs. 10–18: For graphs, check students' work.

For Exercises 10–18, graph each system of inequalities.

10. $x > -1$, $y \geq 2$
11. $y \leq -x$, $x > -3$
12. $x < y$, $y \leq 2$
13. $y > -x - 3$, $y \leq x + 3$
14. $y \leq 2x - 1$, $y > -3x + 2$
15. $y \leq -2x + 2$, $y \leq x - 4$
16. $x + y \leq 2$, $x + y > 1$
17. $y > -\frac{1}{2}x - 1$, $2x - y \leq -3$
18. $2x - y < 4$, $2x + y < 4$
19. Tito Fernandez needs to mix crushed stone and mortar to make a concrete mix to pave his walk. For structural stability he needs to use at least as much mortar as stone, and he wants to end up with at least 40 lb of mix. Write and graph a system of inequalities to model this situation. What combination of mortar and stone will use the smallest amount of mortar?
$y \geq x$, $x + y \geq 40$;
For graph, check students' work.; 20 lb mortar, 20 lb stone

Name ______________________ Date ____________

Practice 66

Cumulative Practice through Unit 8

Find the area of each figure.

1. 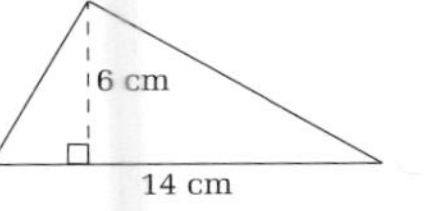

42 cm²

2. 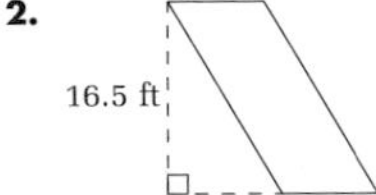

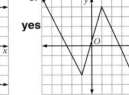

132 ft²

3. 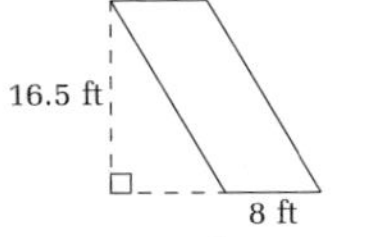
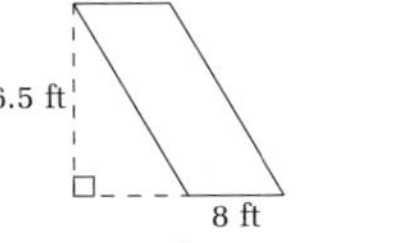

4 in.²

Tell whether each graph represents a function.

4. 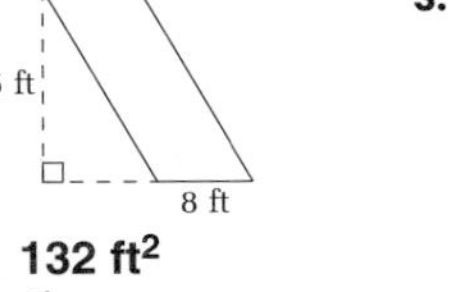 **no**

5. 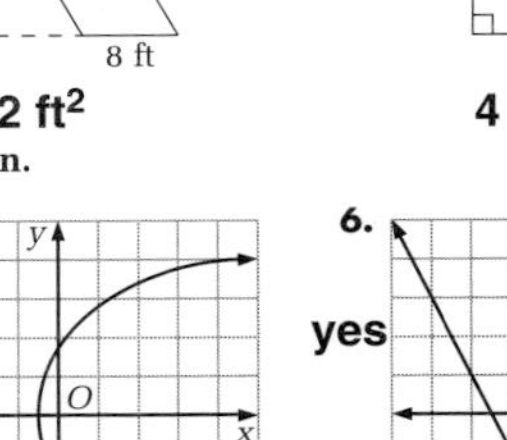
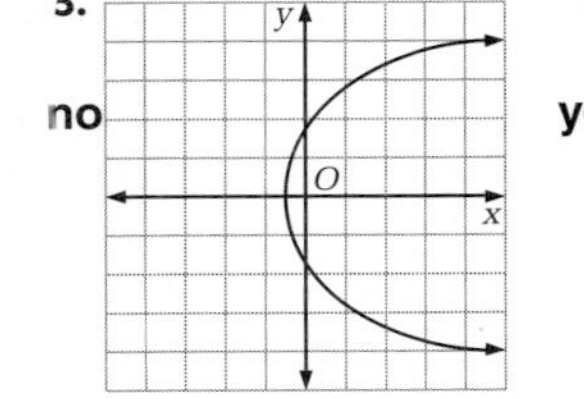 **no**

6. 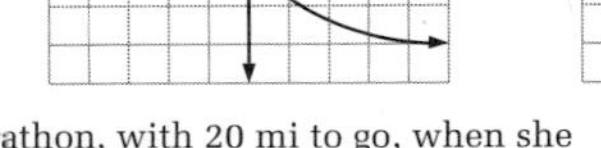 **yes**

7. Felicia had run 6 mi of a marathon, with 20 mi to go, when she stopped for water. What is the ratio of the distance she had already run to the whole distance of the race? $\mathbf{\frac{3}{13}}$

For Exercises 8–10, each expression shows the units of a conversion problem. Use dimensional analysis to find the unit(s) of the answer.

8. $\frac{\text{cents}}{\text{mi}} \times \frac{\text{mi}}{\text{h}} = \underline{?}$ $\mathbf{\frac{cents}{h}}$

9. $\frac{\text{lb}}{\text{in.}^2} \times \frac{\text{in.}^2}{\text{ft}^2} = \underline{?}$ $\mathbf{\frac{lb}{ft^2}}$

10. $\frac{\text{mi}}{\text{h}} \times \frac{\text{h}}{\text{s}} \times \frac{\text{ft}}{\text{mi}} = \underline{?}$ $\mathbf{\frac{ft}{s}}$

For Exercises 11–13, use the following information. Express answers in scientific notation. The distance from the planet Venus to the sun is about 6.7×10^7 mi. Venus travels around the sun in a nearly circular orbit in 225 Earth days.

11. How far does Venus travel in 225 Earth days? How far does Venus travel in one Earth day? **4.21×10^8 mi; 1.87×10^6 mi**
12. Find the length of an arc of Venus's orbit with a central angle of 90°. **1.05×10^8 mi**
13. About how many Earth days does it take Venus to travel 1.31×10^8 mi? **about 70**

Name ______________________ Date ______________

Practice 67

For use with Section 9-1

Find the missing length in each right triangle.

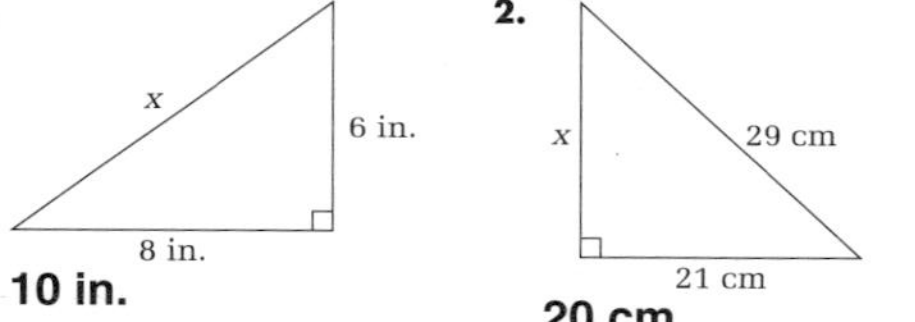

1. **10 in.**
2. **20 cm**
3. 34 ft, 16 ft, x **30 ft**

A right triangle has legs of length a and b and hypotenuse of length c. Find each missing length.

4. $a = 12, c = 20, b = \underline{?}$ **16**
5. $a = 14, b = 48, c = \underline{?}$ **50**
6. $b = 9, c = 41, a = \underline{?}$ **40**
7. $a = 39, c = 89, b = \underline{?}$ **80**
8. $b = 2.4, c = 4, a = \underline{?}$ **3.2**
9. $a = 4.2, b = 14.4, c = \underline{?}$ **15**

Find the value of x in each triangle, then use the value you found to find y.

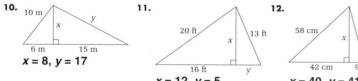

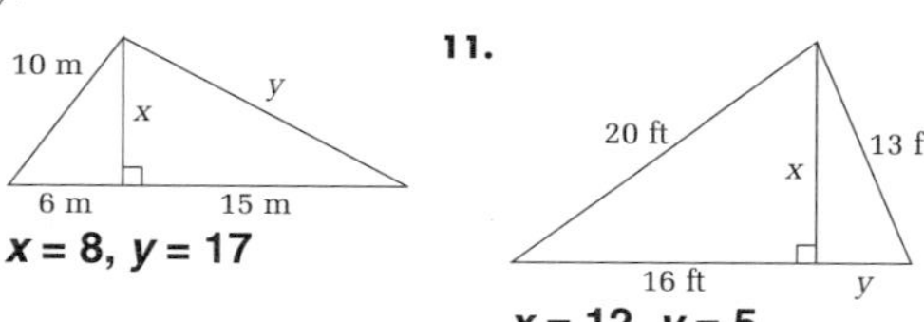

10. **$x = 8, y = 17$**
11. **$x = 12, y = 5$**
12. 58 cm, x, y, 42 cm, 9 cm **$x = 40, y = 41$**

Tell whether each person is using inductive or deductive reasoning.

13. Domingo measures the angles made by the diagonals of several rhombuses. He conjectures that the diagonals of a rhombus will always be perpendicular. **inductive**

14. Vida's favorite major-league baseball player had 17 home runs as of yesterday. This morning he has 18. Vida concludes that the player played in yesterday's game. **deductive**

15. ***Writing*** Suppose you substitute 1, 2, 3, and so on, for n in the expression $n^2 - n + 11$. Marta says that you always get a *prime number* (a number greater than 1 that has no whole number divisors except itself and 1). Is she right? Is she using inductive or deductive reasoning? Is this type of reasoning always correct? Explain. **no; inductive; no; For explanations, check students' work.**

Name ______________________ Date ______________

Practice 68

For use with Section 9-2

Simplify.

1. $\sqrt{40}$ **$2\sqrt{10}$**
2. $\sqrt{75}$ **$5\sqrt{3}$**
3. $\sqrt{80}$ **$4\sqrt{5}$**
4. $\sqrt{108}$ **$6\sqrt{3}$**
5. $\sqrt{150}$ **$5\sqrt{6}$**
6. $\sqrt{98}$ **$7\sqrt{2}$**
7. $\sqrt{700}$ **$10\sqrt{7}$**
8. $\sqrt{60}$ **$2\sqrt{15}$**
9. $\sqrt{450}$ **$15\sqrt{2}$**
10. $\sqrt{245}$ **$7\sqrt{5}$**
11. $\sqrt{128}$ **$8\sqrt{2}$**
12. $\sqrt{242}$ **$11\sqrt{2}$**
13. $2\sqrt{27}$ **$6\sqrt{3}$**
14. $5\sqrt{32}$ **$20\sqrt{2}$**
15. $3\sqrt{175}$ **$15\sqrt{7}$**
16. $4\sqrt{63}$ **$12\sqrt{7}$**
17. $6\sqrt{125}$ **$30\sqrt{5}$**
18. $2\sqrt{54}$ **$6\sqrt{6}$**
19. $7\sqrt{192}$ **$56\sqrt{3}$**
20. $10\sqrt{162}$ **$90\sqrt{2}$**
21. $(\sqrt{8})^2$ **8**
22. $\sqrt{10} \cdot \sqrt{10}$ **10**
23. $\sqrt{6} \cdot \sqrt{2}$ **$2\sqrt{3}$**
24. $\sqrt{13^2}$ **13**
25. $\sqrt{3} \cdot \sqrt{15}$ **$3\sqrt{5}$**
26. $\sqrt{6} \cdot \sqrt{14}$ **$2\sqrt{21}$**
27. $\sqrt{5} \cdot \sqrt{30}$ **$5\sqrt{6}$**
28. $\sqrt{21} \cdot \sqrt{35}$ **$7\sqrt{15}$**
29. $4\sqrt{8} \cdot 3\sqrt{2}$ **48**
30. $10\sqrt{6} \cdot 9\sqrt{6}$ **540**
31. $7\sqrt{15} \cdot 2\sqrt{5}$ **$70\sqrt{3}$**
32. $8\sqrt{7} \cdot 5\sqrt{14}$ **$280\sqrt{2}$**

Exs. 33–44: Assume that variables other than x have only non-negative values.

Solve for x.

33. $x^2 = 44$ **$\pm 2\sqrt{11}$**
34. $x^2 = 27$ **$\pm 3\sqrt{3}$**
35. $x^2 = 96$ **$\pm 4\sqrt{6}$**
36. $3x^2 = 150$ **$\pm 5\sqrt{2}$**
37. $5x^2 = 90$ **$\pm 3\sqrt{2}$**
38. $2x^2 = 360$ **$\pm 6\sqrt{5}$**
39. $3y^2 = x^2$ **$\pm y\sqrt{3}$**
40. $x^2 = 6a^2 + 6a^2$ **$\pm 2a\sqrt{3}$**
41. $x^2 = 10k^2 - k^2$ **$\pm 3k$**
42. $(3b)^2 + (4b)^2 = x^2$ **$\pm 5b$**
43. $x^2 = (4m)^2 - (2m)^2$ **$\pm 2m\sqrt{3}$**
44. $x^2 + c^2 = 19c^2$ **$\pm 3c\sqrt{2}$**

45. A square has a perimeter of $12a$. Write an expression for the length of the diagonal of the square, in terms of a, in simplified radical form. **$3a\sqrt{2}$**

46. A rectangle has length $3b$ and width $6b$. Write an expression for the length of the diagonal of the rectangle, in terms of b, in simplified radical form. **$3b\sqrt{5}$**

Use triangle PQR for Exercises 47 and 48. This triangle is "half" of an equilateral triangle.

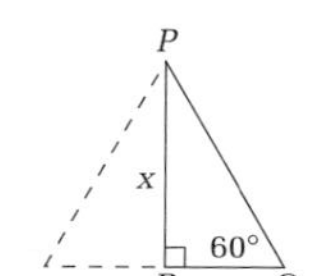

47. Write an expression, in terms of a, for the hypotenuse $\overline{PQ}$ of triangle PQR. **$2a$**

48. Using the Pythagorean theorem, write an equation that relates x and a. Solve the equation for x in simplified radical form. **$x^2 + a^2 = (2a)^2$; $x = a\sqrt{3}$**

Name ____________ Date ____________

Practice 69

For use with Section 9-3

Solve.

1. $(x - 1)(x - 2) = 0$ **1, 2**
2. $n(n - 5) = 0$ **0, 5**
3. $3k^2 = 0$ **0**
4. $(a + 1)(a - 1) = 0$ **−1, 1**
5. $(y - 3)(y + 2) = 0$ **−2, 3**
6. $2w(w - 4) = 0$ **0, 4**
7. $3t(t + 6) = 0$ **−6, 0**
8. $7b(b - 9) = 0$ **0, 9**
9. $-5c(c - 8) = 0$ **0, 8**
10. $z(2z - 7) = 0$ **$0, \frac{7}{2}$**
11. $6m(3m + 4) = 0$ **$-\frac{4}{3}, 0$**
12. $-3v(4v - 18) = 0$ **$0, \frac{9}{2}$**

In Exercises 13–24, the lengths of the sides of a triangle are given. Is the triangle a right triangle?

13. 2 m, 3 m, 4 m **no**
14. 20 mm, 21 mm, 29 mm **yes**
15. 4 yd, 5 yd, 6 yd **no**
16. 8 in., 15 in., 17 in. **yes**
17. 4 ft, 7 ft, 8 ft **no**
18. 5 cm, 5 cm, 7 cm **no**
19. 3 m, 5 m, 6 m **no**
20. 9 yd, 40 yd, 41 yd **yes**
21. 5 m, 10 m, 15 m **no**
22. 2.5 cm, 6 cm, 6.5 cm **yes**
23. 2.1 in., 2.8 in., 3.5 in. **yes**
24. 3.3 m, 3.5 m, 4.8 m **no**

Tell whether each statement is *true* or *false*. If it is false, give a counterexample. **Counterexamples may vary. Sample answers are given.**

25. If you swim, you will get wet. **true**
26. If $x^2 > 16$, then $x > 4$. **false; $x = -5$**
27. If you cannot see your shadow, the sun has set. **false; It may just be very cloudy.**
28. If an animal is a bird, then it can fly. **false; ostrich**
29. If quadrilateral *ABCD* is a square, then it is a rectangle. **true**
30. If two sides of a quadilateral are parallel, then it is a parallelogram. **false; Isosceles trapezoids with just two parallel sides are not parallelograms.**

For Exercises 31–36, write the converse of the statement and tell whether the converse is *true* or *false*. If it is false, give a counterexample. **Counterexamples may vary. Sample answers are given.**

31. If y is even, then y^2 is even. **If y^2 is even, then y is even.; true**
32. If it is raining, then the ground is wet. **See below.**
33. If $a > 0$, then $a^2 > 0$. **If $a^2 > 0$, then $a > 0$.; false; $a = -1$**
34. If you are at school, it is not July 4. **See below.**
35. If $x = 0$, then $xy = 0$. **If $xy = 0$, then $x = 0$.; false; $x = 5$, $y = 0$**
36. $x < 7$ if $x < 5$. **If $x < 7$, then $x < 5$.; false; $x = 6$**
37. ***Open-ended*** Draw several triangles with sides a, b, and c, such that $c^2 > a^2 + b^2$. What can you say about the angle opposite side c? Draw some triangles in which $c^2 < a^2 + b^2$. What seems to be true now about the angle opposite side c? **Check students' work.**

32. If the ground is wet then it is raining.; false; Maybe someone is watering a lawn.
34. If it is not July 4, then you are at school.; false; Thanksgiving Day

Name ____________ Date ____________

Practice 70

For use with Section 9-4

Find the probability that a dart landing inside each shape lands in the shaded region.

1. 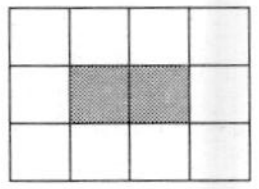 **$\frac{1}{6}$**

2. 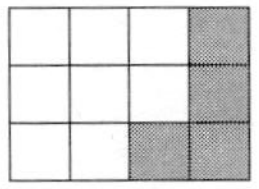 **$\frac{1}{3}$**

3. 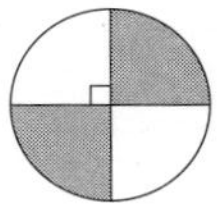 **$\frac{1}{2}$**

4. 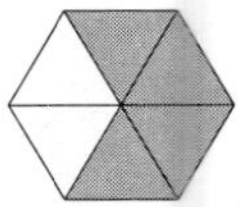 **$\frac{2}{3}$**
(regular hexagon)

5. 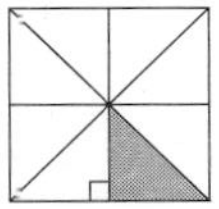 **$\frac{1}{8}$**
(square)

6. 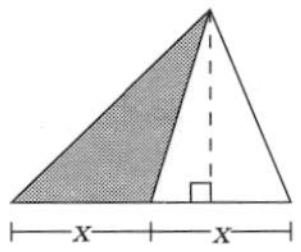 **$\frac{1}{2}$**

7. During each cycle, a traffic light turns green for cars in one direction for 30 s. It is green for cars in the other direction for 25 s. The *WALK* sign is then on for 20 s. Find the probability that when you arrive at the intersection on foot, you can cross without waiting. **$\frac{4}{15}$**
8. A television news program has 18 min of news and 12 min of commercials. Suppose you tune in at a random time during the program. What is the probability that a commercial will be in progress? **$\frac{2}{5}$**
9. A circular target that has a diameter of 48 in. has a bull's-eye with a diameter of 8 in. What is the probability that an arrow hitting the target will land in the bull's-eye? **$\frac{1}{36}$**
10. A running track is as shown. Suppose you run at a constant speed around the track. At a random time, what is the probability that you are on one of the straightaways? **about 0.56**

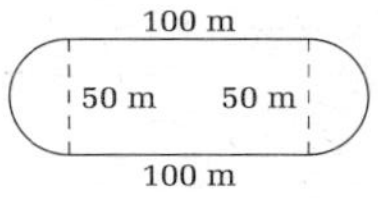

A circular target has a sector marked off and shaded. Find the angle the shaded sector should have so that a dart hitting the target has each probability of landing in the sector.

11. $\frac{1}{3}$ **120°**
12. $\frac{3}{5}$ **216°**
13. $\frac{5}{6}$ **300°**
14. $\frac{2}{9}$ **80°**

15. ***Writing*** The group Endangered Species performed for 12 min at some point during a 2-hour rock concert. Suppose you taped 1 h of the concert. Write a full explanation of how you could find the probability that you taped all of the group's performance. **Check students' work.**

Name ______________________ Date ____________

Practice 71

For use with Section 9-5

Find the surface area of each prism.

1. 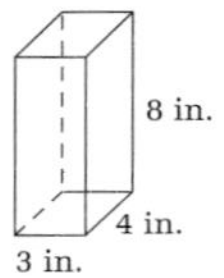

136 in.^{2}

2. 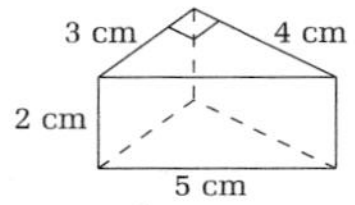

36 cm^2

3. 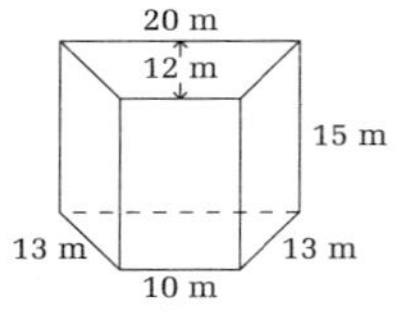

1200 m^2

Find the surface area of each cylinder or half cylinder.

4. 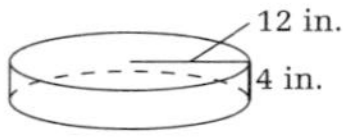

about 1205.8 in.^{2}

5. 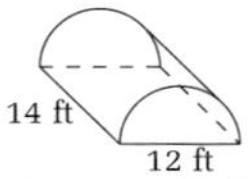

about 545 ft^2

6. 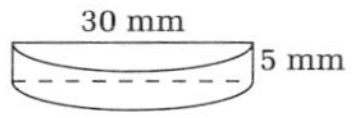

about 1092.5 mm^2

Find the surface area of the regular square pyramid having each set of measurements.

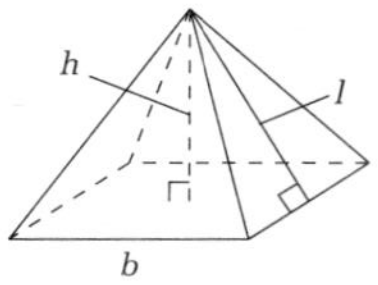

7. $b = 10$; $h = 12$ **360 square units**
8. $b = 16$; $h = 6$ **576 square units**
9. $b = 48$; $h = 7$ **4704 square units**
10. $l = 29$; $h = 21$ **3920 square units**
11. $l = 17$; $h = 8$ **1920 square units**
12. $l = 26$; $h = 24$ **1440 square units**

13. A jewelry manufacturer wants to plate an old coin with silver to make a piece of jewelry. The coin has a thickness of 2 mm and is 25 mm in diameter. How many square millimeters must be plated. Answer to the nearest 10 square millimeters. **1140 mm^2**

14. A prism has bases that are congruent equilateral triangles with sides of length 6 cm. The height of the prism is 8 cm. Find its surface area, to the nearest square centimeter. **175 cm^2**

15. A block of cheese has the shape of a quarter of a cylinder. The bases are quarter circles of radius 5 in. and the height of the block is 6 in. How many square inches must be covered if you wish to coat the outer surface of the block with wax? **about 146.4 in.^{2}**

16. The bases of a prism are trapezoids with parallel sides of length 10 in. and 22 in. Each of the nonparallel sides of the bases has length 10 in. The height of the prism is 11 in. Sketch one base of the prism and use the Pythagorean theorem to find the height of the trapezoid. Then find the surface area of the prism. **height of trapezoid: 8 in.; 828 in.^{2}**

Name ______________________ Date ____________

Practice 72

For use with Section 9-6

For Exercises 1–6, use the space figures below.

A. 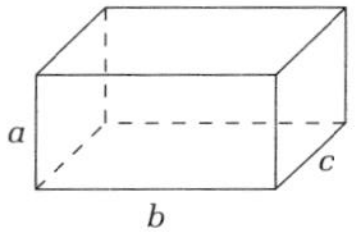

B. 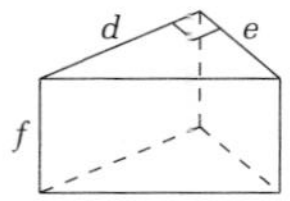

C. 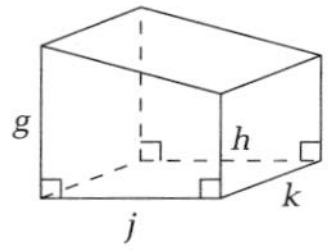

Find the volume of each figure with each set of measurements.

1. Use Fig. A: $a = 8$ in.; $b = 10$ in.; $c = 12$ in. **960 in.^{3}**
2. Use Fig. B: $d = 11$ cm; $e = 8$ cm; $f = 14$ cm **616 cm^3**
3. Use Fig. C: $g = 15$ m; $h = 13$ m; $j = 8$ m; $k = 10$ m **1120 m^3**

Find the missing dimension.

4. Use Fig. A: $a = 12$ mm; $b = 15$ mm; volume = 2340 mm^3; $c = \underline{?}$ **13 mm**
5. Use Fig. B: $d = 8$ in.; $e = 10$ in.; volume = 440 in.^{3}; $f = \underline{?}$ **11 in.**
6. Use Fig. C: $g = 17$ cm; $h = 7$ cm; $j = 5$ cm; volume = 1020 cm^3; $k = \underline{?}$ **17 cm**

Find the volume of each space figure. Answer to the nearest tenth.

7. 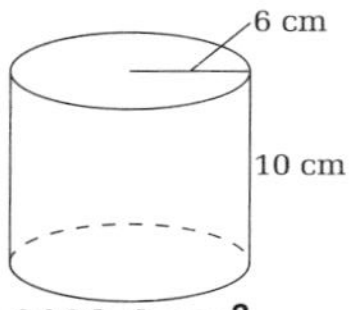

1130.4 cm^3

8. 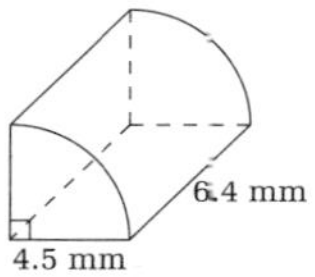

101.7 mm^3

9. 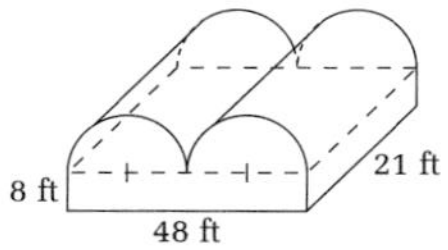

17,559.4 ft^3

10. Andreas has an aquarium with a rectangular base 40 cm × 25 cm. He wants to put in the aquarium a decorative rock in the shape of a cylinder 3 cm tall and having circular bases of radius 8 cm. Suppose he does so. By how much will the water level in the aquarium rise? **about 0.6 cm**

11. *Open-ended* Design your own candy in the shape of a prism, using for a base rectangles, triangles, trapezoids, parallelograms and/or sectors of circles. Find the volume of your candy. **Check students' work.**

Name ____________________ Date ____________

Practice 73

For use with Section 9-7

Find the volume of each space figure.

1.

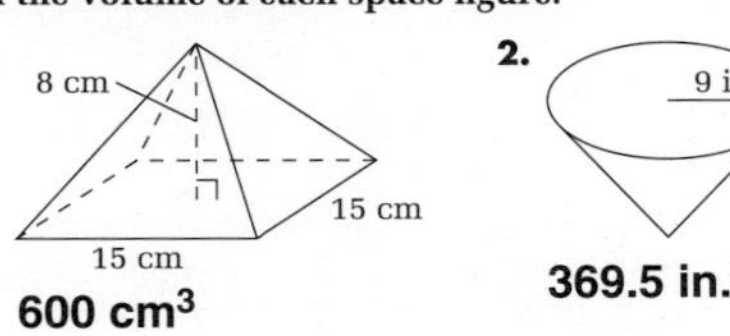

600 cm³

2. 9 in.; 10 in. **369.5 in.³**

3. 8 mm; 10 mm; 3 mm **552.6 mm³**

For Exercises 4–9, use the regular square pyramid at the right. Find the volume of the pyramid, using each set of measurements.

h; l; b

4. b = 42 in.; h = 28 in. **16,464 in.³**

5. b = 25 cm; h = 15 cm **3125 cm³**

6. b = 12 m; l = 13 m **553.6 m³**

7. b = 24 ft; l = 30 ft **5279.1 ft³**

8. h = 11 cm; l = 61 cm **52,800 cm³**

9. h = 48 in.; l = 73 in. **193,600 in.³**

10. A cone has a slant height of 25 cm and a height of 7 cm. Find the volume of the cone. **4220.2 cm³**

11. The slant height of a cone is 26 in. and the diameter of its base is 20 in. Find the volume of the cone, to the nearest cubic inch. **2513 in.³**

12. At a soft-ice-cream stand, the waffle cones for ice cream cones come in two sizes. The smaller size has a radius of 1.5 in. and a height of 4 in. The larger size has a radius of 2 in. and a height of 6 in. Suppose each cone were filled with ice cream and leveled at the top. Find the ratio of the larger volume of ice cream to the smaller. $\frac{8}{3}$

13. A tent manufacturer wants to build a tent in the shape of a square pyramid with a base 8 ft on each side. The tent should have a volume of at least 108 ft³. To the nearest foot, what is the smallest height such a tent can have? **about 5 ft**

14. A popcorn container has the shape shown at the right. The measures shown are approximate. Find the volume of the container. (*Hint:* Think about the difference between the volumes of two cones.) **653.1 in.³**

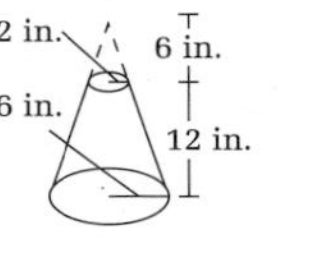

15. Draw a cone and a regular square pyramid with the same height. Suppose the diameter of the base of the cone is the same as the length of a side of the base of the pyramid. Find the ratio of the volume of the cone to the volume of the pyramid. $\frac{\pi}{4}$

Name ____________________ Date ____________

Practice 74

For use with Section 9-8

In Exercises 1–4, for each ratio of the lengths of corresponding sides of two similar figures, find the ratio of their areas.

1. 3 : 4 **9 : 16** **2.** 5 : 7 **25 : 49** **3.** 3 : 8 **9 : 64** **4.** $\frac{1}{13}$ $\mathbf{\frac{1}{169}}$

In Exercises 5–8, for each ratio of the lengths of corresponding sides of two similar space figures, find the ratio of their volumes.

5. 6 : 4 **27 : 8** **6.** 3 : 10 **27 : 1000** **7.** 5 : 12 **125 : 1728** **8.** $\frac{2}{5}$ $\mathbf{\frac{8}{125}}$

Find the ratio of the areas of each pair of similar figures. Then find the missing area.

9.

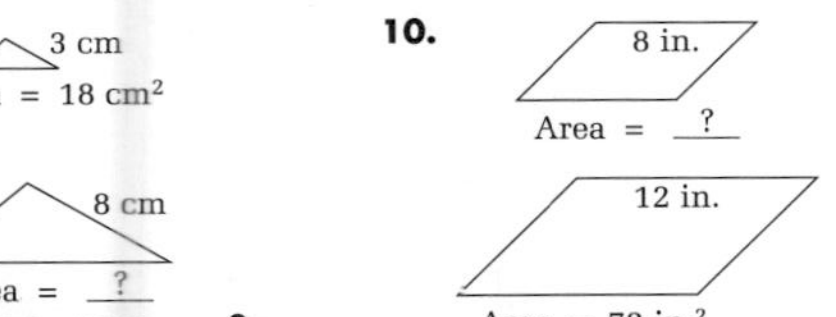

3 cm, Area = 18 cm²; 8 cm, Area = ?

9 : 64; 128 cm²

10.

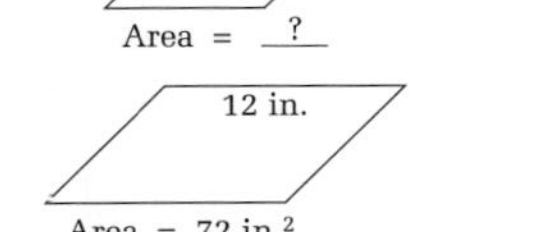

8 in., Area = ?; 12 in., Area = 72 in.²

4 : 9; 32 in.²

11.

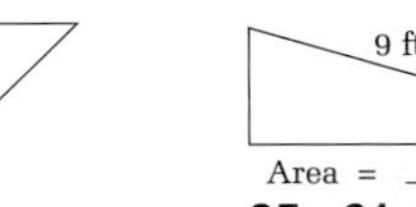

5 ft, Area = 20 ft²; 9 ft, Area = ?

25 : 81; 64.8 ft²

For Exercises 12–14, use the similar pyramids at the right. Find each missing measurement using the given measurements.

I. k; a II. h; b

12. a = 15 cm; b = 10 cm; Volume II = 8 cm³; Volume I = ? **27 cm³**

13. h = 4 ft; Volume I = 54 ft³; Volume II = 16 ft³; k = ? **6 ft**

14. k = 15 mm; h = 6 mm; Volume I = 62.5 mm³; Volume II = ? **4 mm³**

15. Two coins are similar cylinders and contain the same percent of silver. One is 1.5 times as thick as the other. Suppose the silver in the thinner coin is worth \$2.40. How much is the silver in the thicker coin worth? **\$8.10**

16. ***Writing*** Compare all the area formulas that you have learned. How many measurements are multiplied together in each formula? Compare all the volume formulas. How many measurements are multiplied together? Explain the facts about the ratio of areas of similar figures and the ratio of volumes of similar space figures from your answers. **Check students' work.**

Name ______________________ Date ____________

Practice 75

Cumulative Practice through Unit 9

Without graphing, find the slope and the vertical intercept of the line modeled by each equation.

1. $y = 4x + 9$ **4, 9**　**2.** $y = 7 - 2.5x$ **–2.5, 7**　**3.** $y = -0.5x$ **–0.5, 0**

In Exercises 4–7, write an equation for each line.

4. The slope is –3 and the vertical intercept is 8. $\mathbf{y = -3x + 8}$

5. The slope is $\frac{3}{2}$ and the point (4, 7) is on the line. $\mathbf{y = \frac{3}{2}x + 1}$

6. The vertical intercept is 2 and the horizontal intercept is 5. $\mathbf{y = -\frac{2}{5}x + 2}$

7. The points (–1, 6) and (3, 8) are on the line. $\mathbf{y = \frac{1}{2}x + \frac{13}{2}}$

Graph each inequality. **Exs. 8–10. Answers show two checkpoints on boundary of graph and tell where solution points lie relative to boundary.**

8. $y \ge -x + 3$ **(0, 3), (1, 2), above and on**

9. $y < \frac{1}{3}x - 2$ **(0, –2), (3, –1), below**

10. $2x + y \le 5$ **(0, 5), (1, 3), below and on**

Find the area of each sector.

11. 9 cm **63.6 cm²**

12. 17 in. **113.4 in.²**

13. 115°, 11 ft **121.4 ft²**

14. A sign for Monoco gas stations is to have the name MONOCO inside a rectangle that measures 3.5 ft by 10 ft. The rectangle is to be inside a circle. What is the smallest diameter the circle can have? **10.6 ft**

15. A spaghetti sauce can has a height of 10.5 cm. It has circular bases of diameter 7.2 cm. Find the surface area of the can, to the nearest square centimeter. **319 cm²**

16. Find the volume of the can in Exercise 15, to the nearest tenth of a cubic centimeter. **427.3 cm³**

17. A spinner dial has congruent sectors numbered from 1 to 12. What is the probability of spinning a number less than 7? $\mathbf{\frac{1}{2}}$

18. Pisces Rent-a-Car charges $250 for a one-week rental plus $.20 per mile. CPS Rent-a-Car charges $190 for a one-week rental plus $.35 per mile. For how many miles would the two companies charge the same amount? **400 mi**

Name ______________________ Date ____________

Practice 76

For use with Section 10-1

In Exercises 1–6, tell whether each transformation is a reflection. If it is, draw the line of reflection.

1. p | q

2. “ ” **not a reflection**

3. ⇑ ⇒

4. ∩ / ∪

5. C c **not a reflection**

6. W / M

Each diagram below shows a figure and its image.

I. **II.** **III.**

Write an equation of each line of reflection.

7. Diagram I $\mathbf{y = 4}$　**8.** Diagram II $\mathbf{y = -2}$　**9.** Diagram III $\mathbf{x = -3}$

In each diagram, tell the image of each point.

10. For I: D, E, F, G, H **S, Q, P, R, T**

11. For II: H, J, K **T, S, R**

12. For III: U, V, W, Z **Q, R, W, P**

For each ordered pair (x, y), tell the image of the point under each reflection. Give an equation of the line of reflection.

13. $(x, y) \to (x, -y)$: (3, 2), (1, –1) **(3, –2), (1, 1); y = 0**

14. $(x, y) \to (-x, y)$: (–5, 1), (3, 4) **(5, 1), (–3, 4); x = 0**

15. $(x, y) \to (-y, -x)$: (4, –3), (5, 1) **(3, –4), (–1, –5); y = –x**

16. $(x, y) \to (x, 6 - y)$: (2, 5), (–1, 4) **(2, 1), (–1, 2); y = 3**

17. *Open-ended* Look in magazines for ads that picture an object and its reflection. For each ad, trace the object and its reflection and draw the line of reflection. **Check students' work.**

Name ______________________ Date ____________

Practice 77

For use with Section 10-2

In Exercises 1–3, match each function with its graph.

1. $y = x^2 - 2$ **B**
2. $y = (x - 2)^2$ **C**
3. $y = (x + 2)^2$ **A**

A. 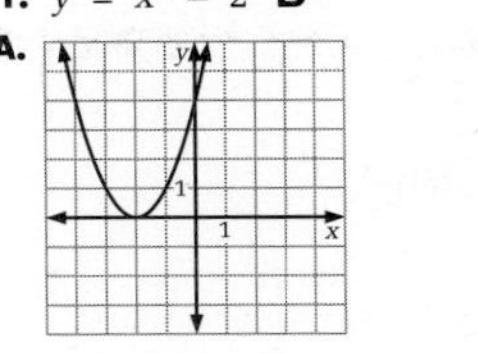

B. 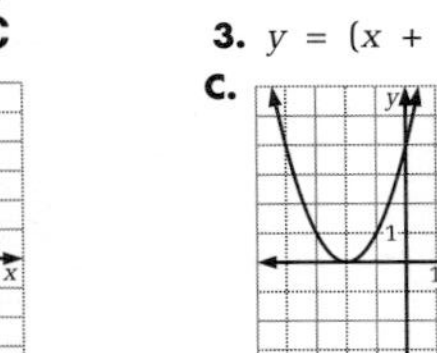

C. 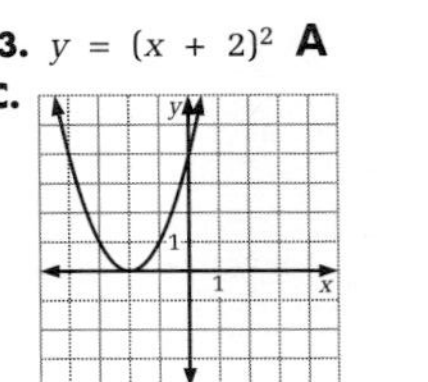

In Exercises 4–9, describe in words the translation of the graph of $y = x^2$ that produces the graph of each equation.

4. $y = (x - 3)^2$ **right 3 units**
5. $y = x^2 + 4$ **up 4 units**
6. $y = x^2 - 1$ **down 1 unit**
7. $y = (x + 5)^2$ **left 5 units**
8. $y = (x - 6)^2$ **right 6 units**
9. $y = x^2 + 7$ **up 7 units**

Exs. 10–18: Answers give equation of graph, direction, and number of units.

Tell how to translate the graph of $y = x^2$ or $y = -x^2$ in order to produce the graph of each function.

10. $y = -x^2 - 2$ **$y = -x^2$, down 2**
11. $y = x^2 + 5$ **$y = x^2$, up 5**
12. $y = -x^2 + 3$ **$y = -x^2$, up 3**
13. $y = -(x - 1)^2$ **$y = -x^2$, right 1**
14. $y = -x^2 - 6$ **$y = -x^2$, down 6**
15. $y = -(x + 1)^2$ **$y = -x^2$, left 1**
16. $y = (x - 4)^2$ **$y = x^2$, right 4**
17. $y = (x - 2)^2 + 1$ **$y = x^2$, right 2, up 1**
18. $y = (x + 5)^2 - 3$ **$y = x^2$, left 5, down 3**

For the graph of each function, find an equation of the line of symmetry and the coordinates of the vertex.

19. $y = x^2 - 5$ **$x = 0$, (0, –5)**
20. $y = (x + 1)^2$ **$x = -1$, (–1, 0)**
21. $y = (x - 10)^2$ **$x = 10$, (10, 0)**
22. $y = -(x - 8)^2$ **$x = 8$, (8, 0)**
23. $y = -x^2 + 11$ **$x = 0$, (0, 11)**
24. $y = x^2 - 7$ **$x = 0$, (0, –7)**

Find a function whose graph fits each description and has the same shape as the graph of $y = x^2$.

25. vertex at the point (3, 0) **$y = (x - 3)^2$ or $y = -(x - 3)^2$**
26. translation of $y = x^2$ up 5 units **$y = x^2 + 5$**
27. translation of $y = -x^2$ left 6 units **$y = -(x + 6)^2$**
28. vertex at the point (–9, 0) **$y = (x + 9)^2$ or $y = -(x + 9)^2$**

Name ______________________ Date ____________

Practice 78

For use with Section 10-3

Match each equation with its graph.

1. $y = (x - 2)(x - 4)$ **C**
2. $y = (x - 3)(x + 1)$ **A**
3. $y = -x(x - 4)$ **B**

A. 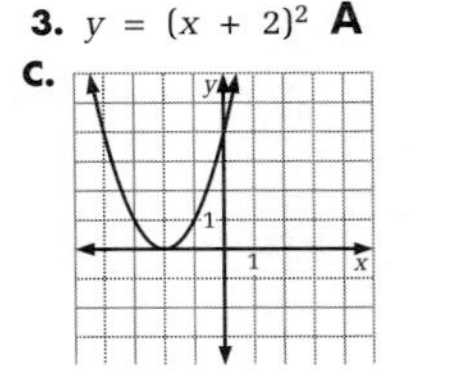

B. 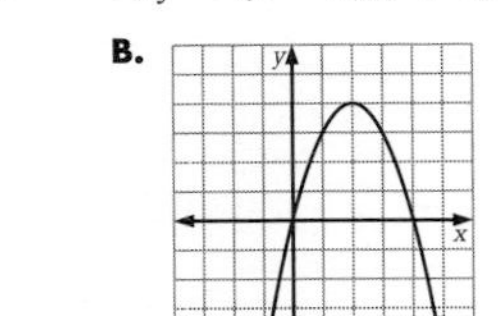

C. 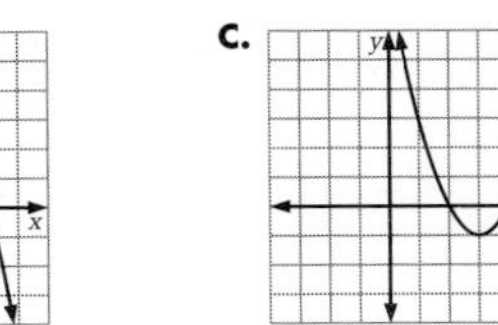

Graph each parabola. **Exs. 4–12: For graphs, check students' work. Three checkpoints are given for each graph.**

4. $y = x(x - 4)$ **(–1, 5), (2, –4), (4, 0)**
5. $y = x(x + 2)$ **(–3, 3), (–1, –1), (1, 3)**
6. $y = -x(x + 4)$ **(–5, –5), (–2, 4), (0, 0)**
7. $y = (x - 1)(x + 1)$ **(–2, 3), (0, –1), (2, 3)**
8. $y = (x - 2)(2 - x)$ **(0, –4), (2, 0), (4, –4)**
9. $y = (x - 1)(x + 3)$ **(–4, 5), (–1, –4), (2, 5)**
10. $y = (x + 2)(4 - x)$ **(–3, –7), (1, 9), (5, –7)**
11. $y = (x - 1)(3 - x)$ **(–1, –8), (2, 1), (5, –8)**
12. $y = (2x - 6)(x + 1)$ **(–1, 0), (1, –8), (3, 0)**

Find the x-intercepts and y-intercept of the graph of each equation.

13. $y = x(x - 3)$ **0, 3; 0**
14. $y = -x(x + 7)$ **0, –7; 0**
15. $y = (x - 1)(x - 6)$ **1, 6; 6**
16. $y = (x + 4)(x - 11)$ **–4, 11; –44**
17. $y = (3x - 1)(x + 4)$ **$-4, \frac{1}{3}$; –4**
18. $y = (2 - x)(4x + 3)$ **$-\frac{3}{4}$, 2; 6**

Dinah Johnson, an economist for a cable TV company, graphed the relationship between total monthly revenue (y) and proposed increase (x) in the monthly fee. The fee is now \$8.00 and revenue is \$128,000.

19. What are the x-intercepts and the y-intercept of the graph? **–8, 16; 128,000**
20. What fee increase will maximize revenue? **\$4**
21. Which equation could represent the graph? **C**
    a. $y = (16{,}000 + 1000x)(8 + x)$
    b. $y = (16{,}000 + 1000x)(8 - x)$
    c. $y = (16{,}000 - 1000x)(8 + x)$
    d. $y = (16{,}000 - 1000x)(8 - x)$
22. ***Writing*** The two factors in the answer for Exercise 21 represent proposed fee and audience size. Describe how one of these quantities affects the other. **Check students' work.**

Name ______________________ Date ____________

Practice 79

For use with Section 10-4

Simplify.

1. $a^3 \cdot a^2$ $\mathbf{a^5}$
2. $n^4 \cdot n^3$ $\mathbf{n^7}$
3. $x^2 \cdot x^6$ $\mathbf{x^8}$
4. $b^6 \cdot b^2 \cdot b$ $\mathbf{b^9}$
5. $r^4 \cdot r^2 \cdot r^3$ $\mathbf{r^9}$
6. $5c^3 \cdot c^5$ $\mathbf{5c^8}$
7. $6p^8 \cdot 4p^3$ $\mathbf{24p^{11}}$
8. $-10z^6 \cdot 3z^4$ $\mathbf{-30z^{10}}$
9. $(8k^7)(-3k^3)$ $\mathbf{-24k^{10}}$
10. $(-7x^6)(2x^3)$ $\mathbf{-14x^9}$
11. $(11y)(-4y^5)$ $\mathbf{-44y^6}$
12. $(-n^7)(-6n^8)$ $\mathbf{6n^{15}}$
13. $x^3y \cdot x^7y^2$ $\mathbf{x^{10}y^3}$
14. $(a^4b^3)(-a^6b^5)$ $\mathbf{-a^{10}b^8}$
15. $(-m^4n^2)(mn^6)$ $\mathbf{-m^5n^8}$
16. $(-5u^2v^3)(4uv^2)$ $\mathbf{-20u^3v^5}$
17. $3xy^2 \cdot 8xy^4$ $\mathbf{24x^2y^6}$
18. $(-3j^3k)(-5j^2k^2)$ $\mathbf{15j^5k^3}$

Simplify.

19. $(x^4)^3$ $\mathbf{x^{12}}$
20. $(y^2)^5$ $\mathbf{y^{10}}$
21. $(c^3)^2$ $\mathbf{c^6}$
22. $(2n)^5$ $\mathbf{32n^5}$
23. $(-2k)^4$ $\mathbf{16k^4}$
24. $(-3r)^3$ $\mathbf{-27r^3}$
25. $(xy^2)^5$ $\mathbf{x^5y^{10}}$
26. $(-m^5n)^2$ $\mathbf{m^{10}n^2}$
27. $(-a^2b^3)^3$ $\mathbf{-a^6b^9}$
28. $(-2r^2s)^4$ $\mathbf{16r^8s^4}$
29. $(4uv^5)^3$ $\mathbf{64u^3v^{15}}$
30. $(-2x^2y^3)^7$ $\mathbf{-128x^{14}y^{21}}$
31. $a^5(3a^3)^2$ $\mathbf{9a^{11}}$
32. $(-2a^4)(2a^2)^5$ $\mathbf{-64a^{14}}$
33. $(4n)(-2n^3)^4$ $\mathbf{64n^{13}}$

34. Write an expression in simplified form for the area of the square at the right. $\mathbf{49n^2}$

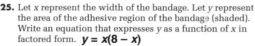

35. Write an expression in simplified form for the volume of the cube at the right. $\mathbf{27p^6}$

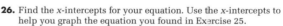

7n
7n
3p²
3p²
3p²

Insert parentheses in the expression on the left side of each equation to make a true statement.

36. $3c^2d^4 = 81c^8d^4$ $\mathbf{(3c^2d)^4}$
37. $2x^3y^5 = 8x^3y^5$ $\mathbf{(2x)^3y^5}$
38. $3a^2b^4 = 3a^8b^4$ $\mathbf{3(a^2b)^4}$

Name ______________________ Date ____________

Practice 80

For use with Section 10-5

Expand each expression.

1. $x(x + 5)$ $\mathbf{x^2 + 5x}$
2. $x(x - 12)$ $\mathbf{x^2 - 12x}$
3. $-x(x - 3)$ $\mathbf{-x^2 + 3x}$
4. $2x(x - 10)$ $\mathbf{2x^2 - 20x}$
5. $-6x(x + 7)$ $\mathbf{-6x^2 - 42x}$
6. $9x(2 - x)$ $\mathbf{18x - 9x^2}$
7. $3x(4x + 5)$ $\mathbf{12x^2 + 15x}$
8. $7x(8 - 3x)$ $\mathbf{56x - 21x^2}$
9. $-2x(4x - 11)$ $\mathbf{-8x^2 + 22x}$
10. $5x^2(x + 3)$ $\mathbf{5x^3 + 15x^2}$
11. $-4x^2(5 - 6x)$ $\mathbf{-20x^2 + 24x^3}$
12. $-5x(x^3 + 2)$ $\mathbf{-5x^4 - 10x}$

For Exercises 13–24,

a. **factor one side of each equation completely.**
b. **find the *x*-intercepts and *y*-intercept of the graph of each equation.**

13. $y = x^2 + 3x$ $\mathbf{x(x + 3); 0, -3; 0}$
14. $y = x^2 - 15x$ $\mathbf{x(x - 15); 0, 15; 0}$
15. $y = x^2 + x$ $\mathbf{x(x + 1); 0, -1; 0}$
16. $y = -x^2 - 6x$ $\mathbf{-x(x + 6); 0, -6; 0}$
17. $y = -x^2 + 7x$ $\mathbf{-x(x - 7); 0, 7; 0}$
18. $y = x - 4x^2$ $\mathbf{x(1 - 4x); 0, \frac{1}{4}; 0}$
19. $y = 2x^2 + 5x$ $\mathbf{x(2x + 5); 0, -\frac{5}{2}; 0}$
20. $y = -8x^2 + x$ $\mathbf{-x(8x - 1); 0, \frac{1}{8}; 0}$
21. $y = 10x^2 - 3x$ $\mathbf{x(10x - 3); 0, \frac{3}{10}; 0}$
22. $y = 3x^2 - 6x$ $\mathbf{3x(x - 2); 0, 2; 0}$
23. $y = 5x^2 + 20x$ $\mathbf{5x(x + 4); 0, -4; 0}$
24. $y = -2x^2 + 2x$ $\mathbf{-2x(x - 1); 0, 1; 0}$

A maker of medical supplies wants to design an adhesive bandage with a square pad in the center, as shown at the right.

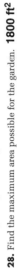

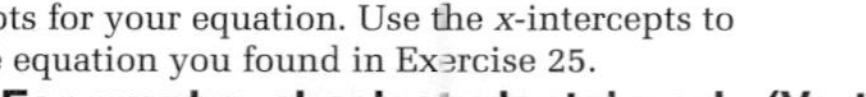

25. Let x represent the width of the bandage. Let y represent the area of the adhesive region of the bandage (shaded). Write an equation that expresses y as a function of x in factored form. $\mathbf{y = x(8 - x)}$

26. Find the x-intercepts for your equation. Use the x-intercepts to help you graph the equation you found in Exercise 25.
***x*-intercepts: 0, 8; For graphs, check students' work. (Vertex is (4, 16).)**

Yoshi is going to build a fence for a rectangular garden that will be alongside a brick wall at the back of his property. He has 120 ft of fencing. He will use the brick wall for one side of the garden. Refer to the diagram to answer Exercises 27 and 28.

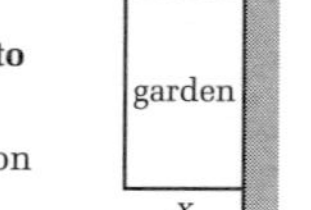

27. Write an equation to express the area y of the garden as a function of x. $\mathbf{y = x(120 - 2x)}$

28. Find the maximum area possible for the garden. $\mathbf{1800\ ft^2}$

Name ______________________ Date ____________

Practice 81

For use with Section 10-6

Expand each product.

1. $(x + 1)(x + 4)$ **$x^2 + 5x + 4$**
2. $(x + 3)(x + 5)$ **$x^2 + 8x + 15$**
3. $(x - 2)(x + 2)$ **$x^2 - 4$**
4. $(x - 6)(x + 1)$ **$x^2 - 5x - 6$**
5. $(-x + 8)(x - 3)$ **$-x^2 + 11x - 24$**
6. $(x - 7)(x + 9)$ **$x^2 + 2x - 63$**
7. $(x - 3)(x + 3)$ **$x^2 - 9$**
8. $(x - 6)(x - 6)$ **$x^2 - 12x + 36$**
9. $(-x - 8)(x - 5)$ **$-x^2 - 3x + 40$**
10. $(x - 11)(x + 7)$ **$x^2 - 4x - 77$**
11. $(-x + 12)(x - 4)$ **$-x^2 + 16x - 48$**
12. $(x - 9)(x - 4)$ **$x^2 - 13x + 36$**
13. $(5 - x)(2 + x)$ **$10 + 3x - x^2$**
14. $(7 - x)(3 - x)$ **$21 - 10x + x^2$**
15. $(x + 8)(2 - x)$ **$-x^2 - 6x + 16$**
16. $(2x - 1)(x + 5)$ **$2x^2 + 9x - 5$**
17. $(-3x + 2)(x + 6)$ **$-3x^2 - 16x + 12$**
18. $(3x - 4)(2x + 1)$ **$6x^2 - 5x - 4$**
19. $(5x - 3)(4x - 1)$ **$20x^2 - 17x + 3$**
20. $(8x + 3)(2x - 5)$ **$16x^2 - 34x - 15$**
21. $(4x - 3)(-7x + 2)$ **$-28x^2 + 29x - 6$**

Match each equation with its graph.

22. $y = x^2 - 4$ **A**
23. $y = x^2 - 2x - 3$ **B**
24. $y = x^2 - 4x$ **C**

A.
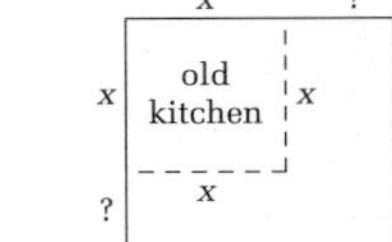
B.
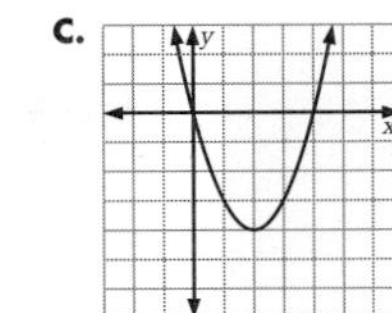
C.

Without graphing, find each feature of the graph of each equation.

a. the equation of the line of symmetry
b. the coordinates of the vertex
c. the y-intercept

25. $y = x^2 - 6x - 5$ **$x = 3$; $(3, -14)$; -5**
26. $y = x^2 + 4x + 7$ **$x = -2$; $(-2, 3)$; 7**
27. $y = x^2 - 8x + 12$ **$x = 4$; $(4, -4)$; 12**
28. $y = -x^2 - 10x - 24$ **$x = -5$; $(-5, 1)$; -24**
29. $y = x^2 - 2x$ **$x = 1$; $(1, -1)$; 0**
30. $y = -x^2 + 6x + 16$ **$x = 3$; $(3, 25)$; 16**
31. $y = 2x^2 + 8x + 10$ **$x = -2$; $(-2, 2)$; 10**
32. $y = -3x^2 - 18x - 5$ **$x = -3$; $(-3, 22)$; -5**
33. $y = 6x^2 - 12x - 10$ **$x = 1$; $(1, -16)$; -10**
34. $y = -2x^2 + 16x + 3$ **$x = 4$; $(4, 35)$; 3**
35. $y = 5x^2 + 40x - 6$ **$x = -4$; $(-4, -86)$; -6**
36. $y = 4x^2 - 24x + 13$ **$x = 3$; $(3, -23)$; 13**

37. ***Writing*** Suppose you examined a small piece of a parabola under a microscope. It would be nearly a straight line segment. Describe how the slope of such line segments would change as you made your way along the parabola. **Check students' work.**

Name ______________________ Date ____________

Practice 82

For use with Section 10-7

Factor each trinomial.

1. $x^2 + 3x + 2$ **$(x + 1)(x + 2)$**
2. $x^2 + 7x + 10$ **$(x + 2)(x + 5)$**
3. $x^2 + 8x + 12$ **$(x + 2)(x + 6)$**
4. $x^2 - 11x + 18$ **$(x - 2)(x - 9)$**
5. $x^2 - 10x + 24$ **$(x - 4)(x - 6)$**
6. $x^2 + 9x + 14$ **$(x + 2)(x + 7)$**
7. $x^2 - 9x + 20$ **$(x - 4)(x - 5)$**
8. $x^2 - x - 6$ **$(x + 2)(x - 3)$**
9. $x^2 - 2x - 15$ **$(x + 3)(x - 5)$**
10. $x^2 + 3x - 10$ **$(x - 2)(x + 5)$**
11. $x^2 + 8x + 15$ **$(x + 3)(x + 5)$**
12. $x^2 - 5x - 6$ **$(x + 1)(x - 6)$**
13. $x^2 + 4x - 21$ **$(x - 3)(x + 7)$**
14. $x^2 - 12x + 27$ **$(x - 3)(x - 9)$**
15. $x^2 - 3x - 40$ **$(x + 5)(x - 8)$**
16. $x^2 - 5x - 24$ **$(x + 3)(x - 8)$**
17. $x^2 + 7x - 18$ **$(x - 2)(x + 9)$**
18. $x^2 - 11x + 28$ **$(x - 4)(x - 7)$**

Factor each trinomial that can be factored using integers, or write *unfactorable*.

19. $x^2 - 6x + 8$ **$(x - 2)(x - 4)$**
20. $x^2 - x + 12$ **unfactorable**
21. $x^2 + 5x - 4$ **unfactorable**
22. $x^2 - 9x + 20$ **$(x - 4)(x - 5)$**
23. $x^2 + 3x - 18$ **$(x - 3)(x + 6)$**
24. $x^2 - 6x + 16$ **unfactorable**
25. $x^2 + 10x - 24$ **$(x - 2)(x + 12)$**
26. $x^2 + 10x + 24$ **$(x + 4)(x + 6)$**
27. $x^2 - 4x + 12$ **unfactorable**

Exs. 28–33: Three checkpoints are given for each graph.

For Exercises 28–33, use the line of symmetry, the vertex, and the intercepts to sketch the graph of each equation.

28. $y = x^2 - 3x - 4$ **(4, 0), (−1, 0), (1.5, −6.5)**
29. $y = x^2 + x - 6$ **(−3, 0), (2, 0), (−0.5, −6.25)**
30. $y = x^2 - 5x + 6$ **(2, 0), (3, 0), (0, 6)**
31. $y = x^2 + 2x - 8$ **(−4, 0), (2, 0), (−1, −9)**
32. $y = x^2 - 6x + 8$ **(2, 0), (4, 0), (3, −1)**
33. $y = x^2 + 8x + 12$ **(−6, 0), (−2, 0), (−4, −4)**

34. The Chens enlarged their square kitchen by a whole number of feet in each direction. Margaret Chen said to her husband, "Suppose the length of each side of our old kitchen was x ft. Then our new kitchen has an area equal to $x^2 + 11x + 30$ square feet." By how many feet did the Chens enlarge their kitchen in each direction? **5 ft and 6 ft**

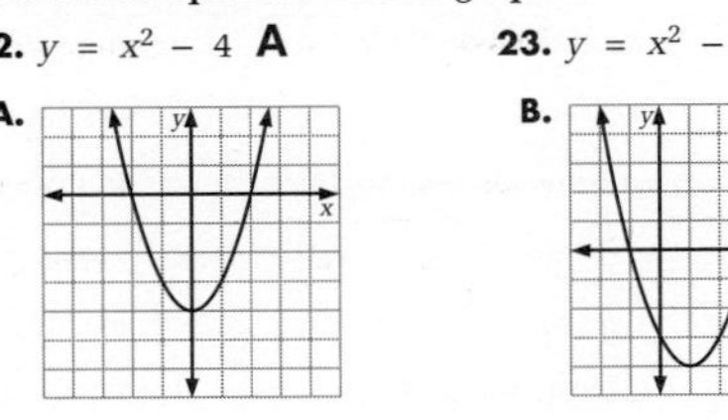

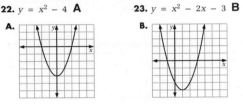

35. Lynn launched a model rocket straight up. The initial velocity of the rocket when it left the ground was 160 ft/s. The height h of the rocket t seconds after launch is given by the formula $h = 160t - 16t^2$. How many seconds will it take the rocket to hit the ground? **10 seconds**

Name ______________________ Date ______________

Practice 83

For use with Section 10-8

For Exercises 1–7, use the graphs below.

A. $y = x^2 - x - 6$

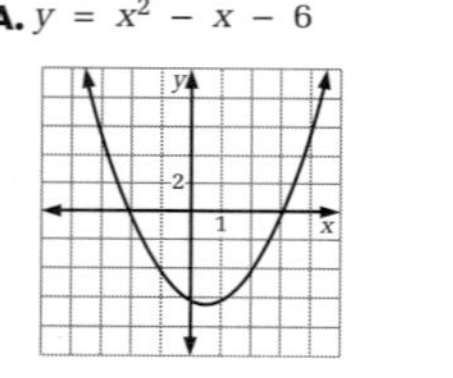

B. $y = x^2 - 5x + 6$

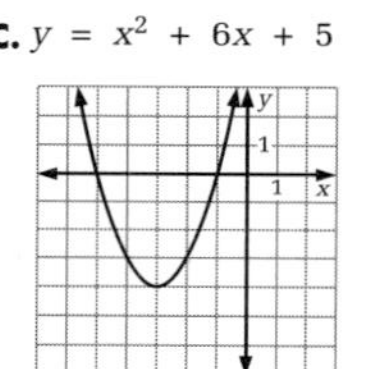

C. $y = x^2 + 6x + 5$

Use Graph A:

1. What are the x-intercepts of the graph? **−2, 3**
2. What are the solutions of the equation $x^2 - x - 6 = 0$? **−2, 3**

Use Graph B:

3. What are the x-intercepts of the graph? **2, 3**
4. What are the solutions of the equation $x^2 - 5x + 6 = 0$? **2, 3**

Use Graph C:

5. What are the x-intercepts of the graph? **−5, −1**
6. What are the solutions of the equation $x^2 + 6x + 5 = 0$? **−5, −1**
7. What are the solutions of the equation $x^2 + 6x + 5 = -3$? **−4, −2**

Exs. 8–13: The x- and y-intercepts are given for each graph.

Solve each quadratic equation by graphing. **The x-intercepts are the solutions.**

8. $x^2 - 3x + 2 = 0$ **1, 2; 2**
9. $x^2 - 3x - 4 = 0$ **−1, 4; −4**
10. $x^2 - 9 = 0$ **−3, 3; −9**
11. $2x^2 - x = 3$ **−1, 1.5; −3**
12. $3x^2 + x = 4$ **$-\frac{4}{3}$, 1; −4**
13. $2x^2 - 7x = -3$ **0.5, 3; 3**

Solve each quadratic equation by using the quadratic formula. Round answers to the nearest hundredth.

14. $x^2 - 4x + 1 = 0$ **3.73, 0.27**
15. $x^2 + 3x - 1 = 0$ **−3.30, 0.30**
16. $2x^2 - 5x + 2 = 0$ **0.5, 2**
17. $2x^2 + 3x + 1 = 0$ **−0.5, −1**
18. $3x^2 - 5x - 2 = 0$ **$-\frac{1}{3}$, 2**
19. $2x^2 - 9x + 7 = 0$ **1, 3.5**
20. $-2x^2 + 11x = 5$ **0.5, 5**
21. $1 = 3x^2 + 3x$ **−1.26, 0.26**
22. $1.4x^2 + 3x + 4 = 6$ **−2.68, 0.53**
23. The height y (in feet) of a baseball thrown from the outfield is $y = -0.0016x^2 + 0.4x + 5$, where x is the horizontal distance (in feet) that the ball has traveled from its starting point. How far will a throw travel horizontally that is caught at a height of 5 ft? **250 ft**

Name ______________________ Date ______________

Practice 84

Cumulative Practice through Unit 10

Find the intercepts of the graph of each equation.

1. $-2x + 6y = 6$ **x: −3; y: 1**
2. $0.4x - 0.6y = 3$ **x: 7.5; y: −5**
3. $-\frac{1}{2}x - \frac{1}{3}y = 5$ **x: −10; y: −15**

Graph each system of inequalities. **Check students' work.**

4. $x - y \ge 3$, $y > -2$
5. $y < 2x - 1$, $x \le 1$
6. $3x + 2y \le 6$, $y \ge x - 2$

Simplify.

7. $(\sqrt{10})^2$ **10**
8. $\sqrt{8} \cdot \sqrt{18}$ **12**
9. $3\sqrt{14} \cdot \sqrt{7}$ **$21\sqrt{2}$**
10. $4\sqrt{50} \cdot 2\sqrt{6}$ **$80\sqrt{3}$**
11. $x^3 \cdot x^2$ **x^5**
12. $p^2q \cdot pq^4$ **p^3q^5**
13. $4y^5 \cdot 3y^3$ **$12y^8$**
14. $(2a^2)^5$ **$32a^{10}$**
15. Write the converse of the statement "If n is even, then $6n$ is even." Tell whether the converse is *true* or *false*. If it is false, give a counterexample. **If $6n$ is even, then n is even.; false; $n = 3$**
16. At a school fund-raising carnival, the target for a beanbag toss is a circle of diameter 10 in. The circle is inside a square that measures 22 in. on each side. Suppose a beanbag falls inside the square. What is the probability that it will hit the target? **about 0.16**

Without graphing, find the equation of the line of symmetry, the coordinates of the vertex, and the y-intercept of the graph of each equation.

17. $y = x^2 - 6x + 2$ **$x = 3$; (3, −7), 2**
18. $y = x^2 + 2x - 5$ **$x = -1$; (−1, −6); −5**
19. $y = x^2 - 12x$ **$x = 6$; (6, −36); 0**
20. A 32-foot ladder leaning against the side of a building makes an angle of 70° with the ground. How high up on the wall of the building will the ladder reach? **about 30.1 ft**

Each diagram shows a figure and a reflection image of the figure. Write an equation of the line of reflection.

21.

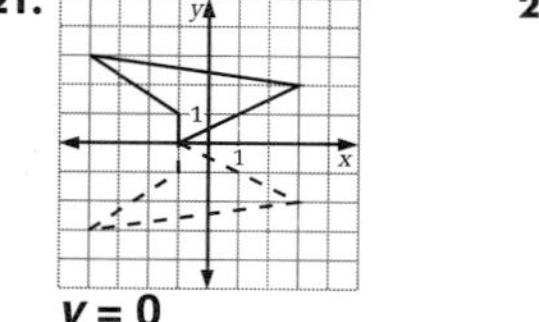

$y = 0$

22.

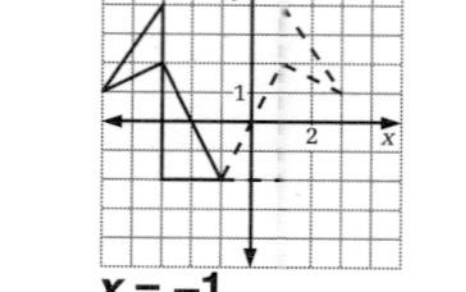

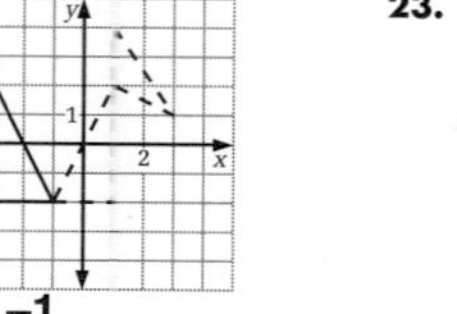

$x = -1$

23.

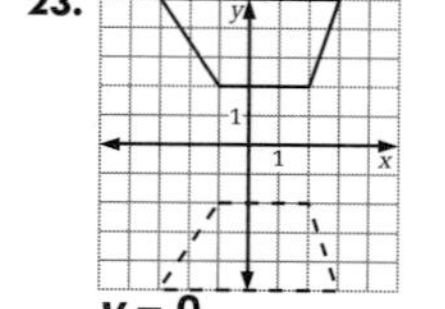

$y = 0$